in

Star Wars in
the Public Square

The Clone Wars
as Political Dialogue

DEREK R. SWEET

CRITICAL EXPLORATIONS IN
SCIENCE FICTION AND FANTASY, 50

Series Editors Donald E. Palumbo *and* C.W. Sullivan III

McFarland & Company, Inc., Publishers
Jefferson, North Carolina

LIBRARY OF CONGRESS CATALOGUING-IN-PUBLICATION DATA [new form]

Names: Sweet, Derek R., 1968–
Title: Star wars in the public square : the clone wars as political dialogue /
    Derek R. Sweet.
Description: Jefferson, North Carolina : McFarland & Company, Inc.,
    Publishers, 2016. | Series: Critical explorations in science fiction and
    fantasy ; 50 | Includes bibliographical references and index.
Identifiers: LCCN 2015042229 | ISBN 9780786477647 (softcover : acid
    free paper)
Subjects: LCSH: Star Wars films—History and criticism. | Politics in
    motion pictures. | Motion pictures—Political aspects.
Classification: LCC PN1995.9.S695 S94 2016 | DDC 791.43/75—dc23
LC record available at http://lccn.loc.gov/2015042229

BRITISH LIBRARY CATALOGUING DATA ARE AVAILABLE

ISBN 9781476623474 (ebook)

Front cover image © 2016 Shutterstock

Printed in the United States of America

*McFarland & Company, Inc., Publishers
  Box 611, Jefferson, North Carolina 28640
    www.mcfarlandpub.com*

To Kathleen and Gareth.
May the Force be with you, always.

Table of Contents

Acknowledgments

There are a number of people I feel called to thank for helping me take my first steps into the book publishing world. My gratitude goes out to Donald Palumbo, the series editor who helped shepherd this project along through his initial feedback and expert guidance. Margie McCue-Enser, Tess Pierce, and Tiffany Knoell have my appreciation for their expert feedback, proofing abilities, and general encouragement.

I would be remiss if I didn't thank Luther College for providing a supportive environment where I am free to explore the intersection of rhetoric and popular culture and share those ideas with students. Many of the ideas presented in this work grew out of my "Hyperspace, Hobbits, and the Hellmouth" class conducted during January term. My enthusiastic and thoughtful students helped me realize my ideas needed to find their way into the public square. Appreciation also goes out to my Communication Studies colleagues—Mark Johns, Thomas Johnson, Kim Powell, and Sarah Wilder—for listening to me prattle on endlessly about the *Star Wars* universe. I am grateful to all of you for making work seem a lot more like play.

I also want to express my appreciation for all those who organize, contribute to, and attend the Science Fiction and Fantasy Area panels, organizational meetings, and social gatherings of the annual Popular Culture Association/American Culture Association conference. Most of the ideas in this book have been vetted, in one way or another, by my fellow scholar fans.

Finally, I want to thank my family for their understanding and support during this process. Kathleen, my partner, deserves tremendous credit for protecting my writing time, listening to me talk through ideas and read sections of my writing out loud, and being my greatest fan. She is, in every possible sense, a true partner. Last, but not least, I want to thank my son Gareth for helping me continue to see the world through the imaginative eyes of a child. He watched every single episode of *The Clone Wars* at my side. I couldn't have asked for a better research assistant.

Preface

In his April 17, 2015, article for *The Telegraph* titled "*Star Wars* Fans: For God's Sake Get a Grip, It's Only a Movie," Martin Daubney commented on the fan fervor surrounding the release of a theatrical trailer for *Star Wars: Episode VII—The Force Awakens*. Comparing grown men to teenage girls who swoon at the sight of Justin Bieber, he wrote, "Like Beliebers, *Star Wars* fans (how can it be that they don't even have a name, like Trekkies?) took leave of their senses, gushed adoringly in quasi-orgasmic tones and posted wildly inappropriate tweets. Some even started dressing as Storm Troopers and body-popping on YouTube." He also made a specific point to chastise several fans who admitted to shedding a tear or two while watching the new trailer. After mentally correcting his spelling—stormtrooper, not Storm Trooper—I wondered why he felt so compelled to criticize this celebration of popular culture and fandom. Did he stop to wonder why the *Star Wars* franchise touches so many people so deeply? This book, a project started long before Daubney decided to deride *Star Wars* fans, is formulated as a response to all those who, like Daubney, dismiss *Star Wars* specifically, and popular culture generally (e.g., books, films, television, music) as "just entertainment." Over the course of several years I've encountered this common refrain on message boards, on Facebook, in the college classroom, in conversations with friends, and even at a recent popular culture conference. When someone starts to discuss the political, social, or spiritual meanings associated with a popular culture artifact, someone eventually chimes in with an admonishment: "You're thinking too hard. It's a television series. It's just entertainment." As someone who teaches, researches, and writes at the intersection of fandom, rhetorical studies, and popular culture critique, I can think of a number of reasons why we, as a culture, should learn to take popular culture more seriously.

I am a *Star Wars* fan. My life was forever changed during the summer

1

of 1977 when, as a nine-year-old boy, I experienced the original film in its theatrical debut. Like everyone else during that fateful summer, I had no idea this science fiction adventure would come to hold such an important place in my life, the popular culture landscape, and the public imagination. Since that time, my love of all things *Star Wars* has only grown with the development of the original text into the sprawling megatext it is today. The six films, scores of books, and thousands of comic books have been a constant companion during my journey from childhood to adulthood. In a sense, I've grown with Luke Skywalker, Obi-Wan Kenobi, Leia Organa, Han Solo, Chewbacca, R2D2, and Yoda (just to name a few). The three *Star Wars* posters that adorned my bedroom walls throughout the 80s morphed into my present collection of action figures and maquettes reminding anyone who enters my home or school office that a *Star Wars* fan resides here. More importantly, however, is the way *Star Wars* captivates my imagination, calls me to consider who I am as a person, and equips me to live my life in particular ways. Am I someone who allows his fiery temper to guide his decisions or am I someone who heeds the wisdom of Master Yoda? "Anger. Fear. Aggression. The dark side are they." Will I emulate the Jedi Knights and strive to serve others selflessly or will I start down the selfish, self-serving path of the Sith?

I am also a rhetorician, someone who studies the way communication, in all its symbolic forms (e.g., writing, speech, visual representation, music), provides a means to influence, negotiate, and transform ourselves, others, and the culture in which we live. People frequently associate rhetoric with political oratory. Congressional debates, presidential inaugural addresses, and political ads stand as excellent examples of rhetorical attempts to address cultural values, affect policy change, and enact national identity. Contemporary rhetorical studies, however, go beyond traditional public address and illustrates how a broad range of texts contribute to conversations about matters of public consequence. How might embodied protests in Ferguson, Missouri, bring attention to the problems associated with police militarization? How might a film like *Catching Fire* enter the public dialogue related to veterans and post-traumatic stress disorder? In my own work as a scholar I have examined Samuel Adams's colonial-era letter-writing campaign, goth fashion, music, and dance, President Obama's campaign oratory, and the television series *Battlestar Galactica* as rhetorical acts. Each of these disparate texts offers insights into how a people constitute knowledge, community, governance, identity, power, and resistance.

As popular culture critic, I am interested in the way various artifacts impact our individual and collective lives. How does my interest in a particular artifact like *Star Wars* influence my sense of self? Conversely, how does *Star Wars* influence my understanding of others? Does my enthusiasm for Marvel comics, *Buffy the Vampire Slayer*, the indie rock band Metric, and specialty coffee culture influence what I buy, how I dress, what I eat, the way I talk, and the way I interact with others? Do pervasive pop cultural narratives encourage me to judge myself and others in certain ways? How do these same narratives call me to accept certain values while rejecting others? In a general sense, focusing a critical lens on the presence of popular culture in people's lives reveals how dominant societal discourses, cultural myths, individual identities, and institutional ideologies are reified and subverted. For someone constantly engaging these questions, popular culture is never "just entertainment."

All three of these identities—*Star Wars* fan, rhetorician, and popular culture critic—intersected on Saturday, January 9, 2010. As was our tradition, my family and I sat in front of our television, captivated by the exploits of Anakin Skywalker, Ahsoka Tano, Obi-Wan Kenobi, and Captain Rex as they protected the Galactic Republic against the Separatist droid army. I found myself startled, however, when this particular episode depicted a brutal terrorist attack on a public square. The bombing itself, the civilian casualties, and the bomber's suicide—all depicted explicitly—unfolded in mere minutes. I turned to my partner, Kathleen, and said, "This isn't just a kids' show. This is critical commentary on contemporary political issues. I think I need to write about this." After the episode ended, we talked about that particular storyline as well as others drawing close parallels to contemporary U.S. politics and foreign policy. During the course of our conversation I realized the television program, a program airing on Cartoon Network, offered a more salient political voice than almost any newspaper editorial, cable pundit, or political speech. This book gives that political voice a broader critical audience.

Introduction:
Star Wars and Politics

"*The Clone Wars* is more about dealing overall with life during wartime, in which there's always political strife."—Dave Filoni

"The topic of a the speaker's speech, regardless of what this topic may be, does not become the object of speech for the first time in any given utterance; a given speaker is not the first to speak about it."[1]—Mikhail M. Bakhtin

In a January 21, 2011, post to Wired.com's *Underwire* blog, Dave Filoni, the supervising director for *Star Wars: The Clone Wars* animated series, responded to a number of questions regarding the ongoing television program. One particular question raised the issue of political content. When asked about the program's relation to current political events, Filoni responded:

> Well, George and I will talk about current events when they come up, but I try to take *The Clone Wars* out of the realm of being too ripped from the headlines. George and I don't talk about what character or event will represent what's happening in the real world. *The Clone Wars* is more about dealing overall with life during wartime, in which there's always political strife.

Despite Filoni's denial of any intentional link to real-world political events, the focus of the series—"dealing overall with life during wartime"—seems particularly relevant to U.S. American culture in the early twenty-first century. Indeed, many of the common controversies playing out in the animated program could be pulled from headlines: cloning, torture, terrorism, political corruption, peace, and even the case for a just war. More important for this project, however, is the way in which the television program inspires a dialogue between Wired blogger Scott Thill and Dave

4

Filoni. As a result of the political echoes resonating throughout the program, Thill continues a consideration of the themes in his conversation with *The Clone Wars* showrunner. And, as Filoni relates in a separate interview, this tendency to engage the political content of *The Clone Wars* goes beyond media critics: "I get a lot of comments from people that they watch *Clone Wars* with their kids and this is a family Friday night, even when the shows are sometimes fun and whimsical and sometimes more intense, they like to sit there and talk about what the show will say."[2]

The fact that *Star Wars: The Clone Wars* might have something to say should come as no surprise. Often recognized as a genre of provocative engagement, science fiction moves individuals to critically interrogate matters of common political concern. For Frederik Pohl, the mere mention of political science fiction is something of a redundancy. He writes, "To speak of 'political science fiction' is almost to commit a tautology, for I would argue that there is very little science fiction, perhaps even that there is no good science fiction at all, that is not to some degree political."[3] Largely allegorical, science fiction encourages individuals to draw connections between fictional portrayals of extraterrestrial encounters, technologically-advanced civilizations, deep space exploration, alternative histories, and interplanetary wars and the non-fictional world in which they presently live. The fantastic elements of science fiction texts—from the plots, to the characters, to the settings—engage the popular imagination, encourage viewers to juxtapose the world as it is with the possibilities and potentialities of a world that could be and, in doing so, gives "voice to our deepest longings, and speak to our hopes about the future of our society and ourselves."[4] This voice, a voice also heard within the characters and narratives of *The Clone Wars*, calls for a critical rethinking of these texts as a form of socio-political deliberation.[5]

Since the debut of *Star Wars: A New Hope* in 1977, numerous scholars have explored the way the voices of the *Star Wars* cinematic universe speak to audiences. Indeed, *Star Wars* has been well examined from a number of critical perspectives. From a mythical perspective, a perspective that illuminates the archetypal narratives contributing to a culture's social institutions and norms, *Star Wars* is a traditional quest narrative woven together from the diverse threads of Saturday afternoon serials, Arthurian legend, Samurai tales, and modern war epics. Interpreted as cultural myth, the *Star Wars* films reinforce the familiar U.S. American cultural tropes of rugged individualism, good versus evil, and the potential for redemption. The rise and fall of Anakin Skywalker, and his ultimate redemption via the efforts of his son, cautions audiences to heed the words of Master Yoda: "Anger, fear, aggression. The dark side are they."[6] Examined through the lens of cultural studies, a critical approach "that seeks to analyze how cultural phenomena intersect with social formations such as economics, technology, race, and gender," *Star Wars* scholars interrogate the way the six films reify and subvert hegemonic cultural ideals.[7] The various critical perspectives aside, scholars who scrutinize the *Stars Wars* films and associated cultural phenomena are, in some sense, acknowledging Filoni's observation concerning the power of the mediated text to incite thought and discussion among viewers.

Inspired by Filoni's comments, this book adds my voice to the body of work focused on the *Star Wars* universe. Rather than exploring the six films, however, I turn my attention to the text with which Dave Filoni is involved directly: *Star Wars: The Clone Wars*. And while *The Clone Wars* displays many of the mythic and cultural elements so frequently associated with the *Star Wars* universe, my critical perspective stresses the political elements of the series. There is no question mythic narratives and cultural phenomena are major influences in the realm of the political. Such widely understood myths as the American Dream, the Wild West, American exceptionalism, myths deeply ingrained in the collective imagination of U.S. American society, shape the way people think about national identity, party affiliation, individual opportunity, and justice. Likewise, realizations of race, gender, and class reveal the underlying ideologies contributing to the creation, reinforcement, and transformation of institutionalized cultural hierarchies and conceptions of power. The definitive focus of this project, however, is not on the mythic narratives embedded within *Star Wars*; similarly, this project does not attempt to reveal how the science fantasy epic reinforces or challenges institutionalized patterns of cultural subjugation and debasement. Rather, my exploration of politics in the *Star Wars* universe engages *The Clone Wars* as an important voice in ongoing deliberations over matters of common interest and public consequence. Put simply, this project is more concerned with the debate surrounding specific political issues than with broader conceptions of belief, party, ideology, or power.

To be fair, politicos, reporters, and scholars have always considered the *Star Wars* franchise a politically-charged science fiction text. Two months prior to the release of *Return of the Jedi*, Senator Edward Kennedy referred to President Reagan's advocacy for the Strategic Defense Initiative—a military research program tasked with developing a space based missile defense system—as nothing more than "misleading Red Scare tactics and reckless *Star Wars* schemes."[8] Kennedy's comparison between the Strategic Defense Initiative and a piece of culturally resonant science fiction was obviously intended as an indictment of the unrealistic technological expectations associated with such a complex system. The Reagan administration, however, "readily accepted the critics' language, welcoming an association with the romanticism and the lure of technological advancement found in the films."[9] Congress and the press were not the only ones who read the original *Star Wars* trilogy as a politically-relevant text.

As early as 1978, one year after the release of the original *Star Wars* film, Dan Rubey touched on the political content of the film. Rubey's essay—a critical review exploring the tensions resulting from the mediated convergence of technology, metaphysics, and humanity—addresses the mythic and cultural implications of the film but also interrogates several political points. The intense visual experience of special effects—laden science fiction spectacle, he argues, positions viewers in a way that dehumanizes the experience of warfare. As he points out, the explosions of Alderaan and the Death Star resulted in billions of deaths that—"Obi-Wan Kenobi's brief attack of heartburn" aside—went largely unacknowledged by the characters in the film and probably weren't given much thought by viewers observing the destruction from the safety of their theater seats.[10] This kind of cinematic experience echoes a form of sterilized, technological warfare emerging from World War II; with the aid of increasingly sophisticated weaponry and war machines, pilots, sailors, and soldiers frequently engaged enemy targets beyond their line of sight. Released just a few years after the conclusion of the Vietnam War, Rubey suggests the science fiction spectacle of deep space warfare imitates the firebombing of Dresden or the long-range jet fighter skirmishes of the 1960s and 1970s in that those who drop bombs, fire missiles, and even unleash the planet-annihilating weaponry of the Death Star rarely see the face of the enemy or the innocents caught in the crossfire.[11]

Like Rubey, Ryan and Kellner argue the original trilogy—*A New Hope*, *The Empire Strikes Back*, and *Return of the Jedi*—emphasizes several political dialectics present during the post–Vietnam 1970s: governmental control versus individual freedom, individual success versus communal responsibility, and "faith and feeling against science and rationality."[12] Embracing the traditional hero's journey—the person of humble beginnings embarks on a quest that ultimately leads to the salvation of the broader community—the films celebrate the ability of the free individual to resist, and ultimately overthrow, the oppressive tyranny of sprawling government. Such ideals, argue Ryan and Kellner, reflect the emergence of the conservative political movement associated with the Reagan revolution. If the Empire is understood as an analogy for government's intrusion into matters of private life and the "curtailment of individual self-control and freedom," then the Rebel Alliance represents conservative political reform and the fight to resist the stifling practices of liberal leaning government.[13]

While some critiques engage the ideological underpinnings of the *Star Wars* films, Stephen McVeigh interrogates what he refers to as "the central trope, the engine that drives the narrative the trilogies: war."[14] Reinforcing the work of earlier *Star Wars* scholars, McVeigh construes the original trilogy as a post–Vietnam critique of military superiority whereby a technological superpower is defeated by smaller, more humanized forces. The films, he argues, present a dual reading of U.S. military might, a reading that helps rehabilitate the damaged U.S. psyche concerning morally just war. In one sense, the Empire reflects the massive technological advantage displayed by the U.S. military machine and even conjures haunting memories of the moral ambiguities associated with Vietnam. Rather than fully embrace those moral ambiguities, however, Lucas offers a multilayered representation of the galactic conflict harkening back to World War II (the Empire's penchant for Nazi-style uniforms) and even the American Revolution (the Rebels as resisting an oppressive regime). Thus, the original trilogy presents a dual image of U.S. military might: one portraying the United States as a morally bankrupt oppressor and another encouraging viewers to rethink U.S. interests and actions as just. If the original trilogy offers an assessment of post–Vietnam America, the prequel trilogy addressed "the fears and concerns over the demands, shapes, and nature of future wars."[15]

The prequel films, suggests McVeigh, reflect an institutional change in both the nature of war and the way in which wars are fought. Produced in the decade following the end of the Cold War, the prequel trilogies reflect a geopolitical anxiety concerning future wars: fifty years of superpower-fueled mutually assured nuclear destruction, stalemated conventional armies, and small conflicts by proxy gave way to an era of indeterminate enemies, counterinsurgency tactics, and global police operations. The post–Cold War era marked "a moment when the American military recognized that the nature of war had changed and sought to embrace new technology in the theater of war, to bring about a change in military practice."[16] Just as the Persian Gulf War, the War on Terror, and the Iraq War featured innovations in military technology—namely the increased use of cruise missiles, smart bombs, and drones—the conflict of the prequels relied on weaponized droids and genetically-manipulated clones rather than conventional soldiers. In either case, Persian Gulf or prequel, McVeigh observes that the respective military strategies involve rapid troop deployment and a reduced involvement of human soldiers.[17] In a passage particularly relevant for this project, McVeigh shows how the content of President George W. Bush's post–9/11 speech to a joint session of Congress—a speech detailing the blueprint for the War on Terror—engages the plot of *Attack of the Clones* in a kind of cultural dialogue. Drawing these kinds of connections between political deliberations and popular culture content is the focal point of my argument. Nowhere is this dialogue between ongoing cultural debate and *Star Wars* more apparent than in the work of Anne Lancashire.

Lancashire's early *Star Wars* scholarship breaks down the narrative complexity of *Return of the Jedi* in relation to the two previous installments of the original trilogy and illustrates how the growth of Luke Skywalker brings a central theme to life: "maturity as the victory of self-knowledge and cooperative love ... over hatred, violence, and fear."[18] Lancashire's work examining the intertextuality of *The Phantom Menace* and the films of the original trilogy, however, moves the discussion of *Star Wars* and political affairs toward the critique of pertinent public issues. Interspersed with the familiar narrative structure, mythic archetypes, and visual spectacle of the *Star Wars* universe is a film grounded not in the epic themes of intergalactic tyranny and rebellion but in more prosaic conflicts concerning "trade, taxation, and political power."[19] The political skirmishes of *The Phantom Menace* provide the foundation for the explicitly political war that breaks out in *Attack of the Clones*: "the economic and political greed and ambition— the dark-side unrestrained appetite—of the political and business classes ... is leading towards the death of democracy (the Republic) and the rise of political dictatorship (the Empire)."[20] Contending that the film is "first and foremost a political—and politically critical—film," Lancashire posits that the *Attack of the Clones* invites a rereading of the entire *Star Wars* narrative from a political perspective.[21] Depicting a Republic affected by corporate interests, oversized political egos, and a complacent constituency, *Attack of the Clones* details the pivotal moment when a well-meaning democracy starts the descent toward political dictatorship. Parallels with the Enron banking scandal, the erosion of individual freedoms in the name of the War on Terror (e.g., the Patriot Act), and the questionable decision to invade Iraq establish *Attack of the Clones* as a kind of mediated allusion for the challenges facing the people of the United States.

Although several scholars provide insights into the political nature of *Star Wars*, some of the most poignant analysis appears in the journalistic assessments of *Revenge of the Sith*. At the time of the film's release (May 19, 2005), the United States military was deployed—in the name of national security and the broader war on terror—in Iraq and Afghanistan and the

Bush administration, an administration that enjoyed broad support post–9/11, faced increasing criticism from an American public tired of prolonged conflict and the policies associated with that conflict (e.g., the Patriot Act, various war spending bills). Given this context, the *Wall Street Journal* commented on how the film's "anti–Bush, anti–Iraq War message" served as an "indictment of the Bush Administration for allegedly abusing power in order to wage war and persuade the American people to abandon central tenets of democracy."[22] Other news sources also detected a link between *Sith* and real-world politics. As David Germain wrote in a May 16, 2005, piece appearing in the *Los Angeles Times*, the Cannes Film Festival premier of *Revenge of the Sith* resulted in several comparisons "between the final chapter of the sci-fi saga and our own troubled times." The most notable similarity, reported Germain, appeared in the form of Anakin Skywalker's line "If you're not with me, then you're my enemy" with President Bush's post–9/11 warning to the nations of the world: "Either you are with us, or you are with the terrorists." In his May 16, 2005, review for the *New York Times* A. O. Scott made nearly the same observation:

> Mr. Lucas is clearly jabbing his lightsaber in the direction of some real-world political leaders. At one point, Darth Vader, already deep in the thrall of the dark side and echoing the words of George W. Bush, hisses at Obi-Wan, "If you're not with me, you're my enemy." Obi-Wan's response is likely to surface as a bumper sticker during the next election campaign: "Only a Sith thinks in absolutes." You may applaud this editorializing, or you may find it over-wrought, but give Mr. Lucas his due. For decades he has been blamed (unjustly) for helping to lead American movies away from their early–70's engagement with political matters, and he deserves credit for trying to bring them back.

In fact, the political commentary of *Revenge of the Sith* became political reality when Senator Frank Lautenberg (D–N.J.) stood on the Senate Floor, pointed to an image of Chancellor Palpatine, and said, "In a far-off universe, in this film, the leader of the Senate breaks the rules to give himself and his supporters more power. I sincerely hope that it doesn't mirror actions being contemplated in the Senate of the United States."[23] Of note here is the way newspaper writers, movie reviewers, and even a senator acknowledged the politically-relevant themes resonating throughout the third film of the prequel trilogy. The political dialogue between *Star Wars* and contemporary politics did not end of with the release of *Revenge of the Sith*.

As I suggested in the opening paragraph of this introduction, *The Clone Wars* animated series continues to implicate the *Star Wars* universe as politically-relevant science fiction. At the conclusion of season four, Scott Thill commented:

Hitting its stride, *The Clone Wars* has become increasingly philosophical and powerful. It's the scariest cartoon on television for any age. It's also perhaps our most relevant animated series, especially for a nation so shocked and awed by perpetual war that it's willing to hand off constitutional rights like due process and habeas corpus for a patriotic song and dance.[24]

Keeping this political resonance in mind, the series emerges as an unexpected voice in public deliberations encouraging viewers to consider, analyze, and judge a wide variety of controversial issues and policy debates. More specifically, my engagement of *The Clone Wars* explores the way in which the series enters into what Hauser and Benoit-Barne describe as "the ongoing conversation about how we shall act and interact—our political relations" and how those conversations encourage "political choice based on a sense of the common good."[25] Viewed as a participating voice in a multivocal public dialogue *The Clone Wars* calls on viewers to consider such varied questions as what constitutes a good citizen, what social beliefs, values, and attitudes should be sanctioned or rejected, or what governmental policies or actions should be deemed just or unjust.[26] Encounters with mediated texts like *The Clone Wars* mark what Mikhal Bakhtin would describe as a dialogic moment of communicative interplay whereby "viewpoints, world views, and trends cross, converge, and diverge."[27]

With Bakhtin's notion of popular dialogue in mind, the remainder of this book examines *Star Wars: The Clone Wars* as a form of political discourse concerning matters of public consequence. My purpose in introducing Bakhtinian dialogics to the rhetoric of science fiction is threefold. First, I hope to add my voice to a growing number of scholars who recognize Bakhtin's dialogics as one way to recast rhetoric as a collaborative, rather than monologic, enterprise. Bakhtin argues the traditional conception of rhetoric advances a communicative exchange whereby an individual attempts to advocate her or his worldview with little regard for the worldview of others. With an emphasis on persuading individuals to accept or reject a particular proposition, traditional rhetorical practice positions listeners as passive recipients rather than active participants and champions "power in the form of individual advancement or personal gain."[28] A rhetoric grounded in dialogics, on the other hand, recognizes all participants of a communicative exchange, speakers and listeners alike, as active rhetorical agents responsible for collaborative meaning-making. As Hatch explains, a Bakhtinian rhetoric posits deliberative interactions "in which distinct cultural voices and generic forms come together in new and complex ways that are transformative (and suasive) toward fuller truths."[29] Each rhetorical encounter, a communicative exchange Bakhtin identifies as an "utterance," is always part of a broader ongoing conversation comprised of a multitude of previous utterances. Historical and contemporary perspectives, ideas, and ideologies continue to clash in perpetuity; ever unresolved and ultimately unfinalized, fleeting dialogic encounters draw on previous and present understandings to generate any number of potentialities.

Second, and closely related to the first, is my desire to recast consumers of popular culture as active, rather than passive, participants. Many contemporary characterizations of media consumption depict audiences as unthinking couch potatoes who zone out the moment they enter a theater or turn on the television. These uncritical viewers fill their leisure time with vacuous mediated entertainments and, as a result, possess less time for pursuits that would help them participate in discussions relevant to the welfare of the community. Fixated on updating a Facebook status, catching up on Sookie's latest vampire tryst, or marveling at the summer spectacle of *The Avengers* or *The Dark Knight Rises,* audiences tune into their popular culture pleasures and tune out from matters of public importance. Or do they? As other popular culture scholars have noted, the engagement of these seemingly guilty pleasures are more active than not. Participating in a kind of indirect communal viewing, individuals might watch a particular television series and then share their excitements, disappointments, and conjectures with friends, classmates, or work colleagues. More active still is the practice of second screen viewing whereby an individual simultaneously watches a television show and interacts with fellow fans via Twitter, Facebook, message board, or text message. Many consumers of popular culture do not turn off when tuning in but assume the role of an active, critical consumer prepared to discuss a text at some level or another. My argument, then, takes this active consumption to another level as I contend some, if not most, forms of popular culture invite viewers to engage politically-salient dialogues. At a time when the U.S. public is accused of political apathy, I want to assert that perhaps the public is just as politically active as ever.

Third, just as Bakhtin championed the nineteenth-century novel as the potential site of complex, multi-voiced cultural discourses that transcend the monologic voice of the author, I want to cast my lot with mediated texts of popular culture. Like Bakhtin, I do not view all mediated texts as multi-voiced and dialogic; there are those moments when an author's voice and artistic vision mutes the sound of other cultural voices leaving a text stilted, contrived, and lifeless. There are, however, those popular culture texts that capture the complex, contradictory nature of human life in all its dialogic vividness. As Bakhtin asserts, the represented world of a fictional text is clearly distinct from the real world of human life; at the same time, however, the "real and represented world" are "indissolubly tied up with each other ... in mutual interaction."[30] Science fiction, with its emphasis on speculation, juxtaposition, and political tension, is a genre particularly rife with Bakhtinian dialogism. Nowhere is the interrelatedness of the "real and the represented world" more obvious than in the narrative of an alien race relegated to an internment camp (e.g., *District 9*), an invasion which positions the United States as an occupied nation (e.g., *War of the Worlds*, *Battle: Los Angeles, Falling Skies*), or an exploration of the human condition through the eyes of an artificial intelligence or clone (e.g., *Battlestar Galactica, Blade Runner, A.I., Moon*). Informed by the culture in which it is created, such an artistic creation challenges viewers to consider their own perceptions of the broader world. In his piece regarding the political rhetoric of the rebooted *Battlestar Galactica*, Brian Ott articulates a similar understanding of science fiction: "I believe that it stages contemporary social and political concerns in a manner that allows for critical self-reflection better than any other television genre."[31] The moment when a character's response to a moral quandary makes a viewer cheer or cringe, particularly when the choice coincides or conflicts with the viewer's own moral sense, is a glimpse into collaborative meaning-making writ large.

With all this in mind, the remainder of this book advances *The Clone Wars* as a text illustrating my argument for reading popular culture artifacts as meaningful utterances within continuing cultural conversations. Chapter One delves into the prospect of a dialogic rhetoric in relation to film, television, and related media forms. To begin, the chapter reviews previous scholarship centered on rhetoric and science fiction by tracing the popular film and television as equipment for living perspective from Kenneth Burke's original essay to the more contemporary conceptualization of mediated texts as a tool for negotiating postmodern Cartesian anxieties. Building on this body of work, the chapter then turns to the collected writings of Bahktin and the task of parsing out the possibility of a dialogic rhetoric rooted in the ideas of intersubjectivity, addressivity, and unfinalizability. Rethinking rhetoric dialogically offers the possibility of a contentious public square populated by multiple voices, perspectives, interpretations, and potential outcomes. More specifically, I argue the politically ambiguous positions represented by *The Clone Wars* elicit a creative perception calling viewers to not only render judgment but to act.

Having established the possibility of a dialogic rhetoric in chapter one, chapter two is the first of five chapters that illuminates how *The Clone Wars* enters the realm of public deliberations. Centered on a topic of polit-

ical contention—cloning, torture, Just War Theory, peace, and drone warfare—each chapter explores a specific issue from a historical perspective,
illustrates how *The Clone Wars* enters the deliberative arena, and discusses
how viewers of *The Clone Wars* are called to engage the ongoing political
dialogue. Such an exploration of the rhetorical dialogue between previous,
historical utterances, the contemporary mediated text, and the active audience member assuming the position of cultural adjudicator and potential
purveyor of future positions highlights the ways in which multiple forms
of discourse traverse the political landscape and contribute to the constitution, negotiation, and transformation of human knowledge, action, and
community.[32]

As the title of the television series suggests, cloning is an obvious
starting point. The issue of human cloning has been a particularly salient
political issue in the late twentieth and early twenty-first centuries. The
debates over therapeutic and reproductive cloning—the former associated
with embryonic stem cells and the later with the creation of a duplicate of
a human being—echoed throughout the halls of Congress and resulted in
formal documents released by both the National Bioethics Advisory Commission and the President's Council on Bioethics. The early pages of chapter two distill the arguments emanating from these public discussions and
suggest four major objections take center stage: eugenics, individuality and
the right to self-determination, clones as manufactured objects, and family.
In the second half of the chapter, I turn to those episodes of *The Clone
Wars* featuring clone troopers as prominent figures of the primary story arc
and analyze the way in which the series, like Congress and the Bioethics
reports, speaks to these very same concerns.

In chapter three, I turn my attention to torture. In the months following the attacks on the World Trade Center and the Pentagon, the U.S.
intelligence agencies, military, and security forces utilized every tool available in an effort to expose the responsible terrorist network as well as prevent any additional terrorist attacks. One of the most problematic weapons
in the war on terror arsenal included the capture and subsequent rendition
of terror suspects to black detention facilities where they were then subjected to what NBC's Michael Isikoff described as "enhanced," "aggressive,"
and "humiliating" interrogation.[33] Soon after the infamous Abu Ghraib
pictures surfaced, as well as evidence pointing to the systematic use of
enhanced interrogation by U.S. intelligence personnel, editorialists and
opinion page writers posed several questions. What is torture? Is there a
difference between "torture" and "enhanced interrogation"? When, if ever,
are these practices permissible? Is torture always off limits or are there

extreme situations which warrant the use of techniques that nearly everyone agrees are morally reprehensible? What does torture say about a nation as well as the people of that nation?

Like the people fighting on the front lines of the battle to stem terrorism, the characters in *The Clone Wars* find themselves faced with the prospect of using torture as a viable intelligence gathering technique. Anakin Skywalker, the troubled Jedi Knight whose future as Darth Vader always looms in the background of *The Clone Wars*, tortures prisoners in several episodes. Although one would expect this from a Jedi Knight who eventually rises as a Dark Lord of the Sith, Obi-Wan Kenobi, Mace Windu, and Ahsoka Tano also turn to questionable forms of interrogation when faced with the ticking time bomb scenario. These moments of moral quandary are the principal point of inquiry for chapter three.

On December 10, 2009, President Barack Obama stood before the Norwegian Nobel Peace prize committee, accepted his award, and declared "the instruments of war do have a role to play in preserving the peace."[34] Although an unusual venue for defending the use of violence to resolve international crises—Howard Fineman of *Newsweek* noted that those in the immediate Oslo audience were not applauding—Obama's Nobel Peace Prize lecture offered a justification for the use of war as an important element of international relations.[35] Not unlike President Obama, a man who once addressed a speech to an anti–Iraq war rally in Chicago, the Jedi Knights of *The Clone Wars* find themselves in the tenuous position of peacemakers functioning as military generals. The stance taken by both the president of the United States and the protectors of the Galactic Republic, a stance that allows one to simultaneously advocate peace and war, is the subject matter of Just War Theory. Obama's speech, which is obviously informed by the central tenets of Just War Theory, outlines "standards that govern the use of force"; a war is just when (1) conducted in self-defense or as a last resort, (2) initiated in the name of humanitarian relief, and (3) governed by moral rules of conduct.[36] With Obama's speech in mind, chapter four develops the idea of Just War Theory, articulates Obama's "just war" arguments, and examines how *The Clone Wars* functions as part of this ongoing dialogue. How do the Jedi Knights justify their involvement in an intergalactic conflict? From the perspective of the Jedi Knights and the Galactic Republic, does the expansive conflict with the Confederacy of Independent Systems (also known as the Separatists) meet the criteria of a just war? How might the moral quandaries of the Jedi Knights invoke viewers to consider the justness of contemporary conflicts like Iraq and Afghanistan?

Although the case for a just war is an obvious focal point of *The Clone Wars*, arguments for peace also appear throughout the series. While a number of characters advocate peace across several episodes, the explicit emphasis on Senator Padmé Amidala and Duchess Satine Kryze seems to suggest, as U.S. Representative Jeannette Rankin once remarked, that "the peace problem is a women's problem."[37] With Rankin's historical efforts in mind, chapter five explores the diplomatic efforts of Padmé Amidala and Satine Kryze as a critique for not only war as a general concept but also in the light of U.S. American foreign policy. To make this dialogue between the series and contemporary events clear, I engage the work of Jeannette Rankin. Rankin—suffragist, pacifist, and first woman elected to Congress—served two terms in the U.S. House of Representatives and is best remembered for being the only Congressperson to cast formal "No" votes against the country's involvement in World War I and World War II. Never opposed to protecting the borders of the United States, Rankin spoke critically of any and all attempts to involve U.S. American troops in armed conflicts around the world. She made her position clear in 1917 when she stated, "I still believe war is a stupid and futile way of attempting to settle international difficulties."[38] Following the format of previous chapters, I evaluate Rankin's arguments regarding peace and diplomacy and illustrate how vestiges of her message resonate through the sentiments articulated by Senator Amidala and Duchess Satine.

In chapter six I turn my attention to one of the most underreported human rights issues of the post–9/11 era: drones. Since President Obama took office in 2008, the use of remotely-piloted aircraft to target and kill high level enemy personnel has become a prominent weapon in the effort to disrupt terrorist leadership. As Mark Lander reported in the January 30, 2012, *New York Times*, the United States government confirms the operation of remotely-controlled drones, as well as the use of these drones to carry out missile attacks, in Pakistan, Afghanistan, Iraq, Yemen, and Somalia. Despite former CIA director Leon Panetta's assurances that the typical drone attack "is very precise, it's very limited in terms of collateral damage," others argue the number of civilian casualties associated with such attacks is unconscionable.[39] Turning to the human rights reports published by such organizations as the Human Rights Clinic at Columbia Law School, the International Human Rights and Conflict Resolution Clinic of Stanford Law School, and the Global Justice Clinic at NYU School of Law, chapter six delves into the calls for a serious reconsideration of the U.S. drone warfare program and the development of autonomous weapons systems. Objections to the current program center around three major areas of contention:

(1) the unreasonable loss of civilian life; (2) the psychological impact on the people living in drone patrolled areas; and (3) the questionable efficacy of the program. Important to note is while all the reports are critical of the program, each also recognizes the drone program as a necessary element of U.S. national security. Having laid out the drone discourse of these human rights organizations, I then illustrate how *The Clone Wars* narrates a cautionary tale regarding unmanned and robotic weaponry. The representations of droids—those that comprise the automated army of the Confederacy of Independent States (the Separatists) and those that function in support roles from the Galactic Republic—serve as the focal points of my discussion.

In the final chapter, chapter seven, I turn back to the questions presented in chapter one. How does rethinking rhetoric through the lens of Bakhtinian dialogics highlight the role of viewer as an active participant in the consideration of important political matters? How does *The Clone Wars* emerge as a potential site of rhetorical dialogism, contributing to our communal task of discerning, constituting, and challenging ourselves, others, the world around us? Weaving together my musings from chapters two through six, I assert that when presented with the unfinalized ethical contradictions of *The Clone Wars* individuals cannot help but find themselves drawn into the various dialogues surrounding human reproductive cloning, torture, Just War Theory, peace, and drone warfare. *The Clone Wars* issues a call that requires a fitting response. To ignore or reject the difficult ethical quandaries presented for consideration is to reject our place as participants in the public square. The response may take any number of forms. A response might manifest immediately in the form of a discussion with one's self, a child, a partner, or other fans, but may also be less immediate. Like the science fiction genre that obviously shaped congressional considerations of cloning technologies, the tensions presented in *The Clone Wars* may inform a viewer's response years down the road. In this way, even those individuals who consider themselves uninformed about political matters may have a better understanding of the underlying moral dilemmas than they realize.

In *Return of the Jedi* a ghostly Obi-Wan Kenobi confronts his apprentice, Luke Skywalker, with a notion that rests at the heart of my work as a rhetorician. Obi-Wan states, "Luke, you're going to find that many of the truths we cling to depend on a certain point of view."[40] As I illustrate in the remainder of this book, I don't think Bakhtin would disagree with Obi-Wan's observation. I do believe, however, Bakhtin would make a slight modification and assert that our truths depend on the communicative intersection of multiple points of view. For Bakhtin, social truths are never as black and white as the heroes of the *Star Wars* universe; instead, the meanings that shape human life emerge from a collective mediation of contradictions, differences, and ambiguities. This "intersubjective quality of all meaning" is particularly true in the morally gray politics of *The Clone Wars* era.[41] When confronted with the unresolved, politically-uncertain viewpoints posited by *The Clone Wars*, the onus falls on viewers to materialize as engaged social interlocutors negotiating the truths we'll cling to and those we'll let go.

ONE

Science Fiction, Rhetoric and Dialogue in the Public Square

"The dialogic orientation of discourse is a phenomenon that is, of course, a property of any discourse."[1]—Mikhail M. Bakhtin

"You've taken your first step into a larger world."[2]—Ben Kenobi, *Star Wars: A New Hope*

In his germinal essay "On the Poetics of the Science Fiction Genre," Darko Suvin identifies cognitive estrangement as a defining characteristic of science fiction texts. A text exhibiting cognitive estrangement is one familiar enough that readers, or audience members, draw parallels with themselves and the world in which they live. In this sense, science fiction texts typify the world inhabited by an author and her readers. At the same time, however, texts exhibiting cognitive estrangement create distance between the reader and the fictional world; the reader encounters differences—sometimes slight and sometimes significant—that remind her the represented place is imaginary. Estranged texts, texts which simultaneously conjure familiarity and distance, implicate a dialogue—mediated by author and readers—between the imagined world and the real world. Cognitively speaking, science fiction texts are not only "reflective of but also on reality."[3] In other words, the interplay of the familiar and the alien calls readers to engage in creative interpretation as she or he considers the differences represented. Typically, such cognitive estrangement functions as a critical commentary wherein fictional representations offer new ways of looking at the real world inhabited by creator and audience. As Suvin suggests, these texts function as a "stimulus for independent thinking," inviting readers to contemplate varying perspectives concerning everything from cultural norms to political policy.[4]

Some forty years after publication, Suvin's understanding of science fiction texts as a form of cognitive estrangement is widely accepted. Few would question that contemporary science fiction participates in broad cultural conversations, discourses, and deliberations. As Kerslake suggests, science fiction texts function as a voice within the "legitimate and strategic cultural discourses" fundamental to uncovering, negotiating, and integrating "the knowledge and awareness humanity has of itself."[5] When an individual engages a graphic novel, book, film, or television program, he or she enters a world other than her own and encounters the social, ideological, and political ideas articulated within. To some degree, she or he makes that initial step into the "larger world" referenced by Ben Kenobi. She might, for example, reevaluate her opinions regarding climate change after viewing *Wall-E* and the title character's ongoing attempts to reclaim a polluted Earth for humanity-in-exile. Similarly, another person might encounter the powerful animal rights theme central to the reimagined *Planet of the Apes* franchise and find his objections to animal testing reaffirmed. Specific examples aside, science fiction narratives present viewpoints that reinforce familiar understandings of the world, challenge the way things ought to be, and sometimes both simultaneously. In the introduction to her edited collection addressing the relationship between science fiction and world politics, Jutta Weldes underscores the deliberative potential intrinsic to science fiction. She writes, "Popular culture, in expressing, enacting, and producing discourses and their specific ideological effects, participates in meaning production, and thus in politics."[6] Whether one is a moviegoer, a professional media reviewer, or an academic, critical reflection provides an opportunity to expose and engage the "vast sense of 'possibilities' conveyed by science fiction as well as ... the 'arts,' sometimes arts of rhetoric, that help us navigate the possibilities."[7] In discerning and navigating the articulated possibilities, a person cooperates in rhetorical knowledge building by entering what Calvin O. Schrag refers to as a "community of investigators and interpreters" participating in "the dynamics of consent and disavowal, agreement and disagreement, acceptance and rejection."[8] Embracing the lively articulation and adjudication of social knowledge, knowledge that shapes human understanding and action in pragmatic and political ways, acknowledges the rhetorical foundation of everyday meaning-making and living. For Schrag, the reciprocal give-and-take between two friends, strangers on social media, or even between a director and audience member is best understood through the lens of Bakhtinian dialogics.[9]

Following Schrag's lead, the remainder of this chapter focuses on my contention that Mikhail Bakhtin's discursive dialogics provides an opportunity to investigate how science fiction texts, particularly *The Clone Wars*, call audience members to interpret and critique matters of political importance in the public square. I begin the chapter by examining the relationship between rhetoric, science fiction, and the dynamic interplay between text, critic, and audience. Starting with Kenneth Burke's classic call to read literature as equipment for living, I unpack how contemporary rhetorical scholars answer Burke's charge and suggest Bakhtinian dialogics may provide a new approach to thinking about popular culture. Next, I turn to the task of parsing out Bakhtinian dialogics proper and offer my reading of how dialogue and popular culture manifest in a communicative public square. Finally, I conclude the chapter by illustrating how science fiction texts, as a form of dialogic rhetoric, call audiences to acknowledge the communal responsibility of participating in publicly salient deliberations.

Science Fiction as Equipment for Living

My exploration of science fiction as rhetorical action begins with the accomplished rhetorical scholar Kenneth Burke. In his essay "Literature as Equipment for Living," Burke offers what he identifies as a "sociological criticism of literature" and explores how written works—from simple proverbs to book- length manuscripts—contribute to the way people navigate their everyday lives.[10] Burke begins by illustrating how proverbs provide advice or wisdom in relation to a commonplace situation. These short phrases, he suggests, are typically offered as a form of encouragement or admonishment and tend to function pedagogically; proverbs teach socially appropriate attitudes, values, and behaviors. When someone experiences some form of psychological injury resulting from the death of a loved one or maybe a breakup with a romantic partner, she or he might receive cultural wisdom uttered via the phrase "Time heals all wounds." This short phrase instructs the recipient to keep plodding forward, that over the course of days, and weeks, and months, the pain will begin to recede. Having established the pedagogical function of these brief pearls of wisdom, Burke then asks whether all literature might be, in effect, "proverbs writ large."[11] Literary works, Burke asserts, present readers with culturally relevant lessons about how one should act when confronted with commonplace occurrences. From Greek mythology, to Shakespeare, to *Harry Potter*, literature invites a reader to understand her or his world, as well as past, present, and future actions within that world, through a specific epistemological lens. An individual who reads *The Hunger Games*, for example, finds herself subjected to a work "designed to organize and command the army of one's thoughts and images" in particular ways.[12] In the case of *The Hunger Games*, several "proverbs writ large" come to mind. One obvious lesson is the belief that "absolute power corrupts absolutely." The portrayals of the Capitol, the governing district whose people live decadent lives of extravagance while the peoples of the surrounding districts struggle with basic survival, reveal a corrupt system of government run by the malevolent president. As the victors of a great war, the government of the Capitol reveled in their newfound power and forced the remaining districts to pay tribute. Rather than attempt to rebuild a society for all, the government of the Capitol exploited all others so that a handful would benefit. For Burke, literature like *The Hunger Games* has sociological value in that the ideas and attitudes presented on the written page also point to a comparable social condition. When I was reading *The Hunger Games*, I couldn't help but draw parallels with arguments emerging from the Occupy Wall Street movement: 1 percent of the population enjoyed ridiculous wealth at the expense of the remaining 99 percent. Although Suzanne Collins could not have predicted the Occupy Wall Street at the time she wrote her trilogy, she did tap into a message of significant cultural resonance. The "absolute power corrupts absolutely" proverb is what Burke would refer to as a recurring "sociological category" that functions as a kind of equipment for living. Versions of the life lesson stand at the heart of such well known literary endeavors as *Macbeth*, *1984*, and *The Lord of the Rings*.[13] When presented with the same sociological category repeatedly, the critic's role is to examine how the particular proverb works to inform readers about the ins and outs of everyday life.

Taking up Burke's cause, Barry Brummett extends the idea of literature as equipment for living to include mediated texts like film and television. As Brummett points out, discourse—whether in the form of literature, television, film, or popular music—encourages individuals to "confront their lived situations, celebrate their triumph and encompass their tragedies."[14] Discourse, then, equips people to live their lives in that it often "articulates, explicitly or formally, the concerns, fears, and hopes of people" and offers a kind of solution to problematic "situations or experiences ... which people actually confront."[15] To illustrate his advancement of Burke's concept, Brummett provides two examples of mediated discourse as equipment for living. The first illustration examines what Brummett names the "xeroxing anecdote" and focuses on the evil aliens attempt to conquer the Earth by slowly replacing human inhabitants storyline found in the *Invasion of the Body Snatchers* novel (1955) and two films (1956 and 1978). Brummett argues the narrative presented in all three versions of *Invasion of the Body Snatchers* functions to help audiences make sense of anxiety producing changes like increased automation, the proliferation of conformist business culture, and Cold War talk of communist sleeper agents living next door. The common theme through all of these concerns is a profound cultural sense that the autonomous individual is no longer distinguishable from an automaton, a coworker, or even the person who lives down the block. Brummett's second illustration turns to haunted house films as a kind of "symbolic medicine" enabling audiences to "confront real life problems."[16] Identifying haunted house films as a mediated genre well suited for representing a culture's collective unease and apprehension, particularly those misgivings associated with issues of time and space, Brummett writes:

> The troubling situation for which haunted house films seem to be prescribed is a situation in which the received order of time and space collapses. The collision in time and space of incompatible duties, social spheres, cultural allegiances, etc., is the real life exigency suffered by audiences who turn to this type of film. Examples of such uncomfortable simulations might include: the urban family whose child is being bused into suburban space to go to school; the American worker who sees his or her job threatened by an immigrant from a radically different cultural and geographic space; the inner city neighborhood undergoing gentrification; the retiree whose values from time past are threatened by values founded in the present; the ahistorical young person who finds himself or herself enmeshed in the hallowed traditions of an old university or well-established business, etc.[17]

Haunted house films, posits Brummett, can have cultural resonance with a wide variety of audience members, from several different segments of society, who still share a commonality in the form of their anxieties related to confusions of time and space. For example, haunted house films frequently feature a ghostly entity from the past manifesting in the present and often include a historical back story (e.g., a house is built on a Native American burial ground or the house was a site of a horrific murder committed years ago) contributing to the sense that present and past events are simultaneously intertwined and at odds. Similarly, the genre also tends to feature main characters out of their spatial element (e.g., city folk stranded in a remote cabin, manor, or hotel) and ghosts who ignore physical barriers and shift between spatial dimensions with ease. According to Brummett, these elements of haunted house films represent the tensions experienced by movie goers in their day to day lives. Popular culture texts, then, capture some of the social problematics resonating within the respective era and, through the resolutions of the narratives, "audiences are armed to accept, reject, or attempt to change the real course of events depicted in the media."[18]

Since Brummett's explication of electric literature as equipment for living, several other rhetorical scholars have applied the idea to mediated texts. For example, Brian Ott and Beth Bonnstetter interrogate *Spaceballs* as a film preparing audiences to negotiate the complexities of postmodernity. Describing the film's central narrative structure as "parodic tourism," a narrative form "which invites viewers to actively participate in structured intertextual allusions," the authors suggest *Spaceballs* provides viewers with the means by which to cope with the disconcerting and rapid changes associated with the cultural shift from modernity to postmodernity.[19] One of the most compelling dimensions of their rhetorical criticism is the argument for rethinking audiences as collaborative participants in the interpretive process. While Ott and Bonnstetter acknowledge the interdependent relationship between the readers and authors of such modern texts as newspapers and early television, they also point out the assumed passiveness of audiences. A reader or viewer must be present if a communicated message is to be received, of course, but many of these early mediated forms situated viewers as participants in a one way conversation. The continual intersubjective references comprising a parody like *Spaceballs*, a film which makes repeated allusions to well known science fiction texts, emphasizes the active role of audiences in the negotiation of meaning. Mel Brooks positioned audiences as dynamic participants in the telling of his space bound narrative; Brooks expected his audience to possess knowledge of prior science fictions. Without the audience's ability to connect *Spaceballs* to the specific science fiction texts being parodied, as well as make connections with broader cultural perceptions, an important aspect of the film is lost. And just as characters within *Spaceballs* disrupt the unfolding narrative—Ott and Bonnstetter suggest Dark Helmet "alters the direction, experience, and outcome" of the plot—audiences may also choose to accept, reject, or reconceptualize the presented textual symbols as well as the presented equipment for living.[20]

Another compelling idea emerging from Ott and Bonnstetter's manuscript is their emphasis on the pedagogical workings of both popular culture and the rhetorical critique of cultural texts. The popular culture as equipment for living approach situates the interactions between text and audience as kind of teacher/student relationship. The text, in the position of teacher, educates the student in how she or he should respond to social problems encountered in the warp and woof of everyday life. As John Seabrock revealed in a January 6, 1997, essay appearing in *The New Yorker*, George Lucas shares this understanding of movie-going as cultural pedagogy. Addressing the lasting impact of *Star Wars* Lucas explained:

> I wanted it to be a traditional moral study, to have some sort of palpable precepts in it that children could understand. There is always a lesson to be learned. Where do these lessons come from? Traditionally, we get them from church, the family, art, and in the modern world we get them from media— from movies.... Everyone teaches in every work of art. In almost everything you do, you teach, whether you are aware of it or not. Some people aren't aware of what they are teaching. They should be wiser. Everybody teaches all the time.

Important to note in Lucas's understanding of popular culture is the relationship between art and audience. As his quote suggests, popular culture imparts specific lessons to viewers. Also implicated in his quote, however, is the role of individual audience members as teachers. If everyone teaches, as Lucas articulates, then each person has a responsibility to decide which lessons to apply in her or his life and also which lessons to teach others. Unlike students studying mathematical or geometric proofs—subjects which tend to have concrete "right" and "wrong" answers—the lessons taught by popular culture are often more subjective. As such, the popular culture as equipment for living approach presumes an active viewer possessing the agency to interpret, and judge, a lesson's veracity.

The interactions between a popular culture critic and people who encounter a critique take on a similar association. Acting as a pedagogical intermediary, a critic's analysis of a particular text "teaches citizens to use media in ways that can enrich their lives and make them more meaningful."[21] When a critic reads the speculative elements of a science fiction text, she participates in a rhetorical process of constituting both the problems faced by individuals within a culture as well as potential solutions. Viewers who find the premise regarding the suggested problem compelling might also utilize the resolutions offered to make sense of their respective lives. Richard Brody's May 4, 2012, blog post on *The New Yorker* online is an excellent illustration of this point. In his piece, Brody asks readers to interpret the superheroic exploits of Captain America, Iron Man, Thor, Hulk, Black Widow, and Hawkeye—*The Avengers*—as a "post–9/11 revenge fantasy that takes place against the backdrop of unpopular foreign wars." Unable to go back and avert the horror, rage, and sadness resulting from the 9/11 terrorist attacks, *The Avengers* offers a way for U.S. American filmgoers to address their sense of helplessness and frustration almost eleven years after the event. As Brody points out in the closing lines of his piece, the only way to save the inhabitants of a New York City under assault by aliens, as well as resolve the continuing post–9/11 anxieties experienced by viewers, is to remain faithful to cultural gods: technology, patriotism, and the righteous indignation of the American people.

Even more salient for this project is a macro interpretation of the entire *Star Wars* theatrical saga posted to the Yahoo! Contributor Network. Dated February 9, 2012, nearly seven years after the release of *Revenge of the Sith*, Timothy Sexton's "Why the 'Star Wars' Prequels Are Better Than the Original Trilogy" compares and contrasts the political themes resonating through both the original trilogy and the subsequent prequel trilogy. Throughout his piece, Sexton argues that while the conflict in the original trilogy (Rebel Alliance verses the Galactic Empire) offered a "simplistic moral perspective" reflective of audiences' understandings of the Cold War (America versus the Evil Empire), the prequel trilogy offered a far more nuanced political dissertation. The prequels, he contends, make a concerted effort to illustrate the dangers of a representative democracy driven by fear, challenged by inadequate leadership, and shaken by unexpected political events. Drawing a parallel between the films and the Bush administration, Sexton invites readers to reconsider the prequels as a political depiction of how citizens willingly relinquish their freedoms (e.g., the Patriot Act) and weaken the democratic state.

Like the popular critics of mainstream media, academic critics fulfill a similar pedagogical role. Academic critics publish their observations in various professional publications and call on their colleagues to read texts in particular ways who, in turn, pass these readings on to other colleagues or students. Michelle J. Kinnucan makes the pedagogical role of academics clear in her essay titled "Pedagogy of (the) Force: The Myth of Redemptive Violence." Kinnucan's essay examines what she refers to as "the most powerful, yet least acknowledged, mythological archetype in the saga": the belief that violence, particularly in the form of war, has a liberating or redemptive function.[22] Drawing on the works of Walter Wink and Roland Barthes, she argues that *Star Wars* contributes to the normalization of warfare, and violence in general, as a means by which human beings resolved international, and personal, disagreements. Focused on Anakin Skywalker's journey from slave, to Jedi Knight, to Dark Lord of the Sith, to redeemed Jedi Knight (his redemption carries a heavy price, obviously), Kinnucan illustrates how violent acts committed in the name of good carry the day in every film of the trilogy and push Anakin's narrative toward an inevitable conclusion. She summarizes his violent character arc as follows:

Violence redeems in *Star Wars*. Violence rescues young Anakin from slavery; it frees Luke from farm life and family obligations; it reclaims the older Anakin/Vader from the Force's Dark Side; and, finally, it liberates the galaxy from Palpatine and his evil Empire."[23]

The result, she contends, is a contemporary rendition of the monomyth that emphasizes violence as desirable and necessary while simultaneously dismissing nonviolence.

Similar to Kinnucan's examination of redemptive violence, Joshua Atkinson and Bernadette Calafell encourage a new reading of *Star Wars* films by exploring the six film narrative arc of Anakin Skywalker's rise, and fall, as Darth Vader. The authors argue that Anakin's character trajectory contributes to a cultural acceptance of hegemonic masculinity that "creates spaces of permissiveness for physical violence, harassment, and various forms of discrimination."[24] The closing line of their rumination emphasizes the prevalence of the pedagogical approach to popular culture as they observe films like the two *Star Wars* trilogies teach individuals to naturalize and internalize characteristics associated with gendered identities.

As someone engrossed by the study of rhetorical practices, I find the idea of popular culture as equipment for living an attractive proposition. Authors and artists—immersed in the same cultural landscape as their audience members—produce novels, television programs, and films depicting social realities and making suggestions on appropriate and inappropriate responses to particular real-life plot complications. At the same time, however, I still see the pedagogical conceptualization of popular culture production, consumption, and critique—particularly from a rhetorical perspective—as an incomplete explanation of the relationship between author, text, and audience. Despite Ott and Bonnstetter's convincing claim that films like *Spaceballs* offer a crash course in Postmodern Agency 101, I am still curious as to how a viewer acting as adjudicator emerges as an agentic self. Granted, the individual viewer possesses far more agency than an approach to rhetorical interaction which situates audience members as automatons waiting to be programmed. Still, the popular culture as a contemporary equipment for living approach implicates a relationship between author, text, and audience reminiscent of the old sender/receiver models of rhetoric; a rhetor puts forth her or his understanding of social problematics, as well as the appropriate responses to enact, and calls on the audience to accept or reject a mediated life lesson. From this view, the onus is almost entirely on the ideas formulated by the rhetor and her or his efforts to relate those efforts to a particular audience. An audience member is reduced to someone who chooses to incorporate the substance of the lesson into her life or she doesn't. If a function of rhetoric is the negotiation of public matters of consequence, does an understanding of popular culture as equipment for living go far enough in positioning audiences as active members of a deliberative community? Brian Ott and Carl Burgchardt share similar concerns in their call for a critical rhetorical pedagogy.

Throughout the history of rhetorical studies, scholars have turned their attention to the critical reading of texts in an effort to reveal the hidden influences of human communication and shed light on how those texts contribute to the reification or transformation of social problems and inequities. The hidden meanings of the text revealed, the critic shares her or his reading with other scholars, students, and a broader public audience. This familiar approach to engaging, reading, and teaching texts, argue Brian Ott and Carl Burgchardt, is flawed. At the heart of their critique is an assumption that most texts, readings, and classroom discussions are the pedagogical equivalent of a political polemic. In other words, texts, critiques, and discussions thereof tend to offer a limited, if not monologic, understanding of ourselves, others, and the world around us. As such, Ott and Burgchardt draw on the works of Mikhail Bakhtin and argue for adoption of a critical rhetorical pedagogy wherein dialogic texts, dialogic criticism, and dialogic classroom discussions "foster agentive citizenship and promote political alternatives."[25]

While they focus much of their commentary on college students as audience, I want to extend their assertions to include the relationship between text, critics (popular and academic), and casual viewers/readers. If one of the primary functions of rhetoric is the negotiation of matters of public importance and consequence, does a fixed reading that presumes a passive audience "stimulate critical thinking, foster political engagement, and promote civic involvement"?[26] How might the relationship between texts, critics, and audiences be reconceptualized so that all three emerge as salient voices in the negotiation of public affairs? How might the popular cultural as equipment for living perspective be transformed to implicate the dynamic interplay occurring between all three elements? Unlike Ott and Burgchardt, who suggest most texts are monologic, I want to make the argument that most texts, although frequently lacking the internal multiplicity of voices described by Bakhtin, can be considered active voices in broader cultural dialogues. My argument, then, moves the focus away from the role of the individual text and embraces a concept of cultural dialogism that highlights texts in conversation with other texts. Before turning my attention to the possibility of a rhetorical dialogism, however, a further explication of Bakhtian dialogics is in order.

Out of the Classroom and Into the Public Square

Any discussion of Bakhtinian dialogics begins with an understanding of the utterance. Bakhtin, as a critic of Sassurean structuralism, makes clear throughout his work that the utterance should not be confused with the formal mechanics inherent in a written sentence, a conversation, and the subsequent linguistic system of which these are a part. Although many, but not all, utterances include sentences, the utterance—which "may be as short as a grunt and as long as *War and Peace*"—is a communicative interaction constituted within the confluence of history, culture, and everyday life.[27] Rather than a formal unit of language, the utterance is more accurately conceptualized as a communicative exchange occurring between uniquely positioned and autonomously acting participants. As he makes clear in his discussion of the novel as literary form, such discursive exchanges display an inherent dialogic quality. What Bakhtin appears to be arguing here is that all human communication responds to previous utterances and, as such, is situated as part of a responsive, never-ending interaction made manifest in the present moment. At the same time, any and all discourse is also oriented toward a particular audience and potential response. With one eye on past utterances and the other on utterances yet to come, a communicator reveals her predilections through the discursive choices she makes in the present.

Bakhtin claims that this "inter-orientation" of discourse is inescapable: all utterances, from individual words to extensive manifestos, are firmly situated within heterglossic dialogue.[28] Describing heteroglossia as the continual discursive clash between hegemonic and counterhegemonic perceptions, institutions, ideologies, and cultural conventions implicated at all levels of linguistic exchange, meaning emerges amidst "a background made up of contradictory opinions, points of view and value judgments."[29] He writes:

> Thus at any given moment of its historical existence, language is heterglot from top to bottom: it represents the co-existence of socio-ideological contradictions between the present and the past, between differing epochs of the past, between different socio-ideological groups in the present, between tendencies, schools, circles and so forth, all given bodily form. These "languages" of heteroglossia intersect each other in a variety of ways, forming new socially typifying "languages."[30]

These tendencies towards solidarity and incongruity, always present in all forms of discourse, call the possibility of fixed meaning into question and suggest a collaborative meaning imbricated with polysemy, malleability, and ephemerality. When people interact discursively, they cannot help but negotiate a multitude of sometimes divergent and sometimes convergent individual, historical, and cultural perceptions as they work toward mutual understanding. As an active, dynamic, and interpretive accomplishing, meaning arises from the intersection of heteroglossic discourses and allows individuals to achieve a sense of linguistic consistency but not constancy. The dynamic interplay of each discursive encounter stands as a unique moment of dialogic human communication; the conversation between two friends at a coffee house or the indirect exchange occurring between a film-maker and audience marks an unrepeatable occasion of dialogic discernment.

Keeping this in mind, Bakhtin describes the traditional sender/receiver, speaker/listener, or author/audience communication models as deeply flawed in that these conceptualizations appear to grant a great deal of agency to the sender but little to the receiver. Rejecting the passivity of the listener, Bakhtin highlights "an actively responsive understanding" that requires full collaborative attention and participation of all those involved in a discursive exchange.[31] While a person might initiate a line of thought in a particular context, she does not expect her interlocutor(s) to sit idly and accept whatever ideas, worldviews, and opinions are articulated. The initiator anticipates, and expects, a response. When a listener encounters an utterance, she or he engages it, mulls it over, analyzes it, and "either agrees or disagrees with it (completely or partially), augments it, applies it, prepares for its execution, and so on."[32] The active scrutiny of an utterance, as well as the formulation and deployment of an immediate, or even delayed response, is the hallmark of responsive understanding:

> Of course, an utterance is not always followed immediately by an articulated response. An actively responsive understanding of what is heard (a command, for example) can be directly realized in action (the execution of an order or command that has been understood and accepted for execution), or it can remain, for the time being, a silent responsive understanding (certain speech genres are intended exclusively for this kind of responsive understanding, for example, lyrical genres), but this is, so to speak, responsive understanding with a delayed reaction. Sooner or later what is heard and actively understood will find its response in the subsequent speech or behavior of the listener.[33]

Bakhtin's insistence that a listener will respond transforms that individual from one toward whom an utterance is directed to one who directs an utterance toward others. Put simply, "the listener becomes the speaker."[34] Thus, in the coordinated give and take of human communication the boundary between sender/receiver, author/audience, creator/viewer becomes blurred; every author is an audience member and every audience member is an author. Understanding, for Bakhtin, manifests in the ongoing call and response integral to every dialogic encounter.

Having detoured into a general discussion of dialogics, I want to refocus attention on Bakhtin's treatment of popular culture. Although he modeled his conception of discursive dialogics on the routine face-to-face exchanges of everyday life—interactions in the workplace, discussions in the classroom, conversations in the home—Bakhtin was interested, primarily, with the dialogism of artistic discourse. While Bakhtin identifies the novel as the artistic form most capable of capturing the complex, dialogic contentiousness of social heteroglossia, an assertion Kay Halasek attributes to the pervasive cultural, historical, and political influences at work within the fledgling Soviet Union, contemporary scholars apply his conceptions to a wide array of popular culture texts.[35] In the early twenty-first century, the narrated realities present in Bakhtin's novel materialize in such wide ranging popular culture texts as film, television, music, public art installations, and social media. Contemporary popular culture, suggests Hirschkop, is awash with narrative "templates for a life worth living," templates that encourage individuals to "savour and enjoy their lives 'aesthetically.'"[36] Had Bakhtin written in the early part of the twenty-first century, I would like to think he would see dialogism at work in an almost limitless number of popular culture texts. Just as the novel calls readers to participate in the constitution of their social world, contemporary forms of popular culture invite individuals "to engage with other aspects of social experience and other members of the interpretive community, generating a network of 'creative perception' and dialogic participation."[37]

The author, argues Bakhtin, stands in a position unique among writers, speakers, and creators as he or she simultaneously resides within a particular historical and cultural context and yet also stands as "omnipresent witness" to the ideologies, social mores, and worldviews intimated within a narrative.[38] When inhabiting an authorial role, an individual is both part of, and apart from, his parent culture. Likewise, he is part of the work he creates yet oddly apart from that same work; the author cannot inhabit the world that springs forth from his own imagination. The author constructs a represented world populated by multiple characters who display a rich polyvocality resonant with the social world at large. Although the author facilitates an ongoing dialogue between the broader culture and the novel's represented culture, his own voice "remains outside the world he has represented in his work."[39]

Despite the inability to inhabit the worlds and voices springing forth from her imagination, the author's creative efforts do impact the social world in which she lives. Conversely, the social world surrounds the author and cannot help but seep into the contours of a creative work. As Bakhtin remarks,

> The work and the world represented in it enter the real world and enrich it, and the real world enters the work and its world as part of the process of its creation, as well as part of its subsequent life, in a continual renewing of the work through the creative perception of listeners and readers.[40]

The dialogic give and take between represented world and real world, between author and listener, underscores the polysemy at work within inter-oriented discourse and illustrates how a particular text takes on multiple meanings and, through the responsivity of audiences, weaves its way into broader cultural conversations. A nineteenth-century novel, for example, takes on new meanings as the text is encountered by twenty-first-century readers immersed in their particular moment of historical, cultural, and personal understanding. The same holds true for contemporary popular culture texts. While one person might interpret the original *Star Wars* film as both culturally and politically conservative, connecting the film's black and white morality to the "renewed American conservatism" of the early 1980s, another might perceive the underdog story of ragtag rebels standing against the immense might of a military superpower as ideologically liberal.[41] Others, like several authors in Douglas Brode and Leah Deyneka's edited collection exploring the cultural resonance of the *Star Wars* franchise, associate the films with such diverse genres as science fiction, the Western, and fairy tales.[42] Depending on one's interpretation, the represented world of *Star Wars* enters the responsive understanding of viewers and makes its way into discussions of politics, fundamental cultural values, and the life lessons of children. As Martin Flanagan points out in his exploration of dialogism and film, whether one is reading a book, listening to music, or watching a movie "we commune with various speaking agents behind the textual utterance."[43]

Also important to note is how the discursive inter-orientation insinuates a creative, dialogic relationship between artistic texts; previous texts "enrich" the real world and, as a result, contribute to the creative emergence of new texts. Building on Bakhtin's work, Julia Kristeva highlights this point when she writes, "Any text is constructed as a mosaic of quotations; any text is the absorption and transformation of another."[44] An example of this intertextuality, and one most relevant for this current project, is Anne Lancashire's examination of *The Phantom Menace* as part of a broader "narrative, mythological, and metaphoric whole."[45] In her piece, Lancashire calls attention to the fact that the first film of the *Star Wars* prequel trilogy is intended to be understood as part of a six film narrative arc. Pointing out numerous parallels in terms of narrative structure, characterizations, and visual symbols, she argues the film calls on viewers to recognize "intertextual patternings" between *The Phantom Menace* and the films of the original trilogy.[46] In doing so, Lancashire makes explicit the intersubjective dialogue occurring between texts as well as between viewers of the texts. Recognizing the responsive understanding at work, she argues, results in a more meaningful filmic experience. Brooker makes a similar argument regarding the mediated constitution of Batman. Giving Bakhtin's dialogism a direct nod, Brooker suggests texts in conversation with other texts are an important, and often overlooked, element of responsive understanding. Batman's meaning and cultural significance does not spring forth from a single text but emerges from a mediated melange. From Batman's first appearance in 1939 to Christopher Nolan's theatrical trilogy the cultural understanding of the Dark Knight arises from the intersection of tens of thousands of texts. Batman is accomplished "between author and reader" and "in the relationship between the text and other texts."[47] Jeffrey Bussolin's observations regarding the constitutive intertextuality of numerous Joss Whedon projects parallel those of Lanchashire and Brooker. Describing constitutive intertextuality as structural, visual, and linguistic dialogue occurring between mediated texts, Bussolini illustrates how *Buffy the Vampire Slayer*, *Angel*, and *Firefly* made significant contributions to the creation, production, and interpretation of such diverse television programs as *Deadwood*, *Eureka*, and *Torchwood*.[48]

These conversations between texts, coupled with the interactions between author/creator, text, and audience, suggest an underlying intertextuality permeating every moment of responsive understanding. Bakhtin describes this space where interlocutors, texts, and culture come together in responsive understanding as the public square. Patterned after the medieval public square, a space that served numerous public functions (e.g., marketplace, festival grounds, political assembly), Bakhtin's public square is a heteroglossic discursive space where the official and vernacular ideologies, viewpoints, lifestyles, and politics of a stratified society mix and mingle, collide and divide, converge and diverge. Unlike Habermas' conception of the public sphere, Bakhtin's public square makes no pretense toward the idealization of rational deliberation. The public square is a messy place, populated by individuals and groups from various cultural segments who employ a variety of official and vernacular communicative forms—face-to-face conversations, public speeches, social media, television, film, radio, novels, newspapers, magazines—to engage matters of communal importance and consequence. To be certain, the dialogic public square is not a space of equal participation and formalized debate where interlocutors square off with the intention of achieving victory or even consensus. As Hirschkop contends, "It's not that the conversation of the public square, now idolised, isn't composed of dialogues, it's just that it is valued not for the equal rights embodied within it, but for its quasi-Nietzschean 'liveliness,' it's earthiness and vulgarity, its imbrication with interests and struggles."[49] Already echoing with the official discourse of political speeches, congressional debates, media pundits, and corporate spokespersons, the public square is the discursive space where the vernacular voices of authors, artists and fans participate in creating a "connection between the interlocking plots of a nation-state, a class, a family, and an individual life."[50] Such a connection brings the Bakhtinian public square into a direct dialogue with rhetoric.

Rhetoric and the Dialogic Public Square

My turn to Bakhtin in an effort to reconceptualize the rhetoricalness of popular culture may, at first glance, seem like an odd choice. As I suggested in the introduction, Bakhtin decries rhetoric as a monologic affair consisting of individual players who wish to impart their particular truths on members of an audience. Monologism, suggests Bakhtin, "pretends to *possess a ready-made truth*, and it is also counterposed to the naive self-confidence of those people who think they know something, that is, who think they possess certain truths. Truth is not born nor is it to be found inside the head of an individual person, it is born *between people* collectively searching for truth, in the process of their dialogic interaction."[51] This emphasis on imparting one particular truth or another and the resulting clashes between the unyielding advocates of these truths implicates a communicative exchange wherein one person is declared a victor and all others are losers. He states, "In rhetoric there is the unconditionally innocent and the unconditionally guilty; there is complete victory and destruction of the opponent."[52] To further his indictment of rhetoric, Bakhtin also characterizes rhetorical practice as displaying an insidious, faux dialogue: it appears dialogic when it is not. In other words, rhetors frequently make use of the language of others—quoting another person, summarizing a particular policy position, or articulating a shared concern—in the course of their utterances. This proves problematic, maintains Bakhtin, when such double voicedness (rearticulating another's position) is employed by an individual pursuing a singular goal. A rhetor might incorporate the voices of other participants in a particular exchange (e.g., a debate over the legality of human reproductive cloning) but, in the final analysis, the political and cultural complexity of these voices is muted in service to the rhetor's every whim. Uprooted and transplanted from the salient discursive context, pseudo dialogue "is not fertilized by a deep-rooted connection with the forces of historical becoming that serve to stratify language, and therefore rhetorical genres are at best merely a distanced echo of this becoming, narrowed down to an individual polemic."[53] Polemic, adversarial, and focused on the personal whims of a rhetor, the rhetoric described in Bakhtin's writings is more about championing individual interests than deliberating the public good.

To some extent, Bakhtin's articulation of rhetoric is a fair assessment. Rhetoric, not unlike the power of the Force, can be used for nefarious or honorable ends. Murphy makes this clear in his assessment of Bakhtin's dislike for the communicative art: "Rhetoric is scary."[54] Bakhtin's apprehension regarding rhetoric is well founded: "Rhetoric crafts languages and voices; rhetoric demands answers; rhetoric noisely intervenes in human affairs."[55] An individual utilizing the art of rhetoric for personal gain may indeed articulate static, reified truths designed to persuade audiences to see the world in particular ways. In making his forceful assertions regarding rhetoric's tendency to manifest monologically, however, Bakhtin runs afoul of his own writings. As Kay Halasek writes, Bakhtin's insistence on depicting rhetoric as a communicative exchange focused on "creating a combative and confrontational relationship between itself and other discourses" illustrates a contradiction within his own works.[56] While Bakhtin criticizes rhetoric for its monologic orientation he also argues that no communicative exchange occurs without an interlocutor who participates in the dialogic formation of responsive understanding. And while I concede there are a great many rhetorical interactions where a self-absorbed individual crafts a text with little or no apparent regard for other voices, Bakhtin's work insinuates that a self-centered rhetor is still situated within the ebb and flow of historical, political, and cultural contexts. Attempting to draw parallels between the world of the face-to-face encounter and the artistic world of creative endeavors, Bakhtin makes clear that all utterances—a conversation, a novel, a television program—display a constitutive quality. Bakhtin centralizes the dialogic socialness of communicative exchanges when he describes discursive utterances as part of an ongoing language game located at the intersection of everything from formal linguistic structures to official/vernacular declarations to cultural norms, values, and expectations. He makes the collaborativeness of dialogism explicit when he states, "Discourse—in any of its forms, quotidian, rhetorical, scholarly—cannot fail to be oriented toward the 'already uttered,' the 'already known,' the 'common opinion' and so forth. The dialogic orientation of discourse is a phenomenon that is, of course, a property of *any* discourse. It is the natural orientation of any living discourse."[57] What emerges from Bakhtin's work, then, is a conflicted account of rhetoric. On the one hand Bakhtin describes all communicative encounters, including rhetorical interactions, as dialogic. On the other hand, he denounces rhetoric as a monologic enterprise. In an attempt to sort through this apparent contradiction, I turn to James P. Zappen's working concerning Bakhtin, rhetoric, and dialogue.

While some rhetorical scholars point out the apparent contradiction in Bakhtin's work, James P. Zappen's approach to rehabilitating the relationship between rhetoric and dialogue hinges on what he suggests is a misreading of Bakhtin's position. Rather than interpreting his work as antithetical to rhetoric, Zappen situates Bakhtin's criticisms as a call to reimagine rhetoric as a dialogic practice infused with a "multiplicity of voices" and oriented toward the "testing and contesting and creating of ideas."[58] According to Zappen, Bakhtin's indictment of rhetorical practice is not directed as much toward rhetoric itself as it is toward the way both rhetors and rhetoricians (rhetorical critics) interpret the practice pragmatically and theoretically. Conceptualizing rhetoric as an isolated, instrumental means of moving an immediate audience dismisses the situatedness of all discourse and denies the collaborativeness that defines dialogism. Thomas B. Farrell makes a similar observation when he writes, "We misunderstand rhetoric if we assume that it begins and ends as merely directive or manipulative discourse."[59] Joining this chorus is the aforementioned Calvin Schrag who, like Zappen and Farrell, rejects a monologic understanding of rhetoric. Conversely, Schrag describes rhetoric as "a creative activity that displays discernment and insight" and characterizes rhetorical communication "as a collaborative and creative activity of deliberation and discourse against the backcloth of the common good of the *polis*."[60]

Linking Bakhtinian dialogics and rhetorical communication directly, Schrag offers an understanding of rhetoric grounded in the supposition that all human communication hinges on responsivity. When a rhetor engages in the act of invention, he references previously articulated meanings, understandings, and discernments; he collaborates with others, albeit indirectly, and incorporates those responsive understandings within the present rhetorical encounter. No matter the subject matter or rhetorical situation, a rhetor draws on previous utterances, anticipates future utterances, and orients his present utterance toward others. And these others, who cannot help but assume the position of rhetor themselves as they formulate a response (this response might be immediate or delayed), participate in these same dialogic acts. James Jasinski describes these responsive understandings as "the need to maintain discursive and deliberative space."[61] Put simply, the participants in a rhetorical performance work together "to make sense of the world inhabited by both."[62] In all the variations of rhetorical accomplishing, interlocutors direct their utterances toward one another and participate in the vigorous activity of self-constitution. As Schrag remarks,

> We converse and write in a variety of manners and modes. In the different involvements of our shared communal existence our words, spoken and written, lend themselves to elucidating, describing, explaining, contesting, critiquing, dissenting, agreeing, praising, consoling, admonishing—and a variety of combinations of each in colorful genres of mixed discourse. We script our lives in poetry and prose, in letters and electronic mail, in diaries and memoirs, in eulogies and orations, in sermons and scientific discourse.[63]

Building on Schrag's work, I would also add non-discourse forms of communication such as television, film, dance, music, and visual art. Schrag himself alludes to additional modes when he makes reference to "images" as part of the human communication repertoire.[64]

If one conceptualizes rhetoric as dialogic, a communicative practice simultaneously responding to previous utterances and anticipating future utterances, then even a political polemic is understood as part of an ongoing process of meaning-making. As self-serving as a particular utterance might be, the invention and declamation never occur within a vacuum; no matter how much a speaker, author, or filmmaker might wish it were so, a rhetorical utterance can never be disconnected from the surrounding historical, political, and cultural context. This shared sense of communal responsibility, which Schrag highlights in his reference to "the common good of the *polis*," distinguishes rhetoric from other communicative acts. Rhetorical communication is always about matters of public concern and, by definition, is directed toward "an understanding, accommodation, and modification of social practices."[65] Whether rhetoric takes the form of a congressional hearing on the potential dangers of human cloning, a presidential speech concerning military action in a foreign land, or a television program representing torture as an effective tool for intelligence gathering the utterance solicits audiences to acknowledge their communal responsibility and participate in relevant public deliberations. What values should the scientific community consider when conducting biogenetic research? When and how should a government use military force in the name of justice? To what ends should an intelligence apparatus go to protect citizens? In a broader sense, the rhetorical dialogue surrounding these questions contributes to important discussions concerning such salient public issues as reproductive rights, civil liberties, and definitions of citizenship.

In the spirit of Bakhtin's public square and dialogic rhetoric, the remainder of this project focuses on how science fiction texts (*The Clone Wars*, specifically) speak with a critical voice, and sometimes multiple voices, on such important political issues as human cloning, torture, and drone warfare. Often dismissed as melodramatic spectacle, the sometimes understated and sometimes forthright speculations, criticisms, and possibilities associated with the science fiction genre rarely engage matters of public interest directly. The thoughtful social commentary offered by a television program or film is not the same as offering testimony before a congressional sub-committee or "taking the floor on the House of Commons."[66] That does not mean, however, that science fiction texts do not contribute thoughtful perspectives on important social and political issues. Chris Pak's examination of the discursive interplay between representations of genetic engineering and ongoing, real-world deliberations about biogenetics, for example, illustrates how science fiction texts provide "metaphorical portals to ongoing debates."[67] Films like *Pacific Rim*, with its subtle denunciation of U.S. immigration policy (e.g., the use of a wall to protect citizens from "aliens"), or *Star Trek: Into the Darkness*, with its direct criticism of a state's legal right to assassinate citizens deemed enemy combatants, are not meant to be engaged directly by policy proponents or opponents. The questions posed by both films, however, do call on audience members to make connections between the political arguments of a represented world and the broader conversations reverberating throughout the public square. Indirectly, then, the speculative viewpoints of science fiction enter the public imagination and become part of the broader political conversation. As Flanagan remarks,

> Consumption of a filmic text, under any set of viewing conditions, gains us entrance into an interpretive community based around that text. Our "take," or reading, on the text is projected outwards into a discourse sustained by other members of that community. There are many outlets for such opinions with varying degrees of "official" stamp—review in magazines and newspapers, polls on websites, academic seminars, fan clubs, informal discussion with

friends and so on. Bakhtin would have it that once we have voiced our opinion on a text—once we have formulated our answer to it—that response becomes part of the discourse associated with the text, becomes on of many framing voices, contending, conflicting, clamouring to be heard.[68]

The important feature of this dialogic exchange is not whether a popular text contributes to an immediate resolution of a public controversy. Such resolutions rarely occur. Instead, the important feature of Bakhtin's dialogic public square is the continued existence of social and political tensions via the articulation of varying viewpoints. Filled with the simultaneously dissonant and harmonious sounds of contention, engagement, and deliberation, the public square resonates with a multitude of inter-oriented voices engrossed in responsive understanding.

In the chapters that follow, I make explicit the inter-oriented voices of the dialogic public square and illustrate how the imagined worlds, characters, and plots of *Star Wars: The Clone Wars* implicate U.S. American post–9/11 realities. Rather than making broad generalizations about the way *The Clone Wars* enters the public imaginary, I make direct connections between real-world rhetorical texts—congressional hearings, news editorials, presidential discourse, pamphlets, and human rights reports—and the perspectives and positions offered by the television series. Concentrating on the emergent themes developed by the creators of *The Clone Wars*, I delve into five politically-salient issues: human cloning, torture, Just War Theory, peace, and drone warfare. By putting the series into direct dialogue with other rhetorical texts, I illustrate how *The Clone Wars* emerges as "a link in a very complexly organized chain of other utterances."[69] Linked to ongoing discussions in the public square, the series presents a number of engaging questions for audience consideration. How do representations of clone troopers address some of the same public concerns articulated during congressional hearings on human cloning? Is Anakin Skywalker's propensity for violent interrogation analogous to Dick Cheney's warning that the U.S. might need to embrace the "dark side" of the war on terror? How might characters like Master Yoda offer a direct criticism of President Obama's justification of military action? Do Senator Padmé Amidala and Duchess Satine Kryze, with their calls for nonviolence and peaceful negotiation, reverberate with the sounds of former congressional representative and peace activist Jeanette Rankin? Like Rankin's efforts in the early to mid-twentieth century, do these two secondary characters in *The Clone Wars* narrative attempt to give voice to frequently silenced arguments of the early twenty-first century? How might the ubiquity of droids throughout the *Star Wars* universe mirror, or challenge, various human rights concerns pertaining to the United States' increased dependence on drone war-fare? In visiting this deeply developed segment of a galaxy far, far away and exploring these questions, I want to suggest that a rhetoric based in Bakhtin's dialogics might provide a new way of thinking about discourse, deliberation, and debate in the public square.

Two

Congress and the Clone Troopers

"We have arrived at that brave new world that seemed so distant in 1932 when Aldous Huxley wrote about human beings created in test tubes in what he called a hatchery."[1]—George W. Bush

"We're not droids. We're not programmed. You have to learn to make your own decisions."[2]—Captain Rex

At a crucial point during *Attack of the Clones*, the second film in the *Star Wars* prequel trilogy, Jedi Knight Obi-Wan Kenobi is surprised to discover a clone army purportedly commissioned by Jedi Master Sifo-Dyas years earlier. Welcomed by the Kaminoan cloners and treated to a grand tour of the cloning facility, Obi-Wan inspects the process by which 1.2 million clone units are in the process of being grown, trained, and prepared for delivery. Obi-Wan, as well as the audience members who travel with him, witnesses human clones in every stage of development: embryos in gestation tubes, adolescents receiving instruction in classrooms, and adults conducting combat drills. The cloners inform Obi-Wan:

> Clones can think creatively. You will find that they are immensely superior to droids. We take great pride in our combat education and training programs.... You'll find they are totally obedient, taking any order without question. We modified their genetic structure to make them less independent than the original host.

As the tour concludes, the camera pulls back to reveal a troubled Obi-Wan looking out over a massive hangar as fully armored and armed clones move in perfect military precision. This initial encounter with the clone troopers of the Grand Army of the Republic is a significant moment in the *Star Wars* mythos that sets not only the climax of *Attack of the Clones* into motion but also lays the groundwork for the decimation of the Jedi Order in *Revenge of the Sith*. The clones encountered by Obi-Wan Kenobi become the primary troops by which the Galactic Republic battles Count Dooku (a fallen Jedi) and the droid armies of the rebellious Confederacy of Independent Systems. These battles form the context for *The Clone Wars* television series.

While the clones appear largely in the background of the two prequel films, the clone troopers emerge as primary characters in the animated *Clone Wars* series. In fact, the theatrical clone troopers and the animated clone troopers seem like almost different characters completely. The clones of the two feature films lack individuality (in both appearance and behavior), obey orders with a curt nod or a "Yes, sir!" and maintain superficial relationships with their Jedi generals. The troopers of the animated series, on the other hand, possess a greater degree of individuality, discuss battle plans with other clones as well as their superior officers, and maintain what can only be described as friendships with their Jedi generals. And while *The Clones Wars* explores the galactic war waged in the years between *Attack of the Clones* and *Revenge of the Sith*, the television series provides a much more complex portrait of clone troopers in the *Star Wars* galaxy. These contradictory representations of clone troopers should come as no surprise as the extended screen time of a serialized television program allows the writers, directors, and animators of *The Clone Wars* to present a vast array of three dimensional characters moving through multiple, intertwined story arcs. A three episode story arc focusing on the attempts of Obi-Wan Kenobi, Anakin Skywalker, and Ahsoka Tano to free one of their Jedi colleagues from a military prison might be followed by a single episode featuring a squad of clone troopers protecting an isolated communications outpost. The clone troopers, characters relegated to the background in the *Star Wars* films, are often front and center in *The Clone Wars*. Indeed, several standalone episodes and story arcs focus on clone troopers as the primary protagonists.

Joining the ranks of such familiar science fiction texts as *Boys from Brazil*, *Old Man's War*, *Moon*, *Star Trek*, *Farscape*, and *Battlestar Galactica*, the depiction of cloning in *The Clone Wars* wrestles with the "metaphysical and ethical challenges" associated with "the prospect of cloning fully-grown human persons."[3] Cloning narratives, no matter the form, call on audiences to consider such questions as the possibility of individuality and uniqueness in the midst of a hegemonic community, the role of science in creating or prolonging human life, and the morality of manufacturing cloned individuals only to harvest their organs or send them into harm's way. The questions inspired by these popular texts, and frequently engaged directly by the characters represented within the texts, "animates the cultural imaginary to explore the meaning of the new biotechnologies in and for our lives and selves."[4] Some critics, like Sheryl Hamilton, go so far as to suggest that science fiction texts focused on cloning and biogenetics may be the primary way many members of the public square acquire the knowledge necessary to participate in cultural dialogues concerning biotechnologies.[5] Fictional accounts of biotechnology, coupled with the occasional round of news stories covering a biotechnical breakthrough, tend to focus attention on the philosophical implications rather than the science. As such, argues Hopkins, most people are far more prepared to discuss the ethical considerations of cloning than they are the actual scientific process involved.[6] It should come as no surprise, then, that political deliberations regarding cloning follow a similar pattern.

The Politics of Cloning

Throughout much of the twentieth century, cloning remained a familiar plot element consigned to the sphere of speculative fiction. All that changed in February 1997 when a team of Scottish scientists announced the successful birth of Dolly, a cloned sheep. Although an admittedly inexact and imperfect scientific method—Dolly was the 277th attempted clone—the cloning of Dolly moved what was once an impossible feat of fictional scientists to a plausible potentiality: the possibility of cloning human beings became a reality. Unaware of the scientific complexity involved with cloning a mammal, some people reacted with a cautious excitement as journalists speculated on the possibility of organ transplants, cures for disease, and transhumanism. "It's unbelievable," remarked Professor Lee Silver, a biologist at Princeton University. "They said it could never be done and now here it is, done before the year 2000."[7] Not everyone saw this event as a reason to celebrate human ingenuity and scientific achievement. Pundits, politicians, and the general public expressed extreme caution and outright revulsion toward what they viewed as the next logical step in cloning research: human cloning. On February 23, a day after the Dolly announcement, *Los Angeles Times* medical writer Thomas H. Maugh II described the revelation as "fraught with moral ambiguities" and "likely to spark an intense debate about the ethics of genetic engineering research in humans." As the content of Maugh's piece illustrates, media sources overlooked the scientific significance of the breakthrough (if the process was discussed at all), and turned immediately to the moral and ethical implications of cloning technologies.[8]

Before turning to an examination of the congressional debates, a quick science lesson is in order. According to the Genetics and Public Policy Center of Johns Hopkins University, cloning technologies cluster around two distinct procedures: (1) reproductive cloning, or the process of creating a genetically identical embryo which is then implanted and gestated within a uterus and (2) therapeutic cloning, the duplication of an embryo for the purpose of harvesting stem cells. While reproductive cloning results in an identical copy of the genetic donor, like Dolly, therapeutic cloning duplicates an embryo with the intention of coaxing stem cells to adopt the properties of a particular kind of cell that might then be used to treat disease. Reproductive cloning produces a genetic twin; therapeutic cloning produces genetically twinned cells and tissue.[9] As *The Clone Wars* presents little commentary on the issue of therapeutic cloning, the contents of this chapter focus on reproductive cloning.

As Maugh predicted, an intense congressional debate ensued over the ethics and uses of cloning technologies. The debates, occurring in two major waves over the course of six years (1997–2003), struggled to come to terms with the new technology as well as the possibility of governmental controls over said technology. The first wave of congressional debate emerged soon after the Dolly announcement. Ten days after the news broke, President Clinton prohibited the use of federal funds for scientific research pertaining to human cloning, encouraged the private sector to declare a moratorium on similar work, and tasked the National Bioethics Advisory Commission with investigating the political, legal, and social ramifications of the process. Acknowledging the potential boon to genetics research and medical treatments, as well as the potential ethical issues involved, Clinton called on the country to evaluate cloning technologies with "caution but also with a conscience" and to consider "the concerns of faith and family and philosophy and values, not merely of science alone."[10] Within six months the NBAC recommended federal legislation banning public or private attempts to clone a human child and also concluded that "the cloning of human DNA sequences and cell lines" (therapeutic cloning) should continue unabated.[11] Congress did not see the issue in the same light and, as a result of the pro-life advocates who demanded a ban on both reproductive and therapeutic cloning, the Cloning Prohibition Act of 1997 was defeated.

For the next several years numerous attempts to revive some form of cloning prohibition surfaced but, despite a unanimous rejection of human reproductive cloning, ideological arguments about the ethics of therapeutic cloning doomed proposed legislation. Shelved by Congress, the cloning debate dropped out of the public eye temporarily. The ethical challenges presented by cloning technologies resurfaced as a matter of public consequence when, over the course of fourteen months (September 2000 to November 2001), several announcements garnered the attention of the news media and the scientific community.

September 2000: Brigitte Boisellier, science director for project Clonaid, revealed plans to impregnate five surrogate mothers with cloned embryos. While the seriousness of the science behind Clonaid's interest in cloning was always in question—Clonaid is the company associated with the Raelianism, a movement that believes life on Earth was engineered by extraterrestrials—the publicness of the announcement, as well as the sensational media coverage, brought the issue of cloning back into the public eye.

January 2001: Fertility specialists Pano Zavos and Severino Antinori announced their intention to clone a human baby within a two year period.[12]

July 2001: Advanced Cell Technology, a respected biotechnology company, acknowledged efforts to clone human cells for therapeutic purposes; on November 26, 2001, the *New York Times* reported ACT had achieved its goal.

On August 9, 2001, President George W. Bush responded to the various announcements and echoed President Clinton's concerns regarding the rapid advances in biotechnology. President Bush stated, "As the genius of science extends the horizons of what we can do, we increasingly confront complex questions about what we should do. We have arrived at that brave new world that seemed so distant in 1932 when Aldous Huxley wrote about human beings created in test tubes in what he called a hatchery."[13] Unlike President Clinton, however, President Bush articulated a nuanced position regarding the use of federal funds for what he termed "research cloning" (therapeutic cloning). Under Bush's order, research involving previously developed stem cell lines (in other words, stem cells derived from previous research cloning) would be eligible for federal funds; research involving the cloning of new stem cell lines would be prohibited. Later that same year (November 28, 2001), Bush formed the President's Council on Bioethics and tasked the council with investigating the ethical and social issues surrounding therapeutic cloning and stem cell research. On April 10, 2002, President Bush voiced his support for congressional legislation banning any and all forms of human cloning, reproductive, therapeutic, or otherwise. Although legislators answered the president's call for action, the second round of congressional deliberations also broke down as a result of pro-life and pro-choice arguments concerning therapeutic cloning. A formal bill never received bilateral support and, to this day, human cloning in the United States is not prohibited by federal law.

Despite the failure to produce a piece of legislation banning reproductive human cloning, the congressional debates did challenge lawmakers, as Senator Harkin suggested, to "ask how human cloning research is going to affect our Nation."[14] Other legislators situated congressional deliberations in the broader context of human existential philosophy as they asked how cloning might impact humanity's understanding of the meaning of life itself.[15] Whether the debate was focused on national implications or implications relevant to a broader view of humanity, most representatives seemed to agree that human reproductive cloning was one of the "most important scientific and ethical issues of the twenty-first century."[16] And even though consensus was never reached on legislative action, Congress remained unified in its opposition to reproductive cloning and expressed its opposition in terms of recurring issues: individuality, the commodification of humanity, eugenics, and family. Given that a clone is a genetic duplicate of another person, the first of these concerns—questions of individuality and self-determination—is the most obvious. The National Bioethics Advisory Commission's report on human cloning, a report frequently cited in the early years of congressional debates, asked: "Is there a moral or human right to a unique identity, and if so would it be violated by this manner of human cloning?"[17] Representative DeMint emphasized the new philosophical and ethical challenges implicated by the possibility of human cloning when he stated, "Our fingerprints are like snowflakes—there is not, nor has there ever been, an exact replica of another human being."[18] This prospect of attempting to duplicate the human fingerprint or snowflake of self-identity, argued Senator Bond, "threatens human dignity, of what it means to be a unique individual."[19] Representative Greenwood went so far as to draw on religious tradition when he described every naturally born human as a unique creation of God and described clones, an artificially created human, as "replicates, the human equivalent of an epilogue."[20]

While much of the legislative dialogue addressed the individuality of the person being cloned, participants in the conversation also raised several questions regarding the individuality and self-determination of clones. To what extent would a clone be given the opportunity to develop her or his own sense of individuality, uniqueness, and autonomy? As a duplicate of another person, would a clone be given the opportunity to explore her own identity or would she be expected to adopt the character traits and behavioral nuances of the original? As several legislators and witnesses in congressional hearings suggested, one can easily imagine the anxiety inducing challenges faced by a clone created as a replacement for a dead child. Nigel M. De S. Cameron, professor of theology and culture at Trinity University, made this point explicit during his testimony at a Congressional hearing: "Think of a child growing up, wondering every time mom and dad look at the child, am I myself, or am I here as a copy of my dead sibling?"[21] Could parents, even with the best of intentions, allow a cloned child to develop her own identity and avoid making subtle comparisons with the original child? Could such comparisons influence the way a parent acts with a cloned child and, thus, put subtle pressures on the identity of that child? Arthur Caplan, professor and director of the Center for Bioethics at the University of Pennsylvania, remarked during his March 28, 2001, congressional testimony, "whether or not you are the same as the person who cloned you, many will treat you that way."[22] To complicate matters further, congressional deliberation brought to light another important question concerning individuality: does a society committed to protecting life, liberty, and the pursuit of happiness for its constitutive members, have a responsibility to "also respect the individual's right to self-determination"?[23] If scientists cloned a person with a brilliant mind, exceptional physical fortitude, or superlative artistic skill, would the clone be manipulated psychologically, or maybe even coerced physically, to excel as an engineer, a soldier, or poet? Even if the cloned individual was allowed to escape the specter of his original, people would "compare his doings in life with those of his alter ego, especially if he is a clone of someone gifted or famous."[24]

The second oft-treated concern in the human cloning debate revolved around the commodification of the human body and life itself. Several dialogue participants questioned whether a cloned individual might receive treatment different than a child conceived naturally; would people be more likely to exploit a manufactured person than one born and raised in a traditional biological sense? Much of the debate surrounding this issue addressed the idea of cloning individuals for medical purposes. How does a society negotiate the complex moral quandaries that arise when duplicating an individual to serve as a living and breathing "spare parts" repository?[25] What about the married couple who decide to store a cloned embryo "as a replacement in case the first child dies"?[26] As Representative Greenwood asked, would the fact that one child might be produced naturally and the other artificially result in distinguishing the two processes wherein one is considered "creation and the other mere construction"?[27] Drawing a distinction between "creation" and "construction" implicates a potential value judgment: one child might be treated as an autonomous person while the other might be exploited and objectified as a manufactured commodity. The report from President Clinton's National Bioethics Advisory Commission made this point clearly and concisely. The report stated, "to objectify a person is to act towards the person without regard for his or her own desires or well-being, as a thing to be valued according to externally imposed standards, and to control the person rather than to engage her or him in a mutually respectful relationship. Objectification, quite simply, is treating the child as an object—a creature less deserving of respect for his or her moral agency."[28] In essence, most of the participants in the dialogue adhered to the notion that a culture allowing reproductive human cloning runs the risk of exploiting these manufactured individuals; the mere potential for creating a class of disposable humans is enough to justify a full ban. "It does not take a fan of science-fiction," commented Representative Tiahrt, "to imagine the scenarios that would ensue from legalized cloning—headless humans used as organ farms, malformed humans killed because they were viewed as an experiment not a person, gene selection to create a supposed inferior species to become slaves, societal values used to create a supposed superior species."[29] Senator Frist summarized the position of most legislators when he said, "Cloning should be strictly prohibited to prevent the commoditization and exploitation of human life."[30]

Closely related to the cloning as commodification concern was the troubling prospect that cloning technologies "could lead to a new eugenics movement" and "the establishment of scientific categories and superior and inferior people."[31] Unlike the commodification argument, an argument which cautioned clones might be singled out as disposable, second class people, the eugenics argument warned non-genetically-modified individuals might be the people at risk of being pronounced inferior. As Stuart Newman, professor of cell biology and anatomy at New York Medical College, testified to the House of Representatives, the field of eugenics focuses on "defining humans as genetically superior or inferior" as well as researching ways to improve human genetic stock in such broad areas as resistance to disease, enhanced memory function, superior artistic ability, physical constitution, beauty, and longevity.[32] Several legislators cautioned that the search for an improved human, even when initiated with good intention, could prove detrimental. For Representative Musgrave the cloning of human life, as well as the genetic therapy associated with the practice, requires the reconceptualization of human life as an object to be improved, manipulated, and perfected. Such pursuits, argued Musgrave, diminish "all human life" and "render certain people desirable and others not."[33] Conjuring the spirits of World War II, Representative Pitts likened the genetic manipulation of cloned individuals to the horrific scientific programs of Nazi Germany: "The Nazis may in fact have been able to create a race of healthier and more capable Germans if they had been allowed to proceed, but eugenics and cloning are both wrong."[34]

The final major point of opposition related to traditional conceptions of family. A handful of congressional witnesses dismissed objections to human reproductive cloning as a threat to family structure and characterized the new relationships as "just another way of creating a family, just like in vitro fertilization."[35] Most of the debate participants, however, disagreed with this opinion and articulated apprehension toward rethinking familial relationships in the age of human reproductive cloning. Testifying before a Senate hearing Leon Kass, chair of the President's Council on Bioethics, cautioned that cloning as a reproductive technology would "enshrine and aggravate a profound and mischief-making misunderstanding" of the meaning and practice of family.[36] Representative Weldon expressed similar misgivings when he stated, "Because human cloning is an asexual form of reproduction, cloning confounds the meaning of 'father' and 'mother' and confuses the identity and kinship relations of any cloned child. This threatens to weaken existing notions regarding who bears which parental duties and responsibilities for children."[37] When employed by an infertile couple, reproductive cloning could give rise to any number of confounding familial relationships. A cloned child, for instance, might find herself in a family unit whereby her mother is also her genetic twin. Similarly, a father might raise a child who is not only his son but also his genetic grandfather. In light of these potential challenges to traditional family connections, Cardinal Keeler warned cloning would "mean a radical rupture of these bonds."[38] One might also envision a case where a clone, an individual replicated for research or performing hazardous tasks, might be raised in an environment quite different than the traditional family structure. Rather than father or mother in the commonly understood sense, a clone might be raised by a team of researchers or biogenetic engineers. Although not a direct participant in the congressional deliberations, Jorge Garcia, a professor of philosophy at Rutgers University, weighed in on the controversy and offered his observations regarding manufactured humans and the absence of family. "She may have many quasiparents," he argued, "but one ground for worry is that none may be tied to her in the role of protector that a child's parents traditionally occupy."[39]

This summary of congressional deliberations makes clear the near unanimous support for an all out ban on human reproductive cloning.

Looking back at the major arguments supporting a ban—individuality, commodification, eugenics, and family—it's difficult to use the term "dialogic" in the Bakhtinian sense. At least at first glance. Congressional opposition to reproductive cloning takes on a monologic appearance when one considers nearly every speaker, whether a senator, representative, or invited guest of a congressional hearing, makes virtually identical arguments. While multiple speakers participated in the ongoing policy debate, multivocality in the sense of varied cultural voices, ideological positions, and deliberative tensions appears absent. In fact, had the discussions regarding therapeutic cloning not been closely associated with reproductive cloning, a federal ban on cloning would surely be in place today. Taking a step back from the actual congressional exchanges and situating the utterances within a broader cultural conversation on cloning, however, might yield a dialogic understanding of the controversy.

Begun the Clone Wars Have

As I suggested earlier in the chapter, cultural representations of cloning inhabited the realm of science fiction prior to the events of 1997. Before the announcement of Dolly and the rapid fire developments of the subsequent four years, very few individuals encountered the idea of human reproductive cloning outside the science fiction genre. Many references throughout the congressional debates illustrated the pervasive influence of the speculative genre. References to "science fiction," *Brave New World,* and *Frankenstein* stand as evidence for the genre's ability to shape public consciousness. In a Bakhtinian sense, these nods to mediated genres (literary and otherwise) implicate a kind of intersubjective responsive understanding; participants in the congressional dialogue call on prior understandings of "cloning" to make sense of the present. Since a Bakhtinian dialogue is unfinalizable, I want to suggest *The Clone Wars* treatment of human reproductive cloning is a continuation of this active form of collaborative meaning-making . The fundamentals of dialogic meaning-making dictate that *The Clone Wars,* with its extended portrayals of clone troopers and the challenges facing clone troopers in a time of extended war, must also reference previous cultural understandings, as well as anticipate audience response, to constitute present meanings. Any present depiction of human cloning, even a series set in the fictional *Star Wars* universe, acknowledges previous utterances as well as the anticipated creative perception of intended audience members. With this in mind, I turn my attention to examining how *The*

Clone Wars references previous utterances, particularly the congressional concerns around individuality, commodification, and family, and solicits serious political consideration from viewers.

From the outset, *The Clone Wars* makes an argument for the individuality of genetically identical troopers. One of the most obvious displays of individuality is the physical appearance of the clone troopers. Although the clones' unadulterated forms make them indistinguishable from one another, the troopers utilize stylistic choices and body modification to indicate difference. Some clone troopers dye their hair or shave their head; others sport stylized goatees and/or head and face tattoos. Captain Rex, a clone trooper who works closely with Jedi general Anakin Skywalker, is represented with a blonde buzz cut. Commander Cody, on the other hand, wears his natural brown hair in a traditional military flat top. ARC Trooper Fives, a clone trooper who appears with some regularity throughout the series, can be distinguished from other clones by his goatee and trademark "5" facial tattoo. And Tup, a rookie clone who participates in the Umbarra campaign, pulls his hair back into a top-knot and has a teardrop tattooed under his left eye. Some clones also adorn their armor with unique stylistic innovations typically in the form of painted emblems or designs (e.g., Wolf head, teardrop, handprint). To some degree, the stylistic variations from one clone to another help the creators of *The Clone Wars* achieve clarity in storytelling. One can only imagine the narrative confusion viewers might experience when watching a conversation between three or four undifferentiated clones. Narrative conventions aside, the varying appearance implicates a degree of autonomy, of individual identity, on the part of the clones.

Clones also display difference through their demeanor. While one clone might be dead serious at all times, another might be gregarious and fun loving. These personality quirks, often presented in moments outside of combat as all the clones display a workmanlike seriousness when in battle, suggest physical duplication does not result in psychological replication. The clones might share a body but they do not share a personality. In fact, these personal idiosyncrasies often play an integral role in a clone's naming process. The troopers of *The Clone Wars* receive a numerical designation as they emerge from the cloning chambers (e.g., CT-27–5555) and proceed through some 10 years of martial training. Echoing the concerns of some of the congressional deliberators, the cloners, educators, and trainers who prepare the troopers for their assigned duties within the Grand Army of the Republic maintain a professional distance from their trainees and typically refer to them by their numerical designation. The clones, however, take it upon themselves to adopt names rather than numerical designations, names often tied to a personality trait. "Clone Cadets," an episode that depicts a squad of clones going through their final tests before entering active duty, illustrates how several clones take names associated with individual behaviors. Clone trooper CT-27–5555 adopts the name "Fives," a wisecracking CT-4040 takes the name "Cutup," and CT-21–0408, a clone with the propensity to repeat every order, rule, and regulation out loud, adopts the name "Echo." CT-782, a trooper who excels with heavy weapons and also carries the emotional burdens of his squad, becomes known as "Hevy."

The treatment of clones as individuals is not limited to their appearance, behaviors, and names but also in the way other characters interact with them. In the initial episode of the series Jedi Master Yoda, the leader and moral center of the Jedi Order, positions clone troopers as unique individuals in spite of their similar appearance. Stranded on an alien moon and hounded by the droid soldiers of the Separatist army, Yoda and three clones take refuge in a cave for some much needed rest. During their respite, Yoda asks the clone troopers to remove their helmets and one of the troopers quips, "Not much to look at here, sir. We all share the same face." Yoda's response strikes to heart of the individuality argument: "Deceive you, eyes can. In the Force, very different each of you are."[40] So while the clones might share genetic material and have a similar purpose as units in the Republic Army, Yoda grounds his assessment in the spiritual authority of the Force and suggests each clone possesses an undeniable uniqueness. Yoda even goes as far as to identify varying behavioral qualities evidenced by each of the three clones: Rhys is continually assessing the enemy opposition, Jek is overly concerned with weaponry, and Thire is always ready to jump into battle. These differences mark the clone troopers, at least partially, as individuals. Important to note, however, is that when Yoda defines the clones as individuals he does so within the limited subjectivity of soldier. The clones might be different in the Force but, when it comes to the pragmatics of war within the *Star Wars* galaxy, the clones are soldiers not farmers, bankers, or artists. Echoing the concerns heard within congressional discourse, Yoda identifies the clones as individuals yet limits their right to self-determination. The clones, as several episodes of the series suggest, exhibit a degree of self-reflexivity about this contradiction.

For a group of individuals literally born into a life of military service, many clones display a surprising level of self-awareness and existential reflexivity regarding their collective lot in life. Important to remember in the context of *The Clone Wars* is the simple fact that the Kaminoans produced the clones for one purpose and one purpose only: to be the combat units of the Grand Army of the Republic. From fighter pilot, to reconnaissance scout, to naval gunner, to marine, clone troopers fulfill a wide variety of military specializations within the Republic force, typically based on their individual strengths and weaknesses, and achieve varying ranks based on distinguished service. Such references to degrees of ability, as well as examples of clone cadets coveting particular assignments, emphasizes the point that clone troopers, despite being bred for a singular purpose, do have some autonomy. Numerous examples of battlefield ingenuity also suggest the clones are not unthinking grunts who act on every order without question. In fact, Captain Rex makes this point clear when he and some of the troopers under his command question the orders of a Jedi general who is, in fact, acting against the best interests of the Republic. When one of the men argues that the clones must follow orders, Rex replies, "We're not droids. We're not programmed. You have to learn to make your own decisions."[41] Fives reiterates this point in the season six episode "Fugitive." When Fives discovers the biological inhibitor chip tied to Order 66–the order compelling the clone troopers to kill their Jedi comrades in *Revenge of the Sith*—the Kaminoan cloners attempt to conceal their involvement by terminating him. Clone trooper Fives objects to his death sentence and shouts, "I am not a piece of hardware. I am a living being!"[42] This demarcation between clones and droids is an important distinction as a comparison between the two is easy to make throughout the series. Rows of clones marching lock step in their white armor look strikingly similar to the rows of battle droids and super battle droids who make up the combat units of the Separatists. Someone unfamiliar with the *Star Wars* universe could easily mistake the armored clone troopers for a kind of humanoid, robotic soldier. And, truth be told, most episodes feature the Republic clones and Separatist droids moving through the background with a mechanical precision, never questioning orders and always doing their utmost to complete an objective.

When the troopers remove their helmets, however, they expose their humanness and come to life as autonomous individuals capable of self-reflection and self-determination. In an episode titled "The Deserter" the tension between autonomy and servitude takes center stage as two clones discuss the issue explicitly.[43] As the title suggests, the episode revolves around an encounter between Captain Rex and Cut Lawquane, a deserter who fled the war effort and eventually settled down to raise a family. Injured during a clash with Separatist forces, Captain Rex is taken to a local farm to convalesce while the remainder of his squad continues a vital search and capture mission. Captain Rex soon discovers that his benefactor is more than just a simple farmer: he's a former clone trooper who deserted his post early in the war and now lives a life of his own choosing. The following account of their initial encounter centralizes the issue of choice.

> REX: What's your number and rank.
> CUT: My name is Lawquane. Cut Lawquane. And I'm just a simple farmer.
> REX: You're a deserter!
> CUT: Well, I'd like to think I'm merely exercising my freedom to choose. To choose not to kill for a living.
> REX: That is not your choice to make. You swore an oath to the Republic. You have a duty.
> CUT: I have a duty, you're right. But it's to my family. Does that count or do you still plan to turn me in?
> REX: Do I have a choice?

Later in the episode, Cut and Rex continue their conversation and Cut explains why he made the choice to desert from the Grand Army. After his troop transport was shot down during a combat mission gone terribly wrong, Cut managed to crawl away, hide, and watch as the droid army sifted through the wreckage and executed all survivors. "It's the day I felt my life didn't have any meaning," explains an obviously pained Cut. "Everyone I cared about, my team, was gone. I was just another expendable clone, waiting for my turn to be slaughtered in a war that made no sense to me. Can you understand that, Rex?" Rex, his voice filled with empathy, responds quietly: "I've been in countless battles and lost many brothers. They were my family. My home." These interactions between Captain Rex and Cut Lawquane present a rich, nuanced account of the issues at work when one considers cloning, individuality, and self-determination.

Unlike the near unanimous group think offered by participants during congressional deliberations, *The Clone Wars* presents a situation whereby individuality is largely respected but self-determination is restricted. The representation of clone troopers, with their diverse personality traits, stylistic innovations, and names, alleges that cloned individuals, even when raised in a controlled environment, develop distinct identities. In this sense, then, *The Clone Wars* challenges the congressional assumption that cloning technologies pose a significant threat to human dignity and the right to maintain one's uniqueness; cloned individuals are more than the human epilogue of a complete memoir. A clone may share her or his genetic makeup and basic physical appearance with another person (or persons depending on the number of replicates), but stylistic innovations and unique personality traits, as well as the complex cultural milieu permeating a community, contributes to the formation of a singular subjectivity for each and every individual. Furthermore, Master Yoda's reliance on the spiritual authority of the Force simultaneously repudiates the argument that a clone is not a unique individual in the eyes of God and yet supports the notion of a transcendent moral authority. Despite their individuality, however, clone troopers find themselves limited to a life of combat. Important to remember is that Cut Lawquane is an exception to the rule and is presented to viewers as a way of bringing the ethical treatment of the clone protagonists to light. The Cut Lawquane character functions as a narrative disruption, reminding viewers that the characters for whom they feel an affinity fight in a war not of their own choosing. Did the clones who swore an oath to the Republic truly choose to swear that oath or were they prodded, cajoled, manipulated, or even programmed? This depiction of individuals who think and act of their own accord, who recognize they are not unthinking automatons like the enemies they often face and yet ultimately possess little or no self-determination is one of the most tragic points brought to light by *The Clone Wars.*

"I am not a number. None of us are!"

Closely related to the arguments presented about individuality and self-determination is *The Clone Wars'* commentary on commodification. As congressional discussion suggested, moral questions arise when considering how a culture, and individuals within that culture, might respond differently to people born naturally or created artificially. Glimpses into the cloning process, particularly in the season three episodes "Clone Cadets" and "ARC Troopers," leave no question that the clones are manufactured commodities. The Kaminoan cloning facility is a massive, city sized complex of sterile laboratories, massive cloning chambers, expansive military training grounds, cramped living quarters, and regimented classrooms. In an obvious visual reference to in vitro fertilization and the related euphemistic "test tube baby" terminology of the late 1970s and early 1980s, thousands of Kaminoan cloning cylinders—each housing a developing human—populate the background of several scenes. The nearly endless rows of oversized test tubes inhabited by developing clones are reminiscent of the stream of goods often associated with an assembly line. In fact, the entire clone breeding and education process functions with assembly line precision: the clones are grown, born, educated/trained, and certified for deployment. Adding to the manufactured feel is the uniform appearance of all clone cadets; until they graduate to the status of clone trooper, all clones dress exactly alike and, with the exception of some distinctive personality traits, are virtually indistinguishable from one another. For all intents and purposes, the clones are nothing more than interchangeable products being assembled and shipped off to a customer.

And once they find themselves in the hands of the customer, the Republic military machine, the commodification of clone troopers is only reinforced. In episode after episode, season after season, thousands of clones are ordered into battle where they meet their onscreen demise. Presented within the context of an animated Cartoon Network series, it's easy to forget that *The Clone Wars* is story about a galaxy at war and the way in which a core group of characters negotiate the cultural changes inflicted by that conflict. When an episode focuses on a diplomatic mission, or the comedic exploits of Jar Jar Binks or C-3PO, the war effort churns relentlessly in the background; while audience members laugh at Jar Jar's bumbling antics, clone troopers continue to fight, and die, off screen. Lost in the myopic narrative vision of viewers, viewers who are compelled to pay attention to foregrounded characters, is the simple fact that nearly every soldier lost in the context of *The Clone Wars* is a clone trooper. When an ARC-170 starfighter is shot down, or a *Venator*-class Star Destroyer (an aircraft carrier analog) is obliterated, or an attack gunship erupts in flames, the casualties are clone troopers. When enemy weaponry vaporizes scores of ground troops, clone troopers bear the burden. Even though Shaak Ti, the Jedi Master who supervises the clone training process on Kamino, describes the troopers as "living beings, not objects" the vast majority of clones appear *only* as objects. Clone trooper deaths become so commonplace, so routine, that characters in the program rarely acknowledge the loss. With the exception of Captain Rex, Commander Cody, and a handful of clones introduced in one particular storyline or another, clones are anonymous and disposable. Viewers rarely get to know the clone who gets caught in an explosion or falls victim to a super battle droid's blaster fire. What viewers do know is that more clones will be available in the next episode. In fact, the disposableness of clones becomes even more pronounced when the Galactic Senate simply votes to fund the production of additional clones.

Nowhere is the issue of commodification more apparent than in season four's Umbara story arc. The story arc opens with the troopers of the 501st Legion and their commanding officer, General Anakin Skywalker, participating in a dangerous ground assault to capture the capital city of Umbara, a planet cloaked in perpetual darkness. Matters go from bad to worse for the clones when General Skywalker is called back to Coruscant, the Republic capital, and legendary Jedi general Pong Krell takes temporary command of the legion. Unlike Skywalker, a leader who treats the clones as near equals and does his utmost to minimize casualties, General Krell shows little respect for the troopers and regards them as little more than tactical units on the battlefield. Krell refers to the troopers by their numerical designation rather than their chosen names (e.g., CT-7567 rather than Captain Rex), views questions or strategy suggestions as a form of insubordination, and shows no compassion for the massive clone casualties incurred during repeated frontal assaults of military targets. For example, when a trooper questions one of Krell's decisions the general turns to the clone and asks, "CT-7567, do you have a malfunction in your design?" After being dressed down by the general, Captain Rex stands his ground and responds, "I followed your orders, even in the face of a plan that was, in my opinion, severely flawed. A plan that cost us men. Not clones, men!" When the general's reckless tactics lead to an alarming death toll, ARC Trooper Fives turns to his fellow troopers and exclaims, "I am not another number. None of us are!" For the general the clone troopers are nothing more than the means by which to accomplish a military objective. For Captain Rex and ARC Trooper Fives, the clones are individual beings—men—deserving of the respect due all people.

In the latter episodes of the story arc the tensions between General Krell and clone troopers come to a head. Frustrated by unimaginative strategies that result in an unnecessary loss of life, Captain Rex, ARC Trooper Fives, and a handful of other clones disobey orders because "it's the right thing to do" and undertake two successful covert operations that benefit not only the soldiers of the 501st but the entire Umbara campaign.[44] As a result of what he deems treasonous actions, General Krell sentences two troopers to death by firing squad. The firing squad scene brings the issue of cloning and commodification into sharp focus as Fives, standing with his hands tied behind his back and staring down the barrels of several blasters, makes an impassioned speech to his comrades in arms.

> This is wrong and we all know it. The General is making a mistake. And he should be called on it. No clone should have to go out this way. We are loyal soldiers, we follow orders, but we are not a bunch of unthinking droids. We are men. We must be trusted to make the right decisions, especially when the orders we are given are wrong.[45]

Fives' speech to his fellow clone troopers is one of the series most overt statements about how a culture might consider the status of clones. For Fives, his role as a soldier is never in question; he is loyal to his brothers and is committed to the ideals of the Republic. He is also a thinking individual capable of making moral judgments of right and wrong and, when necessary, standing up to his superiors when he perceives their judgment as flawed. As the concluding episode of the Umbara arc reveals, Fives' call to disobey orders and confront the general is the morally superior position as Jedi Master Pong Krell has turned to the dark side, betraying both the Jedi Order and the Galactic Republic. While the clones may be manufactured in a facility and given no choice in profession, they are also autonomous individuals. In Fives example viewers see that clones are living, breathing beings and should be treated as such.

The tension between depicting the clones as manufactured objects and living beings illuminates an important issue. If the clones are people who understand such concepts as self-identity, self-determination, and morality, and yet they are born into a life of service without any consideration of their own desires, should they be considered slaves? Slick, a clone trooper who hoped to gain his freedom by passing classified military information to the Separatists, accuses the Jedi Knights of just this thing. When Slick is ferreted out as a turncoat, he accuses the Jedi of treating the clones as slaves: "It's the Jedi who keep my brothers enslaved. We do your bidding. We serve at your whim. I just wanted something more."[46] As Slicks delivers his indictment of the Jedi Order and the government of the Galactic Republic in the sixteenth episode of the first season, the question of slavery percolates in the minds of consistent viewers through the remainder of the series. Are the clones, despite their individuality, self-awareness, and struggles with autonomy, men or are they slaves? When a clone loses his life on the battlefield does he do so of his own volition? This complicated question surfaces numerous times over the course of several seasons.

Like the arguments pertaining to individuality and commodification, *The Clone Wars* also addresses the congressional concerns regarding family. One of the common representations put forth by *The Clone Wars* is that of the clones as a band of brothers displaying the social bonds of combat soldiers. The clones train together, eat together, bunk together, and fight together; they cover each other's back, make sacrifices for each other, and live by a pledge to leave no clone beyond. That these bonds would be emphasized in a television show situated in a prolonged military campaign makes perfect sense. What I want to focus on in terms of social connection, however, is the degree to which the clones appear to address the congressional concerns about cloning and family structures. Grown in a hatchery and raised in the Kaminoan cloning facility, the clone troopers lack what many call a traditional family structure and receive much of their "parenting," as many of the congressional debate participants feared, from scientists and military trainers. The few glimpses into the upbringing of clones suggests an environment not unlike that of a military school. The difference here, of course, is that there is no "home" for the clones to visit during breaks; military school is their home. Nevertheless, the Kamino cloning facility as a home is given serious treatment during the series, particularly when the facility comes under attack from General Grievous, Asajj Ventress, and the droid armies under their command. When Republic forces discover a plot to attack Kamino, Captain Rex and Commander Cody make it clear the upcoming confrontation is more than just another in a long list of battles. Captain Rex turns to General Skywalker and growls, "With all due respect general, if someone comes to our home, they better be carrying a big blaster." Before anyone else can speak Commander Cody adds, "I concur with Captain Rex, sir. This is personal for us clones."[47] These brief comments are of particular note as the clones typically remain emotionally even keeled when speaking of upcoming military actions. This time, however, both Captain Rex and Commander Cody display an uncharacteristic emotional intensity; both officers want to defend their homeland. When the troopers of the 501st Legion arrive on Kamino, Echo and Fives stroll around the facility and reminisce fondly on their experiences as clone cadets. As the two pass a group of cadets Echo remarks, "Ah, look around Fives. Feels like yesterday we were here. Headin' to target practice." Fives chuckles as he responds, "Remember that?" Although a brief exchange between the two characters, the moment reveals the emotional connection the clone troopers have with the place of their birth. The cloning facility is not a home in the sense that most viewers understand the term, but the positive association with Kamino suggests clones will develop new, just as meaningful, understandings of home.

Just as the clone troopers prove capable of negotiating a new understanding of home, they also negotiate a unique family structure. For the most part, the clone troopers "home" experience is one devoid of a recognizable mother or father. A mother figure is completely absent—there are female scientists and engineers on Kamino but they never interact with the clones in a maternal role—and Jango Fett, the genetic "father" from whom all the troopers are cloned, is dead. Still, the clone troopers do manage to make meaningful connections in terms of interpersonal relationships. Yoda, for example, often refers to clone troopers as "friend" and Obi-Wan Kenobi and Anakin Skywalker refer to Captain Rex and Commander Cody simply as "Rex" and "Cody." In the case of Obi-Wan and Anakin, it's clear they consider Rex and Cody more than military personnel under their command; the two clones are more than simple comrades in arms. They are, to the extent Jedi Knights are allowed to develop attachments, true friends. In this sense, the clones make relational connections similar to that of family.

The real familial connections occur, however, between the clones themselves. The clone troopers, as several of my previous examples attest, refer to one another as "brother" on a regular basis. They are, obviously, genetic brothers. As Fives reminds a group of young cadets who find themselves thrown into combat before their training is complete, "We're one and the same. Same heart. Same blood. Your training is in your blood." The portrayal of the clones as brothers goes beyond this obvious genetic connection and develops a sense of the troopers as siblings in a behavioral sense, too. The episode "Clone Cadets," an episode featuring a group of five clones as they attempt to pass their final combat test and become full-fledged clone troopers, illustrates the emotional kinship.[48] The clones of Domino Squad—Cutup, Droidbait, Echo, Fives, and Hevy—treat one another as familial brothers as they tease, encourage, and challenge one another throughout the training process. Droidbait's name, for example, is a result of constant needling about his tendency to be the first member of the squad eliminated during training sessions. Echo and Hevy argue with one another about the squad's lackluster performance, eventually resorting to a brief physical altercation in the barracks; a few hours later, the fight between the two is forgotten and the squad pulls together to complete the Citadel Challenge. And Cutup, as his apt name implies, annoys his brothers with constant wisecracks and his refusal to take anything too seriously. The various moments between the five squad members, and their continued interactions throughout the series (the troopers of Domino Squad, particularly Echo and Fives, become recurring characters), constitute a relationship familiar to many viewers. While adult viewers are no doubt familiar with the "band of brothers" ethos referenced within *The Clone Wars*, the representation of Domino Squad goes well beyond the bond between soldiers. How many viewers might reference their own altercations with a sister or reflect on the unrelenting annoyances of a goofy brother? In this way, the clone troopers represent more than military units or commodities, fighting together for common cause; they represent brothers in every sense of the word.

Further evidence of the relational theme is evident when older clones and younger clones interact in a way indicative of parent and child. Combat veterans offer advice to rookies (often referred to as "shinies" in reference to their brilliant white armor still unmarred by field conditions) or a word of encouragement to clone cadets. The parent/child relationship is most obvious in the interactions between 99, a malformed, hunchbacked clone relegated to cleaning and maintenance duty, and the members of Domino

Squad, a group of five clones struggling to work as a team. Despite Domino Squad's repeated failures, 99 always offers a kind word of encouragement and even comes to the squad's defense when their Master Chief, Bric, dresses down the group as incompetent soldiers. None of the five squad members offers a defense but 99, standing off to the side and not directly subjected to Bric's barking, speaks up and says, "You don't give them enough credit." After yet another humiliating failure on the training grounds, CT-782 packs up his gear and prepares to slip away in the middle of the night. 99, who happens to be working in the barracks, confronts CT-782 about going AWOL and dispenses much needed advice.

> 99: But, you can't do this to your squad.
> 782: My squad? We're nothing but a bad batch. Failures, like you.
> 99: Yeah, but, how can I be a failure, when I never even got my chance? It's a chance you're throwing away. You're always trying to be the anchor, Hevy. You know, do it on your own. Well, maybe you should embrace the fact that you have a team. See, I never had that. But, you need them and they need you. Don't carry such a heavy burden on your own. When you have your brothers at your side, Hevy.
> 782: Hevy? Stop calling me that! We're just numbers, 99. Just numbers.
> 99: Not to me. To me you've always had a name.[49]

The inclusion of this particular scene speaks volumes about the way viewers are invited to think about clone relationships. The vast majority of the screen time devoted to clone troopers show them in combat; this scene, and the entire "Clone Cadets" episode, serves as a break in the typical *The Clone Wars* narrative structure. Rather than following the Jedi Knights and the clones in the context of the broader war, the scene focuses on the humanness of the clones and their ability to make deep, emotional connections with the people in their lives. Instead of offering admonishment and formal instruction, as the trainers of the clone cadets do, 99 speaks to CT-782 on a personal level. 99 refuses to identify Hevy as just another number (CT-782 adopts the name "Hevy" after this conversation), assures the struggling cadet he has value, and reminds Hevy that a Domino Squad committed to acting as a team has what it takes to complete clone training successfully. There is a degree of irony at work when 99, a clone whose adopted name is a number, reminds a clone cadet that his identity, his name, is not tied to a homogenizing, numerical designation. In a nod to the portrayal of clones as more than unthinking combat machines, Cameron Litvack, the writer of "Clone Cadets," depicts 99 as the most human clone of them all.

    As with other depictions of family, the conversation between 99 and

Hevy is one most viewers have likely encountered elsewhere. The interaction between a supportive parent and struggling child occurs regularly across popular culture and, one would assume, is a moment most viewers have played out in their own lives. And that's exactly why the moment between 99 and Hevy takes on crucial significance in the context of *The Clone Wars*. Grown from the DNA of a near perfect physical specimen, genetically modified to produce improved loyalty and creativity, the clones remain deeply human. Intensive training and education might mold them into superior soldiers but they retain the psychological needs of every person: emotional connection, compassion, and a sense of purpose. Born into circumstances where the idea of a nuclear family has no meaning, the clones constitute a new structure wherein the older clones provide support not only for one another but for the younger generation of clones, too. The idea of disparate family structures has particular relevance in the early twenty-first century as single parent households, blended families, same sex parenting, and families of choice become culturally accepted variations on the family theme.

Congress and the Clone Troopers

Trying to parse out the complete cultural dialogue over human reproductive cloning would prove to be a nearly impossible task but examining the points of overlap, agreement, and contention between congressional debates and the namesake characters of *The Clone Wars* offers a glimpse into how members of the public are called to participate in the dialogic public square. The divergent viewpoints put forth by congress and *The Clone Wars* call on active viewers to engage in creative interpretation before reformulating their own utterances in the form of judgment and rearticulation. In other words, *The Clone Wars* presents audiences with ethical positions, and often conflicting positions, that they may accept, reject, and ultimately incorporate into their future understandings and conversations about human reproductive cloning. The congressional debates, for instance, raise concerns about human dignity, about the right of a person to consider herself a unique person in the entirety of the world. The congressional conversation posed several pertinent questions for spectators. What does it mean to be a unique individual? How does a society define individuality? Is individuality defined by biological uniqueness, as Congress seemed to suggest, or is individuality constituted by some combination of biological and psychological factors? Is biological uniqueness a fundamental dimension of being human? Is individuality, biological or psychological, a human necessity? Is individuality a human right? Although participants acknowledged that environment plays an important role in the development of individuality, congressional arguments focused largely on biology and provided little room for disagreement regarding uniqueness as a human right. Cloning, argues much of Congress, violates a cloned person's right to individuality. Congressional consensus on the issue relegates differing opinions, and this includes those reading and watching the debates as participants in the larger public square, as irrelevant to the conversation or flat out wrong. In other words, the congressional conversation attempts to finalize the dialogue, something Bakhtin argues can never truly be accomplished. Congress also questions the potential for individuality and self-determination on the part of the clone. Does a clone ever escape the shadow of her progenitor or is she consigned to living a life that will never be her own?

The Clone Wars, on the other hand, presents the cloning controversy as one riddled with moral complexity. Not addressing the uniqueness of Jango Fett—the genetic template for the clone army is killed in *Attack of the Clones* and receives little more than passing mention in the series—*The Clone Wars* focuses on the clone troopers' individuality and autonomy. As the clone troopers mature they manifest distinct personality traits, adopt specific stylistic innovations, and identify one another by name rather than number. Despite biological uniformity, a highly controlled physical environment, and intense psychological indoctrination, clone troopers develop distinguishable identities. At the same time, the life of a clone trooper is one that lacks any significant autonomy and self-determination; a clone is born and raised to serve as a combat soldier. Few clones seem to question their lot in life. But, as a handful of characters and storylines illustrate, not all clones serve with unwavering conviction. Clones such as Cut Lawquane and Slick, a deserter and turncoat, serve as narrative disruptions and suggest that an unquestionable commitment the Republic is not a notion held uniformly. The tension between self-identity and self-determination, explored through several recurring troopers who possess a strong sense of autonomy, mirrors one of the significant problematics of the human reproductive cloning controversy. To what degree is a clone her or his own person?

The unresolved tensions apparent in the series, and to a much lesser degree in congressional deliberations, result in what Brian Ott calls an "ambivalent frame."[50] In his discussion of *Battlestar Galactica* as allegory for a post–9/11 world, Ott describes the ambivalent frame as a form of narrative that invites the audience to explore the boundaries between conflicting positions. Immersed in the ever present tensions of the ambivalent frame, a viewer is drawn into collaborative engagement with the text and is positioned as a public arbiter who is, at the very least, called to consider divergent positions. The unresolvable conflict of an individual who lacks self-determination entreats the viewer to grapple with how to bring clarity to a morally murky position. Like the senators, representatives, and witnesses who participated in the congressional deliberations, as well as the authors of *The Clone Wars*, the viewer has a responsibility to wrestle with these various utterances and engage the questions posed during ongoing conversation. Addressed as a participant in the public square, the watching and listening individual has a responsibility to consider the allegorical implications of a cloned soldier who fights in war that may or may not make sense to him and connect those implications to the broader cultural dialogue. Thus, the plight of a fictional clone trooper appeals to a viewer's moral sensibilities and challenges her to consider the dynamics of individuality and self-determination associated with the possibility, for example, of cloning a terminally ill loved one.

Similar contradictions surface when examining the viewpoints concerning commodification. The congressional debates raise a reasonable question: will individuals "manufactured" outside of natural conception or, to take it a step further, those produced for a specific purpose (e.g., organ transplant, combat soldier) be treated with the same dignity and respect as a person conceived naturally? The congressional position leaves no room for debate: people will exploit manufactured humans and this, in and of itself, warrants a federal ban on human reproductive cloning. *The Clone Wars* representation of the clone troopers as commodities reinforces this position as a legitimate concern. The clones are, in many ways, depicted as manufactured goods; assembled in a factory and shipped off to various parts of the galaxy, the clone troopers serve as disposable cogs in the Republic war machine. At the same time, however, *The Clone Wars* complicates the viewpoint by suggesting that clones are not simple commodities to be exploited or cast off indiscriminately. The troopers remind one another, as well as their superior officers, that they are more than replaceable parts—they are men, not numbers—and should not be deployed haphazardly. Clone troopers are not the unthinking automatons of the droid army but beings of emotional depth capable of forging meaningful relationships outside the context of battle.

In a direct contrast to the congressional consideration of cloned individuals, the portrayal of troopers as developing a family structure reinforces their presence as affective beings possessing the relational agency to create and maintain intense interpersonal relationships. As mentioned earlier, congressional interlocutors warned of the dire consequences posed by what they described as a radical rethinking of family. Although never able to detail direct harms, Congress questioned whether the absence of a traditional family structure might impact a clone psychologically? Would she or he experience a sense of incompleteness in the absence of an identifiable father, mother, or both? Likewise, what are the long-term cultural effects resulting from the absence of traditional family structure? The speculative fiction of *The Clone Wars* challenges these contentions, contentions resonating with the more recent political debates regarding the threat posed by marriage equality and same sex parenting (particularly in relation to adoption and adoption laws), and presents a different set of possibilities. The story arcs spotlighting Captain Rex or ARC Trooper Fives invite viewers to entertain the possibility that clones, like individuals in contemporary society who manage to negotiate single parent families, blended families, and families of choice, might be quite capable of forging new family structures as well. *The Clone Wars* representation of human reproductive cloning simultaneously reinforces family as a fundamental human need and challenges the normative image of the traditional nuclear family.

These continuous references to individuality, self-determination, and humanity problematize the clone troopers as primary combat soldiers in the war against the Separatists. On the one hand, the clones serve the public good, defending and liberating citizens of the Galactic Republic. On the other hand, the clone troopers find themselves trapped in a form of slavery; forced to further a political agenda that is not of their own choosing, they fight and die for the Republic cause. Watching this contradiction unfold, viewers are called to participate as responsible rhetorical actors. Is the creation of a subservient subclass justifiable if it serves the greater public good? Even if the enslavement of clones is amoral, as is suggested by several episodes, does a culture suspend a degree of morality in order to maintain the security of the majority? At first glance, the idea that a culture might sanction the deployment of a disposable being in the name of the public good might seem outrageous. However, if *The Clone Wars* is positioned as an exploration of political controversy during a time of war, these tensions are not unfamiliar to post–9/11 U.S. Americans who frequently situate military campaigns in Afghanistan and Iraq as actions necessary to protect freedom, democracy, and other national interests. Taking the cultural context into consideration, the symbolization of the clone trooper evokes comparisons with the modern U.S. American soldier who, guided by dress code regulations, proscribed procedures for almost every situation, and a military code of ethics, is "engineered" to look alike, think alike, and act alike. The contemporary soldier is, in a figurative sense, cloned. With this in mind, the ethical dilemma posed by *The Clone Wars* relates directly to the foreign policy debates of the twenty-first century. To what degree are U.S. American constituents, and their congressional representatives, willing to sacrifice "cloned" soldiers to protect national interests? Does the deep humanness suggested by *The Clone Wars* offer a compelling moral argument to not only consider the ethical implications of human cloning but also give increased consideration to the deployment of combat soldiers? I don't want to overstate my case here and suggest that the depiction of clone troopers calls on viewers to support isolationism. What I do want to argue is that *The Clone Wars* asks viewers to remember that an individual person—a daughter, a son, a mother, a father, a sister, or a brother—inhabits the ambiguous idea of "Support Our Troops" and lives within the military uniform.

The specific ethical questions aside, *The Clone Wars* displays a strong Bakhtinian double-voicedness less prominent in the congressional deliberations. According to Bakhtin, double-voiced discourse "serves two speakers at the same time and expresses simultaneously two different intentions: the direct intention of the character who is speaking, and the refracted intention of the author."[51] In the case of *The Clone Wars*, the clone troopers speak for themselves within the context of the narrative at hand; they illustrate the tensions at work in their own lives. They also speak with a voice charged by the relevant perceptions of human cloning as understood by the animators, writers, and directors of the series. Intentional or not, the collaborative artistic efforts of those involved with creating *The Clone Wars* draw on previous dialogic utterances, like the ongoing deliberations in Congress, to make sense of both their world and the science fantasy realm of the *Star Wars* universe. As participants in a mediated dialogue, viewers encounter these double-voiced discourses replete with all the associated issues, concerns, dissonances, and assonances. Science fiction informs congressional debate, congressional debate informs *The Clone Wars*, and *The Clone Wars* informs viewers. The viewer then integrates the ethical quandaries offered by the various characters and narrative arcs as part of her own creative interpretation and draws on those understandings when addressing issues of cloning and biotechnology as they arise in her own life. The viewpoints presented by the multiple, heterogeneous voices of *The Clone Wars* call her to become a dialogic participant in the ongoing cultural discourse. In some respects, the individual viewer becomes a kind of discursive cloner in her or his own right, a participant in the dialogic public square who replicates the DNA of previous utterances within new contexts.

THREE

Torture and the Path to the Dark Side

"We also have to work, though, sort of the dark side, if you will. We've got to spend time in the shadows in the intelligence world. A lot of what needs to be done here will have to be done quietly, without any discussion, using sources and methods that are available to our intelligence agencies, if we're going to be successful. That's the world these folks operate in, and so it's going to be vital for us to use any means at our disposal, basically, to achieve our objective."[1]—Vice President Dick Cheney

"Padawan, terror is not a weapon the Jedi use."[2]—Luminara Unduli

Given Cheney's remarks about "the dark side" and the "shadows of the intelligence world," most people probably envisioned an expanded role for intelligence operatives and special forces soldiers. Not unlike the cloak and dagger exploits of James Bond or *Mission Impossible*'s Ethan Hunt, "the dark side" of the intelligence world entailed undercover psychological operatives, snatch and grab operations, and the possible targeted killing of high level terrorist targets. What most individuals didn't anticipate, however, was a turn to torture. As a signatory of the August 12, 1949, Geneva Conventions, the United States government was bound, by treaty, to refrain from any and all physically violent or psychologically harmful treatment that might be deemed cruel and inhuman. Common Article 3 of the conventions pertains to the detainment of prisoners of war in non-international conflicts and explicitly prohibits any treatment that might be construed as harmful to an individual's "personal dignity, in particular humiliating and degrading treatment." Article 3 also bans "cruel treatment and torture."[3] Furthermore, the United States also signed the United Nations 1984 Convention against Torture and Other Cruel, Inhuman or Degrading Treatment or

Punishment wherein the U.S. government committed to the following definition of inhumane treatment:

> The term "torture" means any act by which severe pain or suffering, whether physical or mental, is intentionally inflicted on a person for such purposes as obtaining from him or a third person, information or a confession, punishing him for an act he or a third person has committed or is suspected of having committed, or intimidating or coercing him or a third person, or for any reason based on discrimination of any kind, when such pain or suffering is inflicted by or at the instigation of or with the consent or acquiescence of a public official or other person acting in an official capacity. It does not include pain or suffering arising only from, inherent in or incidental to lawful sanctions.[4]

In light of the United States official agreement with these humanitarian documents, post–9/11 revelations regarding the mistreatment of Iraqi prisoners of war, the practice of extraordinary rendition, and the waterboarding of at least three Al Qaeda detainees shocked the international community.

Despite the public affirmation and adherence to a no torture policy, the United States government had long utilized "enhanced interrogation techniques" as part of the its intelligence operations. During the Cold War, as Michael P. Vicaro reports in his exploration of U.S. government's definition of torture, the CIA and other agencies systematically explored nonphysical forms of interrogation that would not be easily identified as inhumane or abusive in the traditional sense. The result was a number of enhanced interrogation techniques including "sensory deprivation, dietary manipulation, stress and duress postures, sleep deprivation, and white noise."[5] These shadowy practices came to the public's attention when reports of prisoner mistreatment surfaced at Iraq's Abu Ghraib prison, a prison administered jointly by the United States and Iraq in the aftermath of the 2003 Iraq War. On April 27, 2004, the television program *60 Minutes II* aired on episode detailing an ongoing U.S. Army investigation into the abuse and torture of prisoners held in Abu Ghraib, an Iraqi prison run by U.S. military personnel. The news story included several pictures of U.S. military personnel treating Iraqi prisoners inhumanely. The pictures in question depicted naked prisoners coerced into simulating sex acts, restrained in excruciatingly painful positions, and subjected to dog attacks. Yet another photo, a photo that would become the defining image of the Abu Ghraib scandal, revealed a hooded prisoner standing on a box "with wires attached to his genitals."[6]

While President Bush denounced the "disgraceful conduct by a few

American troops who dishonored our country and disregarded our values," a broader, systematic acceptance and use of torture soon came to light.[7] In an obvious attempt to adhere to the U.N. treaty in name, but not in principle, the Bush administration embraced extraordinary rendition. In the October 30, 2007, edition of the *New York Times*, Scott Shane described the Bush administration's "policy of extraordinary rendition" as a widely employed secret program "in which the United States delivers suspects to other countries, including some that routinely use torture." Similarly, Peter Finn and Julie Tate reported in a September 1, 2011, *Washington Post* article that the CIA routinely shuttled high value terror suspects to and from "covert prison sites" where the prisoners were subjected to various forms of enhanced interrogation. Bob Herbert, columnist for the *New York Times*, described extraordinary rendition as a euphemism for "torture by proxy" and criticized the government for endorsing a program whereby U.S. military and/or intelligence personnel apprehend "individuals, presumably terror suspects, and sends them off without even a nod in the direction of due process to countries known to practice torture."[8] All told, the practice of spiriting detainees to secret black prisons for interrogation reportedly involved 136 individuals and 54 countries.[9] And while President Obama denounced the inhumane treatment of detainees in January 2009 and ordered the closure of covert prison facilities, *The Nation*'s Jeremy Scahill alleged that the CIA continued to operate detention facilities in Somalia.[10]

One of the most hotly debated dimensions of the extraordinary rendition program was the use of waterboarding. Often described as simulated drowning, waterboarding is an interrogation practice whereby an individual is inverted, a cloth is placed over her or his mouth and nose, and water is poured over the cloth. Unable to draw breath through the water saturated cloth, the resulting oxygen deprivation triggers a mental and physical response that compels an individual to escape the life-threatening situation at any cost. The theory behind waterboarding, and all forms of torture used in intelligence gathering, links the cessation of pain with cooperation. When a suspect talks, the pain stops. As Greg Miller reported in the February 7, 2008, edition of the *Los Angeles Times*, the Bush administration confirmed the use of waterboarding as a form of enhanced interrogation, declared the practice legal, and reserved the right to resume the use of the controversial intelligence practice. Confirming what many observers of the post–9/11 landscape suspected, CIA director Hayden admitted the government employed waterboarding on three Al Qaeda suspects during 2002 and 2003. Peter Grier's piece appearing in the April 1, 2014, issue of *The*

Christian Science Monitor revealed that Khalid Sheikh Mohammed, a detainee accused of planning the 9/11 attacks, was waterboarded 183 times. Several months before Hayden's waterboarding admission, an admission that confirmed what many observers had long suspected, Michael Mukasey became embroiled in a congressional debate regarding the controversial tactic. As a nominee for attorney general (he was eventually confirmed), Mukasey was asked by members of the Senate Judiciary Committee to weigh in on the legality of waterboarding. As Evan Perez reported in the *Wall Street Journal* on October 31, 2007, Mukasey stated his commitment to hold the U.S. government accountable to laws declaring torture illegal. At the same time, however, Mukasey also "declined to say if he considers an interrogation technique that simulates drowning to be torture and therefore illegal."

While George W. Bush, Dick Cheney, and Michael Mukasey played language games over the definitions (and legality) of extraordinary rendition, enhanced interrogation, and waterboarding, *The Clone Wars* articulated a clear stand on torture. As Master Unduli states in the ninth episode of season one, "Padawn, torture is not a weapon the Jedi use."[11] Despite the Jedi Master's definitive declaration, a statement even casual *Star Wars* fans would recognize as representative of the Jedi Order's ethical principles, the series revisits the torture controversy repeatedly as some of the most recognizable Jedi heroes—Ahsoka Tano, Anakin Skywalker, Mace Windu, and Obi-Wan Kenobi—appear to heed Dick Cheney's assertion that good ends sometimes justify questionable means. The tension within the series—those opposed to any forms of torture whatsoever and those at least willing to consider the possibility of walking in the shadow—resemble, and intersect with, a similar dialogue carried on between newspaper editorialists. The torture debate, a public deliberation in which *The Clone Wars* and newspaper editorialists give voice to a variety of important pragmatic and principled considerations, revolves around several important questions: What is torture? When, if ever, is torture permissible? If it is permissible, both morally and legally, what kinds of torture and under what circumstances? My interest in this chapter, then, is the way *The Clone Wars* and newspaper editorialists engage this series of politically-relevant questions. I begin the chapter by examining the relationship between post–9/11 cultural trauma and popular culture. Specifically, I explore how popular culture responded, and continues to respond, to the ongoing psychological reverberations from both the initial terrorist attacks and the subsequent counterterrorism and counterinsurgency efforts in Afghanistan and Iraq. Focusing my attention on popular culture representations and dialogues concerning torture, I discuss how newspaper editorials engaged in a lively debate about whether torture should, or shouldn't, be a viable U.S. American intelligence gathering practice. Next, I examine how a similar dialogue plays out in several episodes of *The Clone Wars*. I conclude the chapter by illustrating how these disparate texts address similar issues yet come to different conclusions.

Cultural Trauma, Popular Culture and Torture

While the U.S. government responded to the terrorist attacks of 9/11 by turning to extraordinary rendition, enhanced interrogation techniques, the "suppressions of liberty and free speech in the United States, in bellicose pronouncements of righteous vengeance in the World Court, and ultimately in the Afghanistan and Iraq wars," the psyche of the U.S. American public remained traumatized. Not unlike the events that traumatize people on an individual level (e.g., a car accident, the sudden loss of a loved one, an unhealthy relationship), the concept of cultural trauma describes the way an event has a lasting, sometimes permanent, impact on a community.[12] As Jeffrey C. Alexander states, "Cultural trauma occurs when members of a collectivity feel they have been subjected to a horrendous event that leaves indelible marks upon their group consciousness, marking their memories forever and changing their future identity in fundamental and irrevocable ways."[13] Recognizing the anxiety, fear, and restlessness experienced as a kind of nationwide post-traumatic stress disorder, some contributors to the post–9/11 cultural dreamscape responded by trying to excise all reminders of the cultural injury. As documented in Drew Grant's May 10, 2011, Salon.com article titled "10 Year Time Capsule: 'Spider-Man' and the Erasing of the World Trade Centers," numerous films and television shows released post–9/11 utilized traditional and CGI editing to eliminate the iconic Twin Towers from both large and small screens. While the powers that be at Sony Pictures pulled a *Spider-Man* trailer featuring the twin towers prominently the creators of *Men in Black II* removed a scene featuring the iconic New York landmark. Rather than removing or reshooting scenes, the filmmakers behind *Zoolander* erased the buildings digitally. Zack Snyder, the director of the graphic novel adaptation *The Watchmen*, opted to leave the World Trade Center in his film but chose to shoot a script that changed the climax from one depicting an attack on New York City to one involving multiple attacks around the globe. Symbolically expunging the Twin Towers, or rewriting endings that might hit too close to home, were not the only responses to post–9/11 cultural anxieties.[14]

In her article titled "Rogue Waves, Remakes, and Resurrections: Allegorical Displacement and Screen Memory in *Poseidon*," Claire Sisko King examines film as a means by which to revisit and rethink the cultural memory directly associated with traumatic events. Films that engage culturally traumatic history, whether in the form of direct portrayals of an event or through allegory, encourage audiences to reexamine and rethink the contemporary relevance of past occurrences. She explains, "Texts that replay a traumatic past might be understood, like nightmares or flashbacks, as returning to and repeating traumatic experience in order to manage prior wounds and to make sense of traumatic history."[15] One such text that calls on viewers to consider contemporary political policy issues, as well as notions of national identity, is *Poseidon*, Wolfgang Petersen's 2006 remake of the classic disaster film, *The Poseidon Adventure*. Following the basic plot of its 1972 predecessor (passengers attempt to escape a sinking cruise ship), *Poseidon* simultaneously references the unexpectedness of the 9/11 attacks while also encouraging audiences to work through post–9/11 anxieties by way of a heroic narrative arc that suggests "the nation not only suffered and recovered from tragedy but also was redeemed and improved in the process."[16] While some films, like *Poseidon*, call on viewers to reconsider a rehabilitated national identity, other films urge viewers to consider their own responsibility in relation to national affairs. One such text, according to Vincent Gaine, is the Jason Bourne trilogy.

Gaine interprets the Jason Bourne trilogy—*The Bourne Identity*, *The Bourne Supremacy*, and *The Bourne Ultimatum*—as "political critique" positioning viewers as at least partially responsible for the foreign policy decisions that contributed to 9/11.[17] As an amnesic, Bourne wrestles with his previous life as a CIA assassin through nightmares, hazy memories, and unbidden visions. Traumatized by the violent experiences of his past, Bourne attempts to recover his identity and, more importantly, accepts he is at least partially responsible for the acts he committed as an agent of the U.S. government. Bourne's quest to make some sense out of events that remain largely unfathomable is a thinly veiled allegory for the U.S. American collective consciousness grappling with post–9/11 realities. Gaine explains,

> He is not an unquestioning agent of clarity but, rather, a person like us in the post–9/11 landscape: no longer able to be an unproblematic hero or patriot, but confused, uncertain, and traumatized. In order to work through this trauma, he must become reflective, penitent, and capable of reconciliation, and acknowledge his own culpability."[18]

Insinuating that the overall passivity and silence of the viewing and voting public contributed to the political situation surrounding the evolution and continued conduct of the war on terror, Gaine reads the Bourne trilogy as a text urging audiences to demand more transparency from political officials. Bearing partial responsibility for the actions of their political leaders, Jason Bourne encourages audiences to recognize their own accountability and take an active role in advocating governmental accountability.

Popular science fiction texts also addressed post–9/11 cultural anxieties. As Anna Froula suggests, the *Terminator: The Sarah Connors Chronicles* television series is as much an allegory about negotiating post–9/11 political realities and personal anxieties as it is about anything else. The allegory is most obvious in the basic narrative of the entire terminator franchise: Sarah Connors attempts to save the human race from an artificial intelligence of human design. The parallels between the fictional world of the *Terminator* franchise and the all too real non-fiction narrative of a post–9/11 America are remarkably similar. Confronted by enemies of their own making, Sarah and John Connors attempt to stop a human created artificial intelligence from destroying humanity. Similarly, the U.S. government fights an undeclared war (the war on terror) against allies turned enemies; some members of the anti–Soviet Union mujahideen of Afghanistan—partially funded and trained by the U.S.–eventually became leaders within Al Qaeda. In both instances, the television series and the U.S. government perpetuate what Froula refers to as a "recirculating 'logic' of the preemptive strike as war strategy," a strategy that simultaneously reinforces and assuages cultural fears and anxieties in that it (1) suggests impending future attacks and (2) suggests that the only way to stave off future attacks is to hit the perpetrators first.[19] The preemptiveness of the strategy, however, is an illusion. If one preemptive attack derails a potential threat others continue to lurk just out of sight. And this, of course, calls for another preemptive attack. No matter how many time traveling terminators the Connors stop, they keep coming. No matter how many terrorist leaders the U.S. government kills or captures, new leaders step in to fill the void.

Matthew Hill's reading of *Firefly*, Joss Whedon's science fiction western that premiered one year after the September 11 attacks, offers a non-violent alternative to cultural trauma. Hill draws parallels between Malcolm Reynolds's "experience as a defeated and traumatized" soldier, as well as the various tragic back stories of Reynolds's crew, and the psychological injuries suffered by U.S. Americans.[20] Reynolds and his crew, asserts Hill, represent a rejection of the violent post–9/11 revenge narratives furthered by the Bush administration, the U.S. American public, and popular mediated texts. Rather than attempting to exact revenge on those at least partially responsible for their pain and suffering, a familiar story from U.S.

history and from popular film and television (e.g., *24*), the crew of *Serenity* take refuge in their freedom, mobility, and refuse to be defined by the political and ideological forces at work in the 'verse. Whedon's reconceptualization of the traditional western, suggests Hill, functions as a kind of televisual rupture entreating audience members to envision a post–9/11 landscape wherein people "transcend and overcome trauma" without turning to violent retribution.[21]

While many texts addressed cultural trauma and anxiety in a general sense, others considered specific foreign policy decisions or issues of social justice. Since 9/11, numerous television programs and films have engaged the controversial topic of torture. None of these texts, however, have been more relevant than the televisions shows *24* and *Battlestar Galactica*. Drawing on Umberto Eco's work concerning narrative structure, Aristotelis Nikolaidis unpacks the narrative logic at the center of the fictionalized account of the war on terror put forth by the writers, directors, and actors responsible for *24*. The television series depicts the exploits of Jack Bauer, a member of the U.S. government's Counter Terrorism Unit (CTU), who is continually thrust into the center of various and sundry terrorist plots. Almost always situated within some variant of the ticking time bomb scenario, Bauer finds his investigations stymied by traditional law enforcement techniques and, having exhausted all available options, turns to extraordinary measures to stop an imminent threat. Nikolaidis observes that this race against the clock is "the decisive element of the narrative" providing justification for Bauer's propensity to work outside the law; to foil the terrorist plot in time, Bauer ignores the institutional chain of command, disregards rule of law, and utilizes torture as a primary means of gathering information.[22] The repetitive narrative structure of *24*, argues Nikolaidis, normalizes the use of extraordinary measures in the "war on terror" and marks the program as an important political voice in the post–9/11 debate concerning human rights, torture, and public safety.

While Nikolaidis' work focuses almost entirely on *24* as text, Keren Tenenboim-Weinblatt takes a broader, inter-textual approach to the intersection of television, politics, and public deliberation. Synthesizing the various references to *24* throughout the news media—newspapers, televised interviews, political websites—she makes the claim that the television show illustrates the degree to which fictional narratives and "characters are embedded in the U.S. political culture" as well as the way in which U.S. political culture participates "in shaping and negotiating the effect, meaning, and uses" of narratives and characters.[23] Of particular interest for Tenenboim-Weinblett are moments of vertical inter-textuality, or those moments when a primary text (*24*) is referenced directly by another text, and how the interplay between primary and secondary text simultaneously advance particular understandings while leaving open the possibility of multiple understandings. Drawing on the musings of conservative and liberal columnists her work suggests that "the show is invoked to support and express different political opinions" in a variety of political arguments and contexts.[24] Her point, then, is that engaging fictional narratives may play an important role in making sense of nonfictional deliberations and discussions of public matters.

One such narrative is present in Ron Moore's reconceptualization of the 1970s space opera *Battlestar Galactica*. As a kind of military science fiction meets Noah's Ark, *Battlestar Galactica* recounts the efforts of a lone spacefaring battleship/aircraft carrier analog as the commander and crew attempt to protect the surviving members of their civilization. Decimated by a surprise attack, the ragtag fleet of ships flees across the expanses of space with their attackers—a race of self-aware automatons and bioengineered replicants created by the humans—always in close pursuit. Never shying away from plots addressing foreign policy, national security, or social justice, Karen Randell describes *Battlestar Galactica* as an "erudite and politically motivated space opera" that actively "critiqued the post–9/11 American political landscape."[25] In one particular episode, "Flesh and Bone," a captured Cylon infiltrator named Leoben (a Cylon model indistinguishable from flesh and blood humans) reveals that a hidden nuclear warhead will explode in a matter of hours. The ticking time bomb plot device fully engaged, one of the Galactica's military officers is instructed to extract the whereabouts of the bomb by whatever means possible. Implicated in this order to do whatever it takes is the use of torture. Much of the episode, then, features the psychological and physical game of cat and mouse played between Starbuck, the interrogator, and Leoben. What is unique in this portrayal, argues Randell, is the way Leoben is positioned as a sympathetic character; by the conclusion of the episode, even Starbuck seems to recognize the humanness of her victim. Brian Ott concurs with his reading and suggests that the simultaneous dehumanization and humanization of Leoben is central to the episode's critical ambivalence. The graphic torture of Leoben is intended to repulse viewers, to illustrate the barbaric brutality required to intentionally inflict pain on another. At the same time, however, the parallels with U.S. American foreign policy and the torture of enemy combatants calls viewers to acknowledge their culpability in the practice.[26] Even though the crisis within the episode is eventually resolved–Leoben admits there isn't a bomb in the fleet—the complicated, nuanced representation problematizes torture's efficacy. Although the enhanced interrogation ultimately bears fruit, Starbuck's own humanity stands suspect. In not giving easy "yes" or "no" answers to moral questions, *Battlestar Galactica* "offers philosophical debates rather than easy answers played out to resolve our contemporary problems."[27]

What is important to recognize in these popular culture texts is the way various perspectives and debates resonate in the public square. For many individual viewers, a television program, film, or book may be the only time she or he encounters the difficult ethical questions raised by the prospect of torturing another human being. Truth be told, few people outside the intelligence, military, and law enforcement communities will ever be faced with a situation where torture is the remotest of possibilities. Depictions of torture will, however, influence public perceptions about the practice, perceptions which could influence the way people vote or engage in public activism. As John Ip suggests in his examination of *The Dark Knight* and Batman's use of torture, representations do matter.

> However, popular culture does not simply reflect the societal status quo; it also influences and frames people's views about law, legal institutions, and justice. This is because most people have little direct experience with the law and legal institutions, meaning that much of their knowledge is second-hand and often derived from popular culture. At the same time, popular culture is pervasive and accessible. This gives it the power to shape people's views about the law and legal issues, including views about the war on terrorism and the legal issues that arise out of it.[28]

Although my own work isn't so much concerned with the specific legal issues surrounding torture and the war on terror, Ip's point is well taken. If popular culture is the only experience one has with the ethics of torture, then it stands to reason these texts will play a role in shaping personal belief and, at least indirectly, broader popular opinion. As citizens of a nation participating in their own self-governance, popular culture representations call individuals to consider whether or not they should support or denounce governmental practices. Keeping the relevance of these pop cultural depictions in mind, the next section of this chapter explores the dialogic resonance between two salient texts in the torture debate: news editorials and specific episodes of *The Clone Wars*.

Editorializing the Torture Debate

As Jim Rutenberg reported in the November 5, 2001, issue of the *New York Times,* just a few weeks after the 9/11 attacks, torture emerged as a topic of conversation across various forms of news media. From the *Wall Street Journal*, to *Newsweek*, to CNN, to Slate.com discussions concerning the necessity, morality, and legality of employing torture as a means of coercing information from suspects resistant to traditional interrogation techniques filled the editorial pages. Editorial opinions coalesced around three general positions. First, a number of editorialists offered reluctant support for utilizing both physical and psychological distress to compel a detainee to divulge information particularly when evidence points to a looming terrorist attack. Second, several columnists staked out a more nuanced position limiting torture to more humane forms, techniques they described as less likely to result in significant physical and psychological harms. Finally, a group of editorialists denounced any and all forms of torture. These writers made it clear: turning to torture, no matter the context, means turning away from the virtues and values associated with U.S. American national identity.

Responding to the Congressional debate over the McCain amendment, an amendment to a defense spending bill that banned the use of torture on any and all prisoners, detainees, or enemy combatants, Charles Krauthammer's editorial appearing in the December 5, 2005, issue of *The Weekly Standard* declared a complete moratorium morally irresponsible. According to Krauthammer, an enemy combatant who has knowledge of an impending terrorist attack (the ticking time bomb scenario) or a high-level terrorist operative who could have significant knowledge of an organization's membership, day-to-day operations, and long term strategic plans, should be subjected to both psychological and physical coercion. Krauthammer suggested the debate regarding torture attempts to answer the wrong question. Rather than debating if torture is permissible, a conversation that suggests torture either is or isn't an allowable intelligence gathering tool, the debate should be centered on when. If a government official has reason to believe that a particular prisoner possesses information that might protect U.S. citizens—an instance he referred to as a "legitimate exception"— she or he has "a moral duty" to turn to torture. To be clear, Krauthammer did not call for the widespread and wanton use of torture in the war on terror. In fact, he acknowledged torture as a "monstrous evil" that should result in a troubled national conscience. He also maintained, however, that in particular situations highly trained interrogators could request "written permission for such interrogations from the highest political authorities in the country (cabinet level) or from a quasi-judicial body modeled on the Foreign Intelligence Surveillance Court (which permits what would ordinarily be illegal searches and seizures in the war on terror)."

The idea of torture as a necessary evil appeared as a common refrain from those who offered reluctant support for the practice of enhanced interrogations. Writing in the November 6, 2007, issue of the *Wall Street Journal*, Bret Stephens compared enhanced interrogation techniques, like waterboarding, to the targeting of civilian populations by Allies during World War II. Massive bombing campaigns in Germany and Japan, including the atomic bombs dropped on Nagasaki and Hiroshima, resulted in over a million civilian casualties throughout the war. Stephens editorial characterized both waterboarding and bombing civilians as "evil" acts that should be avoided wherever and whenever possible. There are times, however, when "awful things … have to be done in order to spare great harms." Similarly, a *Wall Street Journal* editorial published on January 6, 2005, also drew on the lessons of history. Waterboarding, the editorial asserted, is a preventative measure, a lesser of two evils designed to protect civil liberties. Without waterboarding and other enhanced interrogation techniques, the United States might need to resort to "Roosevelt's internment camps and Lincoln's suspension of habeas corpus."

In a similar spirit, several editorialists articulated begrudging support for the use of particular kinds of torture in limited circumstances. In his November 4, 2001, article in *Newsweek*, Jonathan Alter, a writer frequently identified as a liberal, argued in favor of some kinds of torture. While he denounced the use of physical torture as "contrary to American values," he asked the reading public to maintain "an open mind about certain measures to fight terrorism, like court-sanctioned psychological interrogation." His call to rethink torture as an interrogation tool suggested the United States public might need to make allowances for such harsh techniques as intense sensory bombardment (e.g., bright lights, loud music) and threatening to harm a detainee's family. Richard Cohen's March 6, 2003, opinion piece for the *Washington Post*, cautioned against the use of torture but admitted, particularly in relation to what he identified as "benign variations (sleep deprivation, shaking, etc.)" of torture that he would "never say never." Having said that, however, he also reminded his readers that "torture is a beast with a rapacious appetite" suggesting that the use of more benign forms opens the door to increasingly malignant practices. *Star Wars* fans may hear the voice of Master Yoda in Cohen's words. As Yoda remarked to Luke Skywalker:

> But beware of the dark side. Anger, fear, aggression; the dark side of the Force are they. Easily they flow, quick to join you in a fight. If once you start down the dark path, forever will it dominate your destiny, consume you it will, as it did Obi-Wan's apprentice.[29]

Wary of torture's dark side, Alan Dershowitz, Harvard Law professor and political commentator, advocated for the establishment of a legal process by which to grant government personnel the official go ahead to employ torture. In the October 17, 2006, *Los Angeles Times*, he described this "torture warrant" as a legal document granting court sanctioned permission, in extreme situations, to utilize non-lethal torture. A request for a warrant would need to (1) demonstrate that time was a crucial factor in stopping an attack (in other words, prove that a ticking time bomb scenario existed) and (2) establish "probable cause that the suspect had ... information" that could lead to thwarting said attack. Instituting such warrants, he reasoned, would actually reduce the amount of torture used by government officials as the process would force individuals to stop and carefully consider their actions. Few people, Dershowitz suggested, would want their names associated with a request to engage in such a morally reprehensible practice. In those extreme situations where officials pushed for such a warrant, the resulting legal record provides ample opportunity for oversight.

While some editorialists supported the use of torture and acknowledged torture should be considered a necessary evil, others denounced the practice in any and all forms. One such editorialist was Bob Herbert. Hebert's February 28, 2005, *New York Times* piece titled "It's Called Torture," recounted the experiences of Maher Arar, an individual wrongly accused of associating with terrorists, subjected to extraordinary rendition by the U.S. Justice Department, tortured by Syrian officials, and released a year later. Maher Arar was never charged, let alone convicted, of any crime against the United States. In light of Arar's experience, Hebert asked, "As a nation, does the United States have a conscience? Or is anything and everything O.K. in post–9/11 America?" Expressing similar disappointment with the actions of his country, Burton J. Lee III, a retired military doctor and George H. W. Bush's presidential physician, added his voice to the anti-torture chorus. Making use of a literary allusion, Lee wrote, "It seems as though our government and the military have slipped into Joseph Conrad's *Heart of Darkness*."[30] For Lee, the reports of prisoner mistreatment at Abu Ghraib, Guantanamo Bay, and other covert prison sites, as well as the Bush administration's admission that enhanced interrogation was a useful tool in the war on terror, indicated a profound shift away from the U.S. American commitment to uphold the highest of ethical standards. In hopes of returning to those ethical standards, he called for medical professionals and others to come together and "clearly state that systematic torture ... is not acceptable." Eugene Robinson made a similar call for the unequivocal end to torture. According to his editorial in the September 19, 2006, issue of the *Washington Post*, the country's debate over the efficacy and morality of torture turns on two important questions: "What kind of nation are we? What kind of people are we?" To make his opposition clear, he referred to President Bush as The Inquisitor. Conjuring images of the Spanish Inquisition, Robinson portrayed President Bush (and the related policies of his administration) as a kind of holy interrogator tasked with discovering, converting, or neutralizing those committed to anti U.S. American heresies. For Robinson, the very fact that the nation engaged in a debate concerning torture depicts the United States as a morally compromised nation unable to lead by example in the international community. The post–9/11 turn to torture provides an uncomfortable response to the question regarding national identity: "This spectacle insults and dishonors everyone." David Luban also questioned the relationship between torture and the U.S. American national identity. He commented in a November 27, 2005, column for the *Washington Post*, "Assaults on human dignity are not who we are or what we stand for." Almost five and a half years later, on May 11, 2011, John McCain made a similar observation in his own *Washington Post* editorial. Senator McCain remarked, "This is a moral debate. It is about who we are."

One of the most direct critiques of the pro torture position addressed the relevancy of the ticking time bomb argument altogether. David Luban, professor of philosophy and law at Georgetown University criticized the use of the ticking time bomb scenario as intellectually dishonest and suggested the initial premise of the ticking time bomb argument deserves significant scrutiny. When, he asked, do intelligence personnel ever have previous knowledge of an impending attack? What is the likelihood that security forces, whether they be police, FBI, or CIA, have prior knowledge that "a bomb is there, ticking away, and that officials know it and know they have the man who planted it."[31] These situations, he argued, are the stuff of popular culture and obfuscate the real torture debate. The real debate revolves around what it means to treat others, even those who may pose a threat to national security, humanely. Where is the dividing line between enhanced interrogation and the cruel, abusive, or degrading treatment the U.S. government professed to abhor? Luban gave John McCain's comment a nod when he concurred that the torture debate contributes to the ongoing performance of national identity and won't be settled until the country takes a long, hard look at what it means to question a prisoner with dignity. Luban was not the only editorialist to criticize the problematic focus on ticking time bomb arguments.

Responding to the justifications provided in relation to ticking time bomb scenarios, Rosa Brooks's editorial published in the May 29, 2005, issue of the *Los Angeles Times* mused that the use of torture says more about the person doing the torture than it does about the need to procure invaluable, time sensitive information. Like Luban, she suggested that the "what ifs" inherent in the ticking time bomb debate distracted from the real questions at hand. She wrote,

> Letting ticking-bomb scenarios set the terms of debate also diverts our attention from the real challenges of the war on terror. Torture is always a weapon of the weak: It's used by those too clumsy to get information any other way. If we had better human-intelligence agents on the ground, with the cultural skills needed to gain the trust of local populations, we wouldn't need illegal interrogation methods to gain information. And if we got serious about preventing the abuse of detainees, we might find more friends when we look for information.

Matthew Alexander, a fourteen-year Air Force veteran and senior interrogator during the Iraq war, wrote an editorial for the November 2008 *Washington Post* agreeing with Brooks's assertion from almost five years earlier. Alexander challenged the assertion "that we need the rough stuff for the truly hard cases" and called for a new approach to interrogation "based on building rapport with suspects, showing cultural understanding and using good old-fashioned brainpower to tease out information."

The voices contributing to the torture debate reflect the complex nature of the moral arguments for and against the practice. As all of the columnists acknowledged, 9/11 challenged U.S. Americans to rethink the world, as well as their place in it, at a foundational level. Are the citizens of the United States willing to compromise their national values to pursue and stop future terrorist atrocities? Columnists like Charlies Krauthammer argued the U.S. should be prepared to use torture, to embrace Dick Cheney's dark side, when reasonable evidence regarding an impending attack surfaces. Indeed, Krauthammer's description of torture as a necessary evil echoed in the rhetoric of editorialists who supported benign forms of torture in limited circumstances. Editorialists like Jonathan Alter described torture as a morally problematic practice but refused to denounce psychological torture outright, suggesting counter terrorism might require the U.S. to concede the battle over moral high ground in order to win the broader war on terror. In contrast to those who accepted torture as an important weapon in the U.S. military arsenal, as well as the editorialists who supported harsher forms of psychological interrogation, writers like Bob Herbert and Eugene Robinson rejected torture outright. Tying torture to U.S. American national identity, nearly all of the editorialists opposed to all forms of torture tied the use of the reprehensible practice to a crisis of conscience. To embrace torture, they argued, is to offer a wholesale rejection of the U.S. position as moral leaders within the global community. What is important to note in this ongoing discussion is that a final position regarding torture never coalesces; in Bakhtinian terms, the conversation remains unfinalized.

The Jedi Turn to the Dark Side

At first glance, suggests Richard Dees, the *Star Wars* universe is "a world with very few shades of gray, much less of brighter, more interesting moral colors."[32] The intertwined stories of Luke Skywalker and Anakin Skywalker/Darth Vader, and their respective associations with the light and dark sides of the Force, certainly follow this axiological pattern. While Luke and Darth Vader have become synonymous with the archetypal struggle between the light and dark, compassion and brutality, love and hate, other characters within the *Star Wars* mythos—Han Solo, Lando Calrissian, Count Dooku—suggest that a galaxy at war isn't always an easy place to negotiate questions of morality. Rather than a fictional universe of moral clarity, I want to suggest *Star Wars* depicts a galaxy rife with moral complexity. This is particularly true in *The Clone Wars*. As David Wiegand wrote in his March 4, 2014, article for SFGate.com:

> *Star Wars* has always been about good versus evil, as have so many melodramas in popular culture throughout history, but knowing which is which isn't always easy. No 'black hat/white hat' signaling here. While hidden identity and secret motivations have always propelled the *Star Wars* saga, the films and *Clone Wars* also explore the moral duality in many of its characters, regardless of whether we initially see them as good or evil.

The Clone Wars, as Wiegand points out, provides extended screen time to explore the various characters and their complex moral development. Characters previously depicted in flat, two dimensional simplicity, emerge as emotionally complex, three dimensional individuals struggling with the ethical dilemmas associated with wartime.

One such dilemma, argues Michael Roston, is the morality of torture. As his December 28, 2009, trueslant.com article titled "Should your Kids Be Watching Cartoon Torture" suggests, television is ground zero in the post–9/11 debate regarding torture's legitimacy. Acknowledging *24* as one of the most frequent voices in the ongoing cultural dialogue, Roston also identifies *The Clone Wars* as an important participant. Roston focuses his

observations on a single episode of the series, an episode I engage momentarily, and questions whether morally ambiguous representations of torture
are appropriate content for Cartoon Network, a cable network targeting
children. Although my examination of torture in *The Clone Wars* does not
address age appropriateness, I want to echo Roston's praise of the program
for engaging complicated issues like torture and depicting the physical,
emotional, and spiritual costs of prolonged war. Like the editorialists who
explored the post–9/11 ethical arguments for and against enhanced interrogation, *The Clone Wars* grapples with whether or not torture might be
used to save lives and protect the public. To that end, my analysis clusters
around the positions articulated in the previous section: support for torture,
support for humane forms of torture, and the denunciation of any and all
forms of torture.

Given the depiction of Jedi Knights as spiritualists and defenders of
the public good, a turn to torture would seem out-of-character. For Anakin
Skywalker, and the character arc that leads to his transformation into Darth
Vader, acts of torture offer a prophetic glimpse into the young Jedi's propensity for treading dangerously close to the dark side. It should be noted,
however, that Anakin's use of torture is not without cause. Echoing the
editorialists who supported the use of torture to prevent deadly terrorist
attacks, Anakin utilizes torture—both psychological and physical—as a
means to an end. In the episode "Mystery of the Thousand Moons," for
example, Anakin and Obi-Wan face a version of the ticking time bomb
scenario. When Padmé, Ahsoka, Jar Jar, and several clone troopers find
themselves exposed to the deadly Blue Shadow Virus, a biological weapon
created by the Separatists, Anakin interrogates a captured Dr. Nuvo Vindi
and demands the antidote. Instead of utilizing traditional forms of questioning, Anakin leaps straight to threats of physical violence. Holding the
tip of his lightsaber to the doctor's throat, an obviously angry Anakin begins
his interrogation.

> ANAKIN: Where's the antidote, Vindi?
> VINDI: You mistake my role, Jedi. My job was to manufacture a plague, not
>   to cure it.
> ANAKIN: We don't have time for games ::thrusts saber closer::
> OBI-WAN: Patience, Anakin. There's more than one way to skin a womp rat.
> ANAKIN: I said "Where!?" ::thrusts closer again::[33]

Although Dr. Vindi never provides the needed antidote, the five-line
exchange is worth considering in detail. Important to note is the way
Anakin ups the threat of physical violence, as well as the psychological distress that frequently accompanies physical posturing, with each repeated

request. An obviously concerned Obi-Wan looks on as Anakin's lightsaber blade inches closer and closer to Dr. Vindi's throat. Obi-Wan's calm admonishment functions to both remind Anakin of his commitments to uphold the ideals of the Jedi Order, ideals that don't condone physical or psychological torture, and suggests there might be other ways to locate an antidote. Above all else, Obi-Wan's idiom functions as an attempt to defuse an interrogation gone awry. As Anakin stands ready to kill Dr. Vindi, Obi-Wan pulls him back from the brink and delays, at least momentarily, his Padawan's descent to the dark side.

Faced with a similar situation in "Brain Invaders," Anakin once again turns to violence. This time, however, he moves beyond threats. Without Obi-Wan to act as his conscience, Anakin crosses the line between the light and dark sides of the Force. Confronted with another time bomb scenario, Anakin rushes to save Ahsoka from mind controlled clone troopers and a fellow Padawan. Attempting to free the mind controlled crew and save Ahsoka, Anakin interrogates a prisoner—Poggle the Lesser—who may know how to counteract the effects of the mind control. As Anakin approaches Poggle's holding cell, a modified version of The Imperial March—also referred to as Darth Vader's Theme—illuminates Anakin's mental state and serves as an ominous omen to the pending enhanced interrogation. When a Jedi mind trick fails to pry the much needed secrets from the detainee, Anakin backhands him across the room and exclaims, "Mind tricks? I don't need mind tricks to get you to talk."[34] Despite Anakin's threat of physical violence, Poggle still refuses to talk. In a moment foreshadowing his future transformation to Darth Vader, Anakin reaches out with the Force, lifts the prisoner telekinetically, and proceeds to Force choke him. The depicted scene—Anakin's face contorted with rage; Poggle clawing at his neck as he struggles to breathe—offers a troubling glimpse into how far the young Jedi will go to save his friends. In his December 4, 2009, review of the episode, IGN.com's Eric Goldman remarked, "Jokes about Jack Bauer interrogation techniques aside, this was obviously a very big deal, as torture is certainly not the Jedi way, and the force choke is of course one of Darth Vader's favorite tricks. Once again, I am impressed and surprised by how dark this show can go." Perhaps even more disturbing is the ease with which Anakin justifies his actions. Confronted by three Jedi Masters who were unable to convince Poggle to talk, Anakin brushes aside their questions and states the important thing is that he obtained the information needed to free their mind controlled comrades and save Ahsoka Tano.

In the final broadcast episode of the series (the final 13 episodes of

The Clone Wars were released on Netflix), Anakin faces yet another variation of the time bomb scenario. When Ahsoka is wrongly accused of a terrorist bombing, expelled from the Jedi Order, and brought before a military tribunal under charges of treason, Anakin follows every possible lead as he tries to uncover the truth and exonerate his Padawan. When his investigation leads him into the Coruscant underworld and a confrontation with former Separatist assassin Asajj Ventress, Anakin turns to torture immediately. Using the Force he slams Ventress into a wall, Force chokes her, pulls her to him telekinetically, and threatens her with his lightsaber. He maintains his physically threatening posture until his captive divulges all she knows about the person behind Ahsoka's wrongful imprisonment. At the conclusion of their conversation, Anakin offers one last psychological nudge as he growls, "If you're lying, you're dead."[35]

As these examples illustrate, Anakin Skywalker repeatedly chooses to ignore his moral compass and turn to the path that he sees as quicker, more powerful, than attempting to remain above the moral fray. Of all the Jedi Knights, Anakin is the one who most often pushes the boundaries of human dignity and resorts to various forms of physical and psychological abuse as a means of coercing prisoners into divulging information. He threatens Dr. Vindi psychologically, tortures Poggle the Lesser physically, and uses both to wrest information from Ventress. In each case, Anakin is confronted with the all-too-familiar ticking tomb bomb scenario and, in a do or die moment, turns to torture. Anakin's actions appear both efficient and expedient as the prisoners succumb quickly to his actions and provide the information needed to save the day. In this sense, then, *The Clone Wars* appears to offer a positive assessment of torture. The message is simple: torture works. What should not be forgotten, however, is Anakin's longer character arc. While Anakin's techniques might appear effective, these actions also contribute into Anakin's descent into darkness. By sacrificing his morality, Anakin loses everything.

Although Anakin Skywalker is the only Jedi Knight portrayed as fully embracing physical torture, other Jedi Knights appear willing to make exceptions regarding psychological torture. Given the centrality of Ahsoka Tano's character, it should come as no surprise that she frequently emerges as a character attempting to make sense of a galaxy at war. As a Padawan learner—a Jedi-in-training who is learning the physical, mental, and spiritual dimensions of the order—she often inhabits liminal spaces. Equally confident and unsure of herself, she sometimes stops and thinks about decisions that might be intuitive to a more accomplished Jedi Knight. Additionally, she acts impulsively and without thinking things through entirely.

Nowhere is this more obvious than in her struggle with the power she wields as a Jedi. When a criminal or military investigation proves difficult, Ahsoka's first response is to attempt to resolve the issues with threats of violence. Her tendency to walk the line between the light side and dark side of the Force becomes evident in the first season episode "Cloak of Darkness." Assigned to help Jedi Master Luminara Unduli transport a captured Nute Gunray, Viceroy of the Trade Federation, back to Corsuscant to face accusations of attempting to assassinate Senator Padmé Amidala, as well as being in league with the leadership of the Confederacy of Separatist planets, Ahsoka participates in the initial interrogation of the detainee. Master Unduli questions the Viceroy about his knowledge of "secret allies, locations of their bases," but when the Viceroy proves resistant to traditional questioning, Ahsoka takes matters into her own hands.[36] Igniting her lightsaber, she rushes toward the prisoner and holds the green blade to his throat. She raises her voice and attempts to force the information from him: "Liar! Liar! I'm tired of all this whining. Tell us what we want to know right now or I will gut you like a Rokarian dirtfish." As the Viceroy screams and cowers, Jedi Master Unduli grabs Ahsoka by the arm and leads her away from the prisoner. She rebukes Ahsoka sternly for her unseemly behavior: "Padawan! Terror is not a weapon the Jedi use."[37] Ahsoka assures the Jedi Master that she never intended to hurt the prisoner but hoped that her actions would scare him into revealing important information.

Ahsoka's encounter with Viceroy Gunray is not the only time she turns to enhanced interrogation. For example, in the episode "Lightsaber Lost," Ahsoka loses her lightsaber while on an investigation in the Corsuscant Underworld.[38] When she locates the pickpocket who lifted her weapon, she immediately resorts to violence. She threatens him, roughs him up, and eventually throws the criminal against the wall via the Force. The Jedi Master accompanying her admonishes her behavior and instructs her to rely on patience, that given time, the solution to her dilemma will surface. The difference in their respective approaches to problem solving is made clear throughout the remainder of the episode. While Ahsoka races across the sprawling spires of the underworld in an extended, parkour inspired chase scene (Ahsoka ultimately loses her suspect), Master Sinube gathers eyewitness testimony. Tera Sinube, an elderly Jedi Master recognized for his abilities as a criminal investigator, plays the perfect foil to Ahsoka's impatient youthfulness. Displaying his skills as a "methodical investigator" and "keen observer of people," Master Sinube teaches the Jedi Padawan that nonviolent interrogation and the thoughtful, thorough review of evidence proves effective.[39] Similar to Matthew Alexander's *Washington Post* editorial advocating interrogations based on affinity building, cultural awareness, and analytical reasoning, Tera Sinube's investigation proceeds humanely, thoughtfully, and levelheadedly. Sinube's painstaking and disciplined approach, an approach that seems agonizingly slow to Ahsoka, leads to the apprehension of a suspect and the return of Ahsoka's lightsaber.

This admonishment of Ahsoka—considering how frequently it occurs—is a pattern that cannot be ignored. When she threatens violence, she receives a stern rebuke: Jedi do not rely on terror as a weapon. These moments of tension between the Padawan and her mentors positions Ahsoka as a learner, as someone trying to figure out how to live one's life by a stringent ethical code. Furthermore, in the Mortis trilogy Ahsoka encounters a Force vision of her future adult self. The future Ahsoka warns the younger Padawan to be mindful of her lack of discipline and her tendency toward impulsive action. The specter urges Padawan Ahsoka to be wary of Anakin's teachings, that continuing to train with the troubled Jedi may result in a turn to the dark side or even death.[40] Privy to Anakin's dark inclinations within the series, as well as his eventual fall to the dark side, viewers once again encounter Ahsoka as someone struggling with difficult moral choices. Will she follow the teachings of her most respected teacher, someone who frequently bends the rules in order to accomplish the task at hand, or will she embrace Jedi values as both a means and an end? I want to suggest here that Ahsoka's struggle to make sense of Jedi teachings parallels some of the same tensions experience by U.S. Americans in regard to torture. At some level, most people understand torture as an inhumane practice. Where the tension arises, as several editorialists pointed out, is whether engaging in questionable moral practices might lead to a greater public good. The second season episode "Children of the Force" reinforces Ahsoka's character as a site of moral conflict.

As part of Darth Sidious's plan to train Force sensitive children in the dark side lore of the Sith, the bounty hunter Cad Bane kidnaps two Force sensitive infants. Despite his efforts to stay one step ahead of the Jedi, Bane is eventually captured and interrogated regarding the location of the abducted children.

BANE: What are you going to do, Jedi, torture me?
WINDU: I think the fear of whoever you work for, outweighs your fear of us.
BANE: This conversation is over.[41]

Windu's response to Bane's question accentuates the immoral logic of torture. The primary assumption behind a threat of torture is fear: the fear that physical pain or psychological distress will be inflicted if one does not capitulate (or the already inflicted pain will continue). Windu's comment implies that one way to compel Bane to reveal the needed information is to increase his fear of his Jedi interrogators.

This turn in the interrogation contradicts the primary teachings of the Jedi Order. As Yoda makes clear in *The Phantom Menace*, "Fear is the path to the dark side. Fear leads to anger. Anger leads to hate. Hate leads to suffering."[42] Despite this core teaching of the order, Windu, Kenobi, and Skywalker opt to utilize fear as a weapon.

ANAKIN: We'll have to use the Force to make him talk.
OBI-WAN: I don't think Bane is that weak.
AHSOKA: Maybe if we all concentrated on his mind together.
OBI-WAN: Using the Force to compel a strong mind to cooperate is ::pause :: risky.
WINDU: There is a danger that his mind could be destroyed in the process.
ANAKIN: Well, do we have another choice?[43]

Determining that they do not have another choice, all three Jedi enter Bane's holding cell. The visual choices in this scene are particularly striking. Throughout the scene, dramatic shadow effects darken the faces of the Jedi implying that their collective action pulls them closer to the dark side. The three stand shoulder to shoulder, right arms extended toward Bane, brows furrowed in concentration. Ahsoka Tano stands behind the three Jedi, her face and body obscured by the foregrounded figures. Anakin begins the psychological interrogation as he states assertively, "You will take us to the holocron." Obi-Wan joins Anakin when the line is repeated a second time; Mace Windu joins for a third repetition. As each Jedi adds his voice to the collective Jedi mind trick, Bane's discomfort grows. He fidgets, he squirms, he exhibits increasing mental incoherence until he shouts, "No! Get out of my head!" His face contorts as he groans, growls, and thrashes about, trying to resist the violent mental probing. At the height of Bane's mental and physical distress, the camera cuts to the startled face of Ahsoka Tano. Her eyes dart back and forth to the three Jedi inflicting pain on their prisoner. She is clearly troubled by the actions of her teacher and two members of the Jedi Council. The Jedi finally end their mental assault and Bane's head slumps to the table. As he struggles to regain his breath, Anakin turns to his fellow Jedi and says, "Perhaps we should try again!" The threat of continued psychological torture proves too much for Bane and he agrees to help the Jedi locate the missing children. An obviously shaken Bane lifts his head slowly, waving off another round of mental punishment: "I, I've had enough of that. I'll take you to the holocron. You'll get your children back." Cade's fear of the Jedi and the pain they can inflict outweighs his fear of his employer.[44]

Based on the actions of many of the lead characters in the series, *The Clone Wars* puts forth arguments for the efficacy of both physical and psychological torture. When Anakin, Ahsoka, Obi-Wan, or Mace Windu resort to enhanced interrogation techniques, they usually get results. On the surface, then, the series legitimates the practice in limited circumstances. When lives are on the line and all other avenues exhausted, torture is fair game. At the same time, however, torture is also portrayed as morally repugnant. Despite the efficacy of the torture techniques employed by Jedi throughout the series, the acts in question are intended to invoke a sense of unease in audience members. Within the purview of the *Star Wars* universe, viewers know these actions run counter to not only Jedi beliefs but also the Galactic Republic's basic ethical principles. These ethical principles, particularly in regard to torture, are brought into sharp relief when compared to the morally impoverished behaviors displayed by many allied with the Separatists. In fact, Separatist military leaders and operatives utilize torture with impunity. Early in season two, for example, mercenary Cade Bane tries to coerce a Jedi, through repeated electrical shocks, into opening a holocron (a holographic archive of Jedi knowledge). Bane's torture kills Jedi Ropal and his body is tossed aside like a piece of refuse. Later in the episode, Bane turns to psychological torture—he threatens to harm a captured Ahsoka Tano—and coerces Anakin to unlock the Jedi archive. Even though Ahsoka implores her Master to let her die—the information Bane is after will endanger children—Anakin capitulates. In another season two episode "Grievous Intrigue," Separatist field commander General Grievous attempts to lure several Jedi Knights into a trap by torturing one of their comrades: Jedi Master Eeth Koth. To underscore the heartlessness of the act, a tactical droid emits a mechanical laugh as it watches the captured Jedi Master writhe with pain.[45] The season four episode "Prisoners" continues to reinforce the idea that Separatist allies lack moral conviction as warlord Riff Tamson utilizes both physical and psychological torture as he attempts to extract information from Anakin Skywalker and Kit Fisto.[46] Even though the warlord acknowledges the Jedi may not have the information, Tamson clearly revels in the pain and suffering of his enemies. The frequency with which villains turn to torture, as well as the pleasure villainous characters seem to derive from inflicting harm on others, reinforces torture as a reprehensible act.

The stark moral contrast between the heroic Galactic Republic and the villainous Separatists is not the only way the series indicts torture. The aforementioned reprimands of Ahsoka, presented by Master Unduli and Master Sinube, are important utterances that invite the audience to evaluate the moral flexibility exhibited by characters. The exchange between Unduli and Ahsoka occurs early in the series (season one, episode nine), thus setting a moral precedent for all ensuing utterances implicating torture. Unduli's declaration is definitive and leaves no room for equivocation: Jedi do not use physical or psychological threats to coerce prisoners into divulging information. All subsequent references to torture are judged by Unduli's— and presumably that of the entire Jedi Order—high standard. The rebuke offered by Master Sinube in season two reinforces the immorality of torture and also emphasizes alternative actions consistent with the principled conscientiousness displayed by Jedi Knights. Presented early in the series, both moments constitute part of the broader cultural conversation regarding torture and, in the tradition of speculative fiction, condemn contemporary counterterrorism practices and related policies. As Bakhtin suggests, any and all utterances are always simultaneously responding to previous utterances and directed toward salient utterances that follow. He states:

> The word in living conversation is directly, blatantly, oriented toward a future answer word: it provokes an answer, anticipates it and structures itself in the answer's direction. Forming itself in an atmosphere of the already spoken, the word is at the same time determined by that which has not yet been said but which is needed and in fact anticipated by the answering word. Such is the situation in any living dialogue.[47]

The intersection of past, present, and future utterances is the nexus of responsive understanding. As a media representation and carefully orchestrated utterance, Unduli's comment addresses the previously uttered remarks that constitute the public dialogue regarding torture, gives voice to a particular perspective (torture is wrong), and becomes part of consequent conversations encountered by viewers. Responding to previous voices in the present, this articulation plays an important part in the responsive understanding of both viewers and those involved in the broader public dialogue.

Torture and the Dark Side

According to Louis Michael Seidman, professor at Georgetown University's Law Center, U.S. American media dropped the ball in terms of covering torture and promoting a sustained conversation on the ethical and legal implications thereof. He wrote, "We need to understand torture and all that it tells us about ourselves, rather than simply outlaw it. We need, in short, to talk about torture."[48] Alan Dershowitz, professor, lawyer, and public intellectual, voiced a similar concern in a September 7, 2011, opinion piece posted to Reuters.com: "Torture, like any other topic, deserves a vigorous debate in a democracy such as ours. Even if government officials decline to discuss such issues, academics and advocacy groups have a duty to raise them and submit them to the marketplace of ideas." Like Seidman and Dershowitz, I acknowledge the need to have a vigorous public discussion regarding torture. Unlike Seidman and Dershowitz, I argue public deliberations concerning efficacy, ethicalness, potential consequences of torture have been ongoing since the Abu Ghraib photographs surfaced. Conversations did take place, and continue to take place, in the public square. In the attempt to come to terms with torture, as well as determine how torture might shape our individual collective identities, the public continues to talk about torture. Editorialists offered thoughts on the matter from a variety of different perspectives. And, as my brief literature review at the beginning of this chapter attests—as well as my substantive exploration of *The Clone Wars*—popular culture texts invited viewers to consider not only the efficacy of torture but also the impact such practices might have on a culture's collective consciousness. Several editorialists made clear calls to include torture as a weapon in the intelligence gathering arsenal. If those tasked with protecting the public from harm uncover a potential terrorist act, they have a moral duty to protect "the people" despite the moral cost. The emphasis on torture's ethical dimension is worth reiterating. For editorialists like Krauthammer and Stephens, the debate over torture's malevolence isn't the issue; both writers identify torture as a necessary evil, a dehumanizing practice that should weigh heavily on the public's conscience. The decision on whether or not to torture another human being involves a figurative moral scale that requires weighing the moral egregiousness of the act with the resulting amount of good that could come about. If the torture of an individual might stop a pending attack, or uncover significant information regarding the personnel, communications, and operations of a terrorist organization, the ends justify the ends. In short, "torture is a dark art that you use because it works."[49]

This same position, at least on the surface, appears to hold true for the Jedi Knights of *The Clone Wars*. When Anakin resorts to threats of violence, and when Obi-Wan Kenobi and Mace Windu join with Anakin to pry information from a resistant prisoner, they do so knowing a significant number of lives hang in the immediate balance. Like the editorialists invoking the ticking time bomb scenario as a criterion for suspending human decency, Jedi Knights utilize torture as a decidedly inhumane means to accomplish a public good. The fact that these practices should trouble Jedi considerably always makes an appearance as part of the text: Obi-Wan suggests to Anakin there are other ways of making Dr. Vindi talk, Master Unduli and Master Sinube remind Ahsoka of her obligations to the tenets of the Jedi Order, and Ahsoka herself expresses misgivings as she watches her teachers torture Cad Bane. Of all the Jedi, Anakin Skywalker is the one individual who employs torture with little or no remorse and even less consideration. In the context of Anakin's broader character arc, his depiction as a Jedi willing to make moral exceptions contributes to his turn to the dark side. One wonders if Anakin's increasingly violent behaviors aren't intended to represent the way U.S. troops and interrogators also felt themselves pulled toward morally repugnant actions. Faced with the perceived threat of imminent terrorist attacks U.S. representatives, who presumably acted in the name of protecting U.S. citizens, turned to Cheney's dark side. So while torture works to save lives in the present—and it always does in *The Clone Wars*—it comes at significant cost.

Anakin's descent into darkness should come as no surprise according to the aforementioned Richard Cohen. As Cohen and other editorialists giving reluctant support to limited torture techniques articulated, even the most humane methods could eventually lead to more violent, physical acts. Torture, even in its benign forms, paves the way for increasingly vicious acts. As Alter, Cohen, and Dershowitz articulated through their reluctant support for psychological interrogation and other non-lethal methods, such costs deserve careful consideration by the U.S. government and public. Involved in a conflict offering few hard targets and the high probability of civilian casualties—that is the nature of terrorism, after all—intelligence gathering becomes the primary means by which to uncover and disrupt terrorist communication networks, strategic planning, and imminent attacks. Unable to rely solely on strategic mobility, high tech weaponry, and superior combat troop training, counterterrorism efforts may require the U.S. people to carry the heavy moral burden of supporting non-lethal torture. The call to weigh these decisions carefully also echoes throughout *The Clone Wars*. Ahsoka's character trajectory details a youngling's evolution from an impetuous adolescent willing to bend the moral teachings of the Jedi Code for the sake of expediency to a thoughtful young adult contemplating the dangers inherent in moral flexibility. The character, who justifies psychological torture early in the series, develops into the eyes through which the audience judges the moral quandaries facing her teachers. Her reaction to Cad Bane's painful, psychological interrogation at the hands of her mentors encourages the audience to question the moral judgment of the respected Jedi Knights. At the same time, however, this particular interrogation also heeds Seidman's and Dershowitz's call for deliberation. Anakin, Mace, and Obi-Wan evaluate the situation, discussing the various possibilities and pitfalls of forcing a prisoner to talk through psychological coercion, and come to the conclusion that the potential payoff—saving children—is worth the risk. Obi-Wan's observation that compelling "a strong mind to cooperate is risky," as well as Mace's acknowledgment that a person's mind might suffer irrevocable damage, epitomizes the sentiments expressed by editorialists who urged caution, but not an outright rejection, of non-lethal torture. Given the visual depiction of the scene, Obi-Wan's assertion goes beyond the risk to their prisoner and extends to the risk of walking so close to the dark side. Even Windu's remark regarding the "danger that his mind could be destroyed," a line obviously directed toward Cad Bane's well-being, also implicates the danger to the interrogators' minds. As Cohen wondered in his editorial, how long will it be before the torture's "rapacious appetite" urges the Jedi to bend the moral rules yet again? In this particular instance, the Jedi Knights seem painfully aware of the "risky" moral implications and, in a calculated effort to gain information expediently, choose to act anyway.

While those open to non-lethal forms of torture argued on the basis of expediency, those opposed to any and all forms of torture focused their arguments on questions of identity. Editorialists like Herbert, Lee III, and Robinson shifted the debate away from discussion of expediency and efficacy and toward a discussion of post–9/11 national identity. For these participants in the public square, the debate at hand did not revolve around a complicated moral calculus intended to evaluate whether an immoral act might result in a tangible public good but around the assertion that the articulation and enactment of communal values is fundamental to collective identity. Put simply, a people are what they say and do. The columnists urged their readers to take a long, hard look at the actions of their government and evaluate whether or not those actions coincide with commonly accepted national values. Several questions emerged from the content of their respective columns. What does it mean to be a U.S. American? What does the United States, frequently described as the "shining city on the hill," represent to other nations? What values, morals, and beliefs define the nation? What does it mean when the nation's actions conflict with its moral principles? How have intentional excursions into Cheney's dark side tarnished U.S. American national identity and global reputation? Is it possible for the United States to maintain a position of international leadership when engaged in immoral acts? Debates over these questions have, according to Lubin and Brooks, been obfuscated by misguided conversations over how government representatives might respond to a ticking time bomb scenario. As both writers make clear, arguments addressing "what ifs" and popular fictions draw attention away from the debate over what it means to suspend one's commitment to treat people—even if they are considered an enemy of the state—respectfully and humanely.

This same question concerning the intertwined relationship between discourse, action, and identity also surfaces, although not explicitly stated, in *The Clone Wars*. The central characters of the extended narrative, characters like Obi-Wan Kenobi, Anakin Skywalker, Mace Windu, and Ahsoka Tano, all utilize torture, in one form or another, as they fight what most would describe as a just war against the Separatists. And, as I pointed out earlier, the ubiquity with which Separatist characters embrace torture clearly demarcates the practice as a morally compromised act. The reproachful remarks and actions of Jedi Masters Unduli and Sinube stand as a criticism and suggest, like David Luban, that "assaults on human dignity are not who we are or what we stand for." These characters remind viewers that Jedi Knights answer to a higher calling, that to be a Jedi Knight requires one to live a principled life. When considered dialogically, the representations of Unduli and Sinube reinforce the unprincipled actions of those Jedi who embrace, sometimes decisively and sometimes hesitantly, actions which cause pain and suffering for others. Granted, the techniques do work in the context of the narrative but there is also the understanding that the Jedi Knights are selling their souls in the process. In other words, the contradictory depictions of the Jedi Knights—those who refuse to utilize enhanced interrogation and turn to alternative measures and those who choose to willingly torture prisoners—come together dialogically and encourage audience members to engage questions of identity. What does it mean to be a Jedi Knight? Does a Jedi Knight torture? When directed toward a culture living in a perpetual wartime state, questions of Jedi identity clearly intersect with questions of U.S. American national identity.

In his book *Captain American and the National Superhero*, Jason Dittmer argues that popular culture representations, and superheroes specifically, play a role in reinforcing, reconceptualizing, and rejecting national consciousness, governmental policy, and political subjectivity. He states, "Superheroes are co-constitutive elements of both American identity and the U.S. government's foreign policy practices."[50] Given torture's frequent depiction within *The Clone Wars*, I find little reason to think the series does not fulfill a function similar to that of Dittmer's superheroes. Joining the ranks of editorialists, the creators of *The Clone Wars* articulates a response to the U.S. government's official discourse and join the dialogic exchange concerning security, expediency, and national identity. The editorialists, it should be noted, with their multiple voices and perspectives, direct their ideas toward the inhabitants of the public square and participate in the responsive give and take that characterizes communal deliberation. Similarly, *The Clone Wars* offers a complex representation of the torture debate complete with characters and storylines that encourage viewers to wrestle with multiple positions, justifications, and potential consequences. Each editorialist advocates for one position or another—sometimes in a agreement with her or his fellow columnists and sometimes in disagreement—but a consensus never emerges. Some columnists value national security above all other considerations and call for utilizing any and all means to protect the public. Others try to walk a fine line between security, expediency, and national identity by staking out a nuanced position that simultaneously supports the use of non-lethal interrogation and maintains commitment to treat prisoners humanely. Formulating a response to those who advocate torture in any form, physical or psychological, opponents place the utmost value in maintaining a national identity founded on handful of immutable human rights. *The Clone Wars* differs from the editorialists in this regard. Although several perspectives regarding the morality of torture weave throughout the text, the final message is decidedly monologic: torture is reprehensible. Every act of torture, no matter how effective, is intended to evoke shock, dismay, and disappointment. In this way, *The Clone Wars* reinforces the sentiments expressed by the editorialists who denounce torture outright and asks viewers to judge the U.S. American actions with the same sense of shock, dismay, and disappointment. As the fall of the Jedi Order and Anakin's transformation to Darth Vader suggest, the turn to torture marks a rejection of collective moral principles and an acceptance that the ends sometimes justify unconscionable means.

FOUR

Obama, Obi-Wan and the Contradiction of Fighting a Just War

> "We must begin by acknowledging a hard truth: We will not eradicate violent conflict in our lifetimes. There will be times when nations, acting individually or in concert, will find the use of force not only necessary but morally justified."[1]—President Barack Obama, "Acceptance of the Nobel Peace Prize"

> "No longer certain that one ever does win a war, I am. For in fighting the battles, the bloodshed, already lost we have."[2]—Jedi Master Yoda, "Sacrifice"

The opening minutes of *The Clone Wars* theatrical film, a ninety eight minute film comprised of what amounted to a four episode story arc of the television series that followed, left no question that big screen and small screen depictions fit within the overarching narrative of the *Star Wars* universe. Capital ships exchanged cannon fire, starfighters engaged in dogfights reminiscent of World War II, clone troopers clashed with battle droids, and Jedi Knights slashed across screen with their unmistakable lightsabers. Most importantly, *The Clone Wars* established itself as a worthy addition to the ongoing story of a galaxy that never seems to have a moment's peace. In fact, of all the on screen *Star Wars* texts, *The Clone Wars* offers the most complex examination of life within a society plagued by constant warfare of one kind or another.

Of particular interest for this chapter is the role of the Jedi Knights within a galaxy plagued by war. Committed to the principles of peaceful deliberation, justice, and thoughtful action, the canonical texts of the *Star Wars* universe (the six films and *The Clone Wars* series) depict the Jedi as spacefaring diplomats and peacekeepers who turn to violence only as a last resort. In *The Phantom Menace*, for example, Qui-Gon Jinn and a young Obi-Wan Kenobi attempt to resolve a trade dispute between the Trade Federation and the planet Naboo. When negotiations fail and the parties engage in military conflict, Master Qui-Gon Jinn turns to Queen Amidala, the leader of the Naboo, and informs her, "I cannot fight a war for you, your Highness. I can only protect you."[3] Several episodes of *The Clone Wars* reinforce the representation of Jedi as negotiators first and warriors second. The episodes "Trespass," "Voyage of Temptation," and "Heroes on Both Sides" involve plots whereby the Jedi act as mediators of a direct conflict or as diplomatic security for peace negotiations. These examples aside, the vast majority of episodes involve the Jedi Knights as generals, as ranking soldiers leading their clone troopers on the front line of the war against the Separatists. The discussion in these episodes rarely centers on issues of peace or, at the very least, exploring ways to cease hostilities, but focuses on the possible military tactics needed to achieve the next objective.

The people of the Galactic Republic, however, are not unthinking masses who support the war against the Confederacy of Independent Systems blindly. Instead, many citizens call the Jedi to task for failing to uphold their communal identity as peacekeepers. In the episode "Sabotage," for example, hundreds of protestors gather outside the Jedi Temple and call for an end to the ongoing conflict.[4] The fictional protestors of *The Clone Wars* are portrayed as part of an ongoing public dialogue about when, and how, a government should (or shouldn't) wage war. These fictional conversations have significant political resonance for post–9/11 audiences. While inhabitants of the *Star Wars* universe grapple with the impact of prolonged war, post–9/11 audiences wrestle with the cultural impact of ongoing wars in Iraq, Afghanistan, and widespread counterterrorism actions around the globe. What I want to argue in this chapter, then, is that the conversations occurring within *The Clone Wars* are one way in which viewers are called to consider issues of wartime justice. According to Michael Walzer, these calls to engage the questions of what constitutes a just war, as well as just conduct within war, remain particularly relevant for contemporary audiences. He remarks, "What happens, or does not happen, on the ground is radically affected by what happens in what we might think of as the moral/political surround."[5] The actions of those considering the possibility of war, as well as conducting a war, must "pay attention to public opinion, our opinion, because we decide, or we have a part in deciding, the benefits and costs of fighting well or fighting badly."[6] It is on these moments of dialogic tension I wish to focus.

According to Dave Filoni, the exploration of the tension between the Jedi as peacekeepers/mediators and the Jedi as generals is one of the series' major thematic elements. As Filoni explains during a March 18, 2014, discussion with IGN.com's Eric Goldman, Yoda's metaphysical journey during the series' four final episodes seems to suggest that the Jedi Order's willingness to become embroiled in a war resulted in their ultimate downfall. Speaking of Yoda directly Filoni observes:

> He knows, frankly, that the Jedi of the time have lost their way and that it's going to be a path that very few of them are going to be able to walk out of the Clone Wars and into whatever the future may hold. Basically, they're all going to have to pay a price for their own role in the violence and the destruction and the things that have happened in the galaxy, which turns out to be true.

Given Filoni's reflections on the concluding arc, Yoda's uncertainty regarding the possibility of winning a war—quoted at the beginning of this chapter—emerges as a significant point of allegorical consideration. In watching Yoda and the other Jedi Knights struggle with their actions during wartime, viewers are drawn into an ongoing cultural dialogue about when a nation and its people should, or should not, turn to war.

In many ways, *The Clone Wars'* philosophical challenges regarding war and peace exemplify those faced by a real-world leader: President Barack Obama. As his quote at the beginning of this chapter suggests, President Obama espouses a position significantly different than Grand Master Yoda. In the years during his rise from the Illinois Senate, to national Senate, to president of the United States, Obama articulated a nuanced position regarding military force. Although some characterized Obama as an antiwar candidate, Obama always maintained the need to assess each geopolitical situation carefully before committing to violent conflict. For example, while Obama supported the use of military resources and personnel in the hunt for Osama Bin Laden, he opposed the Bush administration's invasion of Iraq. This opposition to the Iraq War become one of the defining foreign policy positions of his initial campaign for the presidency. In a February 26, 2007, *New York Times* article titled "As Candidate, Obama Carves Antiwar Stance," Jeff Zeleny spelled out the way Senator Obama differentiated himself from the field of Democratic presidential hopefuls by adopting an antiwar stance. Unlike Senators Clinton and Edwards, two senators who voted to authorize the use of force to topple the despotic regime of Saddam Hussein, Obama had yet to begin his political rise on the national stage when the Bush administration was given the congressional go ahead to wage war. As early as October 2, 2002, Obama took a principled stand against what he referred to as "a dumb war. A rash war. A war based not on reason but on passion, not on principle but on politics."[7] A little more than seven years later (December 10, 2009), President Obama stood in front of the Nobel Peace Prize committee and explained his reasoned approach to waging a just war.

Obama and the World as It Is

Early on the morning of October 9, 2009, Barack Obama awoke to the news that the Nobel committee had selected him as a Nobel Peace Prize recipient. The committee justified the surprise selection by citing Obama's "extraordinary efforts to strengthen international diplomacy and cooperation between peoples" and commitment to resolving global conflicts through the "United Nations and other international institutions."[8] Considering that Obama's tenure in the White House started at the beginning of 2009, many interpreted the award as a political statement intended to pressure the new president to distance himself from the hawkish policies of the Bush administration and embrace international diplomacy. For his part, Obama accepted the award with humility. Standing in the White House Rose Garden he remarked, " I do not feel that I deserve to be in the company of so many of the transformative figures who've been honored by this prize—men and women who've inspired me and inspired the entire world through their courageous pursuit of peace."[9] He also acceded to the perception that the Nobel Committee granted the award more as a call to continue his diplomatic efforts than a recognition of past accomplishments. Despite his acknowledgment of the surprising timing of the award, as well as his sparse resumé when compared with others, some politicos and commentators used the award as an opportunity to criticize both the president and the Nobel Peace Prize committee. As Janet Hook and Mark Silva reported in the October 10, 2009, *Los Angeles Times*, Marc Theissen—a conservative author and former speechwriter for George W. Bush—denounced the award. He stated, "There's literally nothing that he has done to earn the award.... There's no accord of any kind—no treaty. He has literally been in office for nine months and accomplished nothing in terms of peace. He hasn't even withdrawn from Iraq." In a piece titled "Obama's Nobel Peace Prize Hangs with a Heavy Weight," and published on the same day as the peace prize announcement, *The Christian Science Monitor* editorial board simultaneously recognized the paucity of the president's accomplishments and lauded his ability to inspire hope on an international scale.

Considering the public disagreements surrounding Obama's peace prize nomination, surprisingly little public controversy surfaced regarding the content of his contentious Nobel Peace Prize lecture. As Howard Fineman observed in his December 10, 2009, *Newsweek* blog post, Obama's speech— a speech more focused on the justification of war than a call for peace— received a cool reception from the Norwegian Nobel Committee. Observing that Obama's successful run for the Presidency was always considered a defining moment in the legacy of Martin Luther King, Jr., Fineman wrote, "But Obama wanted to make it clear that he was NOT Martin Luther King. He was a commander in chief leading two wars, confronting an implacable terrorist foe." In a December 10, 2009, interview on NPR's *All Things Considered*, Katrina vanden Heuvel also underscored the way in which the speech turned away from matters of peace and toward a justification of U.S. military involvement around the globe: "It was a kind of speech that could be taught in a college course on just war and America's role in the world."

Despite the lack of significant public debate, Obama's Nobel Peace Prize speech highlighted a curious tension within the president's position. Throughout his campaign for the presidency, Obama acknowledged his place in U.S. American history as a beneficiary of Martin Luther King's civil rights legacy. Obama's campaign oratory, as well as a number of speeches after he took office, revealed an individual cognizant of his position as a black candidate running for, and eventually assuming, the highest seat in the land. He tied himself directly to Martin Luther King, Jr., by calling on many of themes developed by King himself. Obama's political rhetoric is riddled with references to King's call for urgency, unity, and beloved community. For example, in a January 20, 2008, speech at Ebenezer Baptist Church, Obama took U.S. Americans to task for failing to reach out to those in need, to care for one another in a spirit of communal responsibility. He remarked, "I'm talking about an empathy deficit, the inability to recognize ourselves in one another, to understand that we are our brother's keeper and our sister's keeper, that in the words of Dr. King, 'We are all tied together in a single garment of destiny.'"[10] Obama called on King's legacy, particularly his conception of the beloved community—a community Martin Luther King, Jr., himself referred to in his denouncement of the Vietnam war as "a worldwide fellowship that lifts neighborly concern beyond one's tribe, race, class, and nation is in reality a call for an all-embracing ... and unconditional love for all mankind"—in an effort to craft a national community willing to move beyond political, economic and social disparity and pursue the public good.[11] Obama's vision for a United States transcending Red State/Blue State dichotomies and coming together to address such salient social issues as poverty, inadequate healthcare, unequal access to education, and unemployment was built, in significant part, on Martin Luther King's commitment to embracing unconditional love as a means of addressing societal injustice. Writing of his intellectual and political evolution concerning nonviolence, King Jr., reflected on his experience as a came to terms with "love-force" (he would later refer to this in the famous "I Have a Dream Speech" as soul force). Over time, particularly after his experience with unconditional love expressed by way of nonviolent resistance in the Montgomery bus boycott, King embraced nonviolence as an ethical imperative.

The content of Obama's Nobel Peace Prize lecture reveals a speaker who, once again, recognizes he stands in the shadow of Martin Luther King's teachings and accomplishments. Obama referenced King, Jr., by name, six times throughout the speech. In response to the many critics who questioned whether Obama, so early in his career as an international leader, deserved the revered honor, admitted he did not measure up to such notable recipients as "Schweitzer and King; Marshall and Mandela."[12] From that point forward, however, Obama pivoted away from King's legacy of nonviolent resistance by describing himself as a conflicted Commander-in-Chief responsible for overseeing two ongoing wars, yet also wrestling with "questions about the relationship between war and peace, and our effort to replace one with the other."[13] Even as someone who benefits from "Dr. King's life's work" and someone who understands "the moral force of nonviolence," Obama argued his position as president of the "world's sole military superpower" requires him to utilize military force in the name of national defense and international justice.[14] Stepping out of King's shadow he rejected nonviolence as an ethical imperative in international affairs and stepped into the light of Just War Theory. He stated:

> We must begin by acknowledging the hard truth that we will not eradicate violent conflict in our lifetimes. There will be times when nations—acting individually or in concert—will find the use of force not only necessary but morally justified.
>
> I make this statement mindful of what Martin Luther King said in the same ceremony years ago—"Violence never brings permanent peace. It solves no social problems: it merely create new and more complicated ones." As someone who stands here as a direct consequence of Dr. King's life's work, I am living testimony to the moral force of non-violence. I know there is nothing weak—nothing passive, nothing naive—in the creed and lives of Gandhi and King.[15]

That Obama turned from King's unwavering commitment to nonviolent strategies should come as no surprise, argues James T. Kloppenberg.

President Obama, he asserts, has always displayed an intellectual penchant for philosophical pragmatism. Kloppenberg's examination of Obama's upbringing, education, and public service detailed an individual who rejects inflexible, universal truths and accepts the "uncertainty, provisionality, and the continuous testing of hypotheses through experimentation" that constitutes U.S. American political life.[16] Obama's Nobel lecture, observes Robert Terrill, reflects his proclivity for pragmatic policy making as he negotiated the seemingly irreconcilable differences between war and peace. Terrill writes, "Obama is calling for, and modeling, a peculiar combination of realism and prudence that may indeed present the ameliorative yet proactive stance that seems right for these uncertain times."[17] Obama reiterated his political pragmatism when he created a clear dividing line between the world as he sees it and the illusory, and never attainable, goal of lasting peace. He stated clearly, "I face the world as it is" and not the world as King wished it to be, particularly in respect to international relations.[18] Obama's rhetorical distinction between a "world as it is" and King's global community founded on the principles of nonviolence and unconditional love, implicates a president resigned to maintaining military force as a major weapon in the U.S. American diplomatic arsenal.

Obama described "the world as it is" as a place where war is deeply intertwined with the human experience. In fact, early in the speech Obama devoted a significant portion of his Nobel Peace Prize lecture to reinforcing his understanding of war as a normal, yet tragic, dimension of human nature. "War," he observed, "in one form or another, appeared with the first man."[19] Situating the emergence of war with the rise of the human species, Obama positioned violent conflict as a naturally occurring phenomenon— "like drought or disease"—that devastates human communities from time to time.[20] Important to note here is Obama's insistence that war has been with humanity since the very beginning. As humanity moved from a tribal existence to relationships based on loosely formed social contacts and then on to more formally organized nation states, humans continued to war with one another. No matter the context—tribal conflict, the world wars of the twentieth century, or the counterterrorism operations in the twenty-first century—human beings all too often turn to war as they attempt to settle disputes. This behavior is due, he argued, to humanity's inherent flaws. To acknowledge violence has always been a part of human society is to understand the "imperfections of man and the limits of reason."[21] Imperfect, flawed, and "fallible," people "make mistakes" and "fail to right the wrongs before" them.[22] As a result of humanity's imperfections and violent tendencies, it should come as no surprise that Obama stated definitively, "War is sometimes necessary" and there "will be war."[23]

In addition to proclaiming war as inevitable, Obama also positioned peace as unattainable. Once again returning to history as a means of supporting his contention, Obama speculated that nonviolent action could not have halted Hitler's march across Western Europe and that diplomacy would bring no compromise in the struggle against Al Qaeda. He remarked succinctly, "belief in peace is rarely enough to achieve it."[24] While unattainable, the promise of peace should be an ideal—a "possibility" or a kind of "moral compass"—toward which the global community strives. Relegated to the unachievable world as it ought to be, the fantasy constructs of nonviolent action and lasting peace become part of Obama's rhetorical horizon calling the global community to action. Peace, although an impossibility, functions as the "North Star that guides us on our journey."[25]

The dialogic tension between the two positions—the inevitability of war and the impossibility of piece—gives rise to what many would no doubt describe as a depressing portrait of a world doomed to endless violent conflict. As Obama reiterated time and again, wishing to live in times of peace will not make it so. At the same time, Obama's speech issued a challenge to continue to move toward the never to be reached horizon of peace, nonviolence, and diplomatic conflict resolution. Calling on listeners to emulate the actions of NATO and UN soldiers and assume the role of responsible "wagers of peace," the president utilized humanity's propensity for violence as evidenced by historical and contemporary conflicts, as well as ongoing efforts for peace and the hope for an improved human condition, to constitute a world where violence is simultaneously normalized and challenged.[26] Nowhere is the dialogic interplay of war and peace more apparent than in the closing remarks of his speech. Obama stated,

> We can acknowledge that oppression will always be with us, and still strive for justice. We can admit the intractability of depravation, and still strive for dignity. We can understand that there will be war, and still strive for peace. We can do that—for that is the story of human progress; that is the hope of all the world; and at this moment of challenge, that must be our work here on Earth.[27]

These historical tensions between oppression and justice, depravation and dignity, war and peace, resulted in the development of Just War Theory.

As civilizations grew in wisdom, observed Obama, so too did societal understandings of war. Over time, religious, political, and academic leaders formulated principles concerning when and how wars should be fought. In light of the inevitability of war and the impossibility of peace, the emergence of Just War Theory offered the hope that armed conflict might be conducted in ways that could minimize the associated personal, psychological, and material harms. In the traditional sense, Just War Theory typically consists of two components: *jus ad bellum*, or the right to wage war, and *jus in bello*, or appropriate conduct when waging war. Like Michael Walzer's classical call to distinguish *"jus ad bellum*, the justice of war, from *jus in bello*, justice in war,"* Obama made a clear distinction between the two practices.[28] As Walzer's discussion of Just War Theory makes clear it is entirely possible to wage a justified war in unjust ways. To that end, Obama defined the standards for justified military force as threefold: self-defense, aiding another nation threatened by an aggressor, and humanitarian intervention. Obama also commented on appropriate wartime conduct. When a nation chooses to go to war, he argued, that nation must embrace the idea that there are particular ground rules for the way war ought to be waged. Given the political context in which his speech was given, Obama reminded a global audience of his commitment to discontinue torture (a practice, as I pointed out in chapter three, utilized by the Bush administration), close Guantanamo Bay prison, and "abide by the Geneva Conventions."[29] He linked a nation's foreign policy decisions with the people of that nation when he declared, "We lose ourselves when we compromise the very ideals that we fight to defend. And we honor those ideals by upholding them not just what it is easy, but when it is hard."[30]

Obama's acceptance of the inescapable certainty of war should not be misconstrued as ignoring the pain and suffering associated with violent conflict. Obama repeatedly observed that inevitable war results in inevitable suffering, all too often in the form of civilian harms: "economies are wrecked, civil societies torn asunder, refugees amassed, and children scarred."[31] Despite ongoing efforts to ensure warring parties abide by particular rules of engagement intended to reinforce just actions in wartime, civilians typically bear the brunt of military action. Even the most just war, he warned, incurs significant cost; as an integral counterpart to pragmatic peace, "war promises human tragedy."[32] He also cautioned against confusing the bravery, self-sacrifice, and patriotism embodied by soldiers, admirable qualities in and of themselves, with a celebration of war. Obama presented a nuanced appraisal of the distinction between the soldier serving her or his country and the practice of war itself when he remarked, "The soldier's courage and sacrifice is full of glory, expressing devotion to country, to cause and to comrades in arms. But war itself is never glorious, and we must never trumpet it as such."[33] The distinction between the heroic ethos exhibited by the soldier and the abhorrent human hardships engendered by war paralleled similar arguments articulated at the onset of the Iraq War. Attempting to portray themselves as patriotic Americans—a rhetorical move necessitated by the post–9/11 tendency to label protest as unpatriotic—many Iraq War dissenters attempted to distinguish their criticism of governmental policy from criticism of the individual soldiers ordered to carry out that policy. As an individual who opposed the Iraq War back in 2002, it should come as no surprise that Obama articulated a similar stance.

Obama's exhortation to eschew the horrors of war while celebrating the selflessness of those serving in the armed forces reconstitutes the familiar "support the troops" call that became so ubiquitous during the 1991 Gulf War. In his exploration of the "support the troops" phrase, Roger Stahl suggests that the contemporary usage of the expression deflects attention away from just war policy debate. Instead of having conversations about the war in which the soldiers are involved, discussion turns to how the public at large might contribute to troop morale by displaying yellow ribbons, writing letters, and sending care packages. Additionally, Stahl argues the phrase is sometimes used to create "symbolic distance between citizen and soldier, doing so mainly by coding dissent and deliberation as immoral threats to the soldier body. As such, dissociation extracts the citizen subject from rightful participation in the public deliberation of state violence."[34] Within the context of his speech, Obama's rearticulation of the "support the troops" rhetoric doesn't deflect attention away from just war policy debate–Obama's entire speech is an attempt to add his presidential voice to the debate regarding the possibility of just wars—but reaffirmed the legitimacy of those who criticize war. While a soldier's service to her or his country should be commended and admired, the waging of war is always a tragic affair. To commend a soldier's actions is not an endorsement of the campaign of which she or he is a part.

In the final analysis, Obama's Nobel Peace Prize speech made an unequivocal assertion: "the instruments of war do have a role to play in preserving the peace."[35] Thus, Obama takes what he initially described has a human imperfection and transforms it into a potential tool for justice. And while peace may not be possible in the ideal sense, a practical peace of nonviolent coexistence is something toward which the nations of the world should aspire even if that means enforcing that peace through military action. According to Terrill, Obama's calculated arguments produce a synergetic conception of just war driven by the practical pull of war and the idealistic draw of peace. The two seemingly contradictory notions emerge as intricately intertwined parts of a dynamic whole, a whole that raises the constituted meanings beyond simple black or white depictions. War and peace cannot be easily categorized as malevolent or benevolent, immoral or moral, evil or good but materialize as integral elements in the practical discernment of what it means to be just. Terrill explains,

> They are encountered as complementary, rather than opposite; that is, the audience is invited to contemplate both war and peace as ever-present modes of human conduct rather than as two starkly delineated options between which a choice must be made. War and peace are in this way figured in a play of signification, so that their meanings remain distinct while the precise moment when one shades into the other is considerably blurred.[36]

Important to note in Terrill's reading is his characterization of the speech as an "invitation to contemplate" a new understanding of war and peace as constituted in the dialogic interplay of the two concepts. Obama redefines the two terms, two words typically considered mutually exclusive, as interrelated elements coming into sharper definition as situational pragmatics dictate. Some critics, however, did not share Terrill's reading and described the speech as monologic and completely dismissive of prospects for peace.

Responding to Terrill's assessment of Obama's speech as "a novel and suggestive vision of the relationship between war and peace," Joshua Reeves and Matthew S. May argue that Obama uses his vision of a perpetually violent world to turn away from the possibility and responsibility of pursuing lasting peace.[37] Obama, they observe, "finesses the necessity of perpetual warfare as he glosses over the raw violence that is its condition of possibility."[38] His address constitutes a president and policymaker fully committed to violent actions around the globe. From Afghanistan, to Libya, to the ubiquitous use of drone strikes, many of Obama's subsequent foreign policy decisions support their reading of the speech as a conscious choice to depict "the world as a global theater of war" requiring U.S. intervention.[39] An understanding of the world as a perpetually violent place requiring constant military intervention in the name of justice, they argue, forecloses possible arguments for peace. In comparing Obama's lecture and Martin Luther King, Jr.'s criticism of the Vietnam War, Denton Borhaug explores the ethical, religious, and political dimensions of each speech and takes Obama to task for claiming to be part of King's legacy. While Obama situates himself as part of King's social justice legacy, "his Nobel speech denigrates nonviolent action, theology, and philosophy as inefficient in its strategies to achieve piece, and unrealistic in its assessment of evil."[40]

Guardians of Peace or Wagers of War?

In 1977, when audiences encountered Jedi Knights during *Star Wars'* original theatrical release, Obi-Wan Kenobi describes the nearly extinct order to a starry eyed Luke Skywalker. He explains, "For over a thousand generations, the Jedi Knights were the guardians of peace and justice in the Old Republic. Before the dark times. Before the Empire."[41] Since then, audiences have come to understand the Jedi Order through a number of mediated texts. Part samurai, part Knights Templar, part Shaolin monk, and part Wild West sheriff, Jedi range across the *Star Wars* galaxy protecting the people of the Republic from pirates, crime bosses, Sith lords, and political tyrants. As members of a diplomatic, spiritual, and martial order, Jedi possess the "political standing of warriors between the ruling class and the ordinary people, and they had an ethical aspect that placed them as actual defenders of good in service of justice and the proper authority of a galactic government."[42] Committed to mediating conflicts, stopping wrongdoers, and providing protection to all those threatened by injustice, the Jedi Knights of *The Clone Wars* (e.g., Obi-Wan Kenobi, Anakin Skywalker, Plo Koon, Aayla Secura) resolve local disputes, rescue abducted children, protect hyperspace lanes from pirates, and conduct humanitarian aid missions. Similar to President Obama, however, the guardians of the peace find themselves drawn into situations where violence seems to provide a clear path toward justice. In "Bounty Hunters," an episode that is an obvious tribute to Akira Kurosawa and his *Seven Samurai* film, Obi-Wan, Anakin, and Ahsoka come to the aid of a small farming village threatened by pirates. When Obi-Wan's attempt to broker a peaceful resolution to the conflict is rebuffed by a determined and devious Hondo Ohnaka and his band of spacefaring picaroons—Hondo is extorting a percentage of the community's nysillin crop, a valuable medicinal herb—the three Jedi join with four mercenaries to protect the village. Reluctant to join the battle initially, the Jedi train the farmers to fight for themselves. Once the battle ensues, however, Jedi, farmers, and mercenaries work together to repel the marauding band and ensure the community's safety.

Obi-Wan's attempt to negotiate a solution to the dispute is one example of *The Clone Wars* consistent representation of Jedi Knights as diplomats and conflict negotiators. Although *The Clone Wars* series revolves around the unfolding story of a galactic civil war, viewers encounter reminders that the Jedi Order favors peaceful resolution over armed conflict. In the episode "Trespass," for example, Obi-Wan and Anakin find themselves thrust into the middle of a territorial dispute between the Pantoran government and the tribal leaders of the Talz. Even when the tensions between the factions erupt into violent conflict, the two Jedi Knights continue to search for a mediated resolution and ultimately bring an end to hostilities. With an uneasy truce in place, Obi-Wan turns to the Pantoran representative and states, "Now that you've created peace between your people and the Talz, remember one crucial thing…. Make it last, Senator. Make it last. And be an example to others so not only this war but every war waged may come to an end as well."[43] Similarly, Padawan learner Ahsoka Tano reminds her master, Anakin Skywalker, that the Jedi Knights are as much about peaceful, political negotiations as they are about leading clone troopers into battle. When Anakin refuses Padmé Amidala's request to approach the Jedi Council and push for a diplomatic resolution to the war, Ahsoka remarks, "Aren't we Jedi Knights? Isn't it our duty to speak our minds, to advise the Chancellor?"[44] When Anakin rebuffs his apprentice for not understanding politics, Ahsoka agrees to help Senator Amidala sneak behind enemy lines and engage in secret peace negotiations. In another episode, "The Academy," Ahsoka receives orders from the Jedi Council to serve as a teacher at a Mandalorian educational academy and instruct the "leaders and peacekeepers of tomorrow."[45] Whether serving as a member of Senator Amidala's security retinue or acting as an extension of the Jedi Council, Ahsoka's character provides viewers a glimpse into the diplomatic efforts that continue throughout the war.[46] She directs the audiences' gaze toward the behind-the-scenes negotiations that attempt to cultivate peace or bring aid to distressed populations. In doing so, she serves as a reminder of who the Jedi ought to be as opposed to who they are in morally compromised context of the Clone War.

That is not to say that Obi-Wan and Ahsoka are the only Jedi characters who provide audience members insight into the diplomatic side of *The Clone Wars*. Anakin Skywalker is another Jedi whose presence helps audiences see the connections between war and peace. For example, in the first episode of season three Anakin accompanies Senator Amidala on a mission to try and avoid a civil war between the Mon Calamari and Quarren, two species inhabiting the water world Mon Cala. While their efforts are not successful—conflict does break out briefly—they do manage to reunite the warring factions and expel occupying Separatist forces.[47] The next episode, "Shadow Warrior," continues the diplomacy theme when Anakin, Senator Amidala, and Senator Jar Jar Binks manage to defuse a similar situation on Naboo.[48] What should also be noted in these examples, however, is that the resolutions to the conflicts almost always benefit the military position of the Republic.

These repeated narrative moves problematize the representation of Jedi Knights as diplomats. Even when engaged in the art of war directly, Jedi frequently rely on diplomacy to further the ends of the Republic. The importance of diplomacy in the context of the war effort is established in the opening battle scene of *The Clone Wars* film, a film that served as a premiere for the ongoing series. In an effort to stall an advancing droid army and provide Anakin Skywalker time to knock out an impenetrable defense shield, Obi-Wan Kenobi allows himself to be captured by Separatist general Whorm Loathsom.

GENERAL: You must be the infamous General Kenobi.
KENOBI: I surrender.
GENERAL: Now, Master Kenobi, order your troops to stand down.
KENOBI: General, have a seat.
GENERAL: Have you gone mad?
KENOBI: I've conceded the battle. Now we simply have to negotiate the terms of surrender.
GENERAL: Don't try any of your tricks,
KENOBI: Surely there's no reason we can't be civilized about this.[49]

An important element of this conversation is Kenobi's assertion that diplomacy, even when discussing terms of surrender, is a civilized act. Obi-Wan's invitation to sit down in face to face negotiations, and the general's subsequent charge that the Jedi's behavior is absurd, creates a dividing line between the two combatants. Obi-Wan, with his ability to cease hostilities and treat his opponent with respect and dignity, appears to represent the actions of an enlightened, thoughtful individual. The general's disbelief and distrust implicate a person unused to setting aside one's animosity and engaging in reasoned deliberations. To be civilized, in other words, is to sit across the table from an interlocutor and negotiate a humane resolution to hostilities. Even more important, however, is the fact that Kenobi's attempt to negotiate is actually a ruse; the only reason he sits down with the Separatist general is to buy time for Anakin's military efforts. Kenobi's deception is successful, the defense shield is deactivated, and the Republic forces quickly force the Separatists to surrender. From the outset of the series, diplomacy is situated in service to the military campaign.

Hoping to liberate the capital city during the battle of Ryloth, Mace Windu—often recognized as the Jedi Order's most proficient warrior—must settle a political dispute between a Rylothian freedom fighter Cham Syndulla and Rylothian Senator Orn Free Taa. The dispute mediated, Mace Windu and his clone troopers work with Cham Syndulla's freedom fighters and hand the Separatist army a resounding defeat. Obi-Wan, Anakin and

Ahsoka face a similar situation on the planet Onderon. When the Jedi Council is contacted by rebels attempting to overthrow the Separatist aligned legal government of Onderon, Obi-Wan, Anakin, and Ahsoka are sent on a covert mission to train and advise the insurgents. What is made clear during the discussion is that the Jedi Order will not get involved in the politics of toppling legitimate governments. Concerned that assisting the rebels might be perceived as sanctioning terrorism, the Council agrees to aid the insurgents with several restrictions: (1) the Jedi Knights must not get involved in the conflict directly; (2) they must limit the training to tactics directed toward the Separatist's droid army; and (3) they must stress the importance of minimizing civilian casualties. As Obi-Wan states succinctly, "We must not train terrorists."[50] Obi-Wan's insistence that the Jedi Knights not instruct insurgents in the ways of terror is but the first of several admonitions throughout the four episode story arc. Echoing the cautions his former Master uttered to a young Queen Amidala in *The Phantom Menace*, Obi-Wan clarifies Jedi support for the Onderonian insurgency when he cautions, "Now to be clear we are not here to fight your war. Rather to show you how to conduct it in the most efficient and successful way possible."[51] Similarly, when the insurgent's hidden training camp is attacked by Separatist droids, Obi-Wan reminds Anakin and Ahsoka, "We can only protect them. We cannot fight this war for them."[52] The three Jedi stand at the periphery of the battle, providing protection and non-confrontational assistance where they can, while the insurgents fend off the advancing droid troops and battle tank.

Such moments, and these are not the only moments portrayed in *The Clone Wars*, underscore the Jedi commitment to maintaining their role as negotiators and protectors even in wartime. At the same time, however, the Jedi actions suggest they are becoming more and more military minded. While they maintain the role of protectors and attempt to retain their position as galactic peacekeepers, the Jedi Order finds itself in something of an identity crisis. Can the Jedi Knights maintain their status as the defenders of peace and justice while mired in a prolonged war?

The Onderon arc is important moment in the series for another reason, too. Although implicated via actions of various Jedi Knights this particular arc makes it clear the peacekeepers made generals hold themselves to a particular moral standard concerning war. During the aforementioned deliberation over whether or not to send aid to the insurgents, Obi-Wan reminds everyone, "How we conduct war is what distinguishes us from others." A clear parallel to Just War Theory and the idea of *jus en bello*— justice in war—Obi-Wan gives voice to the Jedi Order's moral commitment to fight war in as humane way as possible. The representation of the ethically grounded Jedi Order is made plain when contrasted with the Separatist war machine. The Separatist war efforts seems to have no moral center. The Separatists research biological and biogenetic weapons, torture with abandon, use civilian populations as shields, kidnap and attempt to conduct experiments on Jedi infants, and design and deploy various weapons of mass destruction capable of ravaging populations on a planetary scale. Conversely, the Jedi commit their troops carefully, protect civilian populations whenever possible, and discourage the development and deployment of superweapons. The Jedi, as well as the clone troopers under their command, adhere to a strict code of wartime conduct. As Kit Fisto reminds his former Padawan and fellow Jedi Knight Nahdar Vebb, "Those who have power should restrain themselves from using it."[53] An episode from season two, "The Zillo Beast," reinforces the Jedi Order's commitment to an ethical wartime conduct. When the Republic army begins testing a new doomsday weapon, an electroproton bomb, Mace Windu cautions against unintended consequences. Master Windu's worst fears come true when the weapons test, in an obvious nod to the original *Godzilla* film, awakens a long-thought-extinct creature known as the Zillo beast. As the inhabitants of the planet prepare to destroy the monster, the Jedi Master comes to the defense of the creature and states, "We cannot allow the destruction of an innocent lifeform." At another point in the episode he reiterates his position: "It is not the Jedi way to take an innocent life."[54]

Every one of these cautions serves to remind audiences that Jedi Knights are constantly confronted with threats to their way of life. As Obama pointed out in his Nobel acceptance speech, war always results in tragedy. War in the *Star Wars* universe is no exception. Battles go awry, clone troopers lose their lives needlessly, civilian populations suffer, Jedi turn to the dark side, and other Jedi die in action. For every representation of the Jedi Knights as wagers of peace striving to adhere to a higher moral calling, another reminds viewers the Jedi are mired in the midst of a prolonged war. No matter how hard they fight to maintain their moral center, the physical, psychological, and spiritual costs threaten to undermine their ethical responsibility. The temptation to turn to the tactics practiced by the Separatists always looms large. Issuing a caution that foreshadows Obama's Nobel Peace Prize remarks, Yoda warns, "In this war a danger there is of losing who we are."[55] I want to emphasize the point that Yoda's line appeared on Cartoon Network nearly a year prior to Obama's speech. And while I suspect Obama's speech is not a direct response to the dialogue written by Henry Gilroy, it is important to note both of these texts emerge from, and contribute to, the same public square. It doesn't take much imagination to suggest Yoda's words are, in effect, oriented toward the same wars as Obama's. Master Yoda is not the only individual who observes the Jedi Knights travel a problematic path.

One of the most meaningful points of contention regarding the Jedi involvement in the Clone Wars comes from the broader galactic community. Inhabitants from many different segments of the population confront the Jedi Knights regarding their role as generals. As the war drags on, it becomes more and more difficult for the Jedi to maintain their moral standing as protectors of the peace. Describing Obi-Wan Kenobi as "the peacekeeper who fails to keep the peace," a bounty hunter takes the Jedi Knights to task for their role in the war. Sugi's indictment is a powerful one as it calls the moral principles at the heart of the Jedi Order into question. Lurmen leader Tee Watt Kaa offers a similar rebuke: "Violence breeds violence. Jedi are no peacekeepers."[56] Like Sugi, Tee Watt Kaa's criticism raises an important question: can an individual preach peace and practice war? Can a martial organization resist the temptation to settle disputes violently or does the organization's preparation for combative engagement portend future conflict? Is one truly a peacekeeper if she turns to warfare as a means of settling disputes or is she contributing to a culture of violence?

This very topic emerges during a discussion between Obi-Wan Kenobi and Duchess Satine Kryze, the legal ruler of Mandalore.

> KENOBI: A peacekeeper belongs on the front lines of conflict otherwise he wouldn't be able to do his job.
> SATINE: The work of a peacekeeper is to make sure that conflict does not arise.
> KENOBI: That's a noble description but not a realistic one.
> SATINE: Is reality what makes a Jedi abandon his ideals or is it simply a response to political convenience?[57]

The interaction between Obi-Wan and the duchess mirrors the dialogic positions articulated by Obama. Is a peacekeeper, a person allegedly committed to non-violent dispute resolution, obligated to act pragmatically or idealistically? Does a peacekeeper situate the prospect of peace on the horizon and look toward that unreachable horizon as he makes practical decisions in the present moment? Does he recognize the world as it, a world where peaceful resolution is not always possible, or, as Satine argues, should a peacekeeper try to enact the world as it ought to be? Satine's position can also be read as a criticism of the Jedi Order's attempt to conduct a just war. Rather than focusing on justice in war, Satine argues true peacekeepers initiate proactive efforts to resolve disputes before reaching the point of violent conflict. Rather than focusing on the ways to wage war ethically, the Jedi Knights ought to focus their efforts on avoiding war altogether. To do otherwise is to betray one's commitment to peace as a guiding principle.

To bring the question of Jedi justice into even sharper resolution, the authors of *The Clone Wars* depict the Jedi Order itself as divided. Members of the Jedi Council, the twelve member governing body of the Jedi Order, frequently engage in dialogue concerning appropriate courses of action before achieving consensus (which should not be confused with agreement). The deliberations, while civil, indicate council members do differ in their assessments and recommendations. As a conversation between Anakin and Ahsoka makes explicit, rank and file Jedi also express differences regarding the war. Tasked with investigating a bombing within the Jedi Temple, Ahsoka doubts whether a Jedi could have carried out an attack on her or his colleagues. In a response that foreshadows his own eventual turn to the dark side, Anakin notes, "Not every Jedi agrees with this war, Ahsoka. There are many political idealists amongst us."[58] To emphasize his point Anakin reminds Ahsoka that Count Dooku, the leader of the Separatist Confederacy, was once an honored member of the Jedi Order who became increasingly dismayed with what he believed to be a failing Galactic Republic. In *The Star Wars Heresies: Interpreting the Themes, Symbols, and Philosophies of Episodes I, II, and III*, Paul McDonald observes Dooku "was particularly frustrated that the Jedi shackled themselves to a corrupt political system."[59] As if one political idealist turned dark Jedi wasn't enough to make his point, Anakin also references the more recent fall of General Krell. Foreseeing the eventual demise of the Jedi Order and the Galactic Republic, General Krell hoped to gain the attention of Count Dooku and rule as part of the soon-to-be-established Galactic Empire.

The examples of Dooku and Krell within *The Clone Wars* narrative provide an opportunity to illustrate the misguided actions of the Jedi Order. Dooku's exit from the Order, and subsequent leadership of the Separatist movement, stands as a direct criticism of the Jedi Order becoming too mired in galactic politics and too intertwined with the machinations of the Galactic Republic. Instead of acting in harmony with the transcendent spiritual ideals of the Force and acting out of a sense of justice to bring order and balance to the people of the Republic, the Jedi Order acts as the military branch of government. Embroiled in the fog of war, the Jedi are unable to see that each small step down the road to militarism brings them farther away from their own guiding principles. Dooku and Krell are interesting character studies in that while they recognize the slow and steady movement way from traditional Jedi ideals and values, they choose to burn the house down rather than attempt repairs. For Dooku, the redemption of the Jedi Order is impossible; the only viable path is to embrace the dark side of the Force and cleanse the Galactic Republic via the violent ritual of war. General Krell, on the other hand, sees the impending destruction of the Jedi Order as an indictment of their core principles. He rejects the Jedi commitment to selflessness and embraces a doctrine of self-preservation. In both cases, the restoration of order by way of all out war is preferable to the continued chaos all but guaranteed by the just war approach.

Nowhere is the division among Jedi more apparent than in the concluding, four episode story arc of season five. As I alluded to earlier, the story arc concerns what can only be described as a terrorist bombing within the Jedi Temple and the efforts of Anakin and Ahsoka to find the person responsible. Letta Turmond, a civilian, is fingered as the guilty party (she admits to being involved with the bombing) and remanded into Republic military custody. While in custody, Letta confesses to knowledge of a larger conspiracy:

> There are some citizens of the Republic, like myself, who believe the Jedi Order is not what it used to be. Jedi have become warmongers. They've become military weapons. And they're killing when they should be keeping the peace. One of these Jedi agreed with us. One of you wanted to make a statement and was willing to attack your own order to do it.[60]

Before she can identify her co-conspirator Letta is murdered and Ahsoka is wrongly accused of the crime. Escaping military custody, Ahsoka goes on the run in the hope of clearing her name. Her attempt fails, however, and she is eventually recaptured. Expelled by the Jedi Order (the decision was not unanimous) and convicted by a military tribunal, Ahsoka's life is spared when Anakin uncovers the true killer's identity: Jedi Padawan, and friend of Ahsoka Tano, Barriss Offee. In a public admission of her guilt, Barriss Offee offers an impassioned condemnation:

> I did it because I've come to realize what many people in the Republic have come to realize: that the Jedi are the ones responsible for this war. That we've so lost our way that we have become villains in this conflict. That we are the ones that should be put on trial. All of us! And my attack on the Temple was an attack on what the Jedi have become, an army fighting for the dark side, fallen from the light that we once held so dear. This Republic is failing. It's only a matter of time.[61]

In what would be the final broadcast episode of the series—a shortened, 13-episode season six became available on Netflix in Spring 2014—the animators took great care to depict the emotions experienced by the characters. Barriss scowls with righteous indignation while members of the Jedi Council, particularly Obi-Wan Kenobi, communicate their uncomfortableness with furrowed brow.

Barriss's face to face confrontation with members of the Order is one of the only moments when the Jedi's involvement in the Clone Wars is questioned directly. The perspective offered to viewers provides unique insight into this confrontation. Provided glimpses of the behind-the-scenes machinations of Chancellor Palpatine (who is also Sith Lord Darth Sidious), as well as the knowledge that *The Clone Wars* is a prequel era text (most viewers know *The Clone Wars* ends with the rise of the Galactic Empire), viewers understand that Offee's accusation are 100 percent true. The question isn't "Will the Jedi Order fall?" but "How will the Jedi Order fall?" Offee's speech, along with such moments as Anakin's refusal to pursue a diplomatic resolution to the war and Obi-Wan's repeated attempts to defend the Jedi as peacekeepers rather than generals, answers the question I posed earlier in the chapter. Can the Jedi Knights maintain their commitment to peace and justice in the midst of prolonged war? Given the events of *The Clone Wars*, the answer is clearly "no." For all their efforts to remain true to their foundational ideals the Jedi have, as Barriss makes clear, "fallen from the light that we once held so dear." In her March 6, 2014, essay titled "Why Ahsoka Tano Is the Best Thing to Happen to Star Wars in 20 Years," io9.com's Laren Davis observes:

> At some point, it has to become clear that for all their talk of being peacekeepers and fighting the Dark Side, the Jedi are really terrible at being the good guys. They use slaves as their infantry. They're so caught up in their role as knights of the Republic that they can't see that they're fighting a bogus war. And they put far too much trust in the will of the Force and too little in reason and the value of their young people. You can't spend all of those years telling kids that war is complicated without exposing the Jedi's flaws as well.

While I agree with Davis's basic point I would articulate it differently. On the whole, the Jedi are accomplished heroes. Where the Jedi stumble is when they allow themselves to become intertwined in politics and embroiled in a prolonged war. As such, I'd amend Davis's point to read "the Jedi are really terrible at being" generals.

In the season five finale, Ahsoka comes to Davis's assertion all too well. When Barriss Offee's confession clears her of any wrongdoing, the Jedi Council invites her back into the Jedi Order. In what might be the most dramatic moment of the series, Ahsoka refuses the invitation and walks away from her life as a Jedi Knight. Her exit is significant for several reasons. First, she's the only Jedi who chooses to leave the temple and, as far as the audience knows (perhaps the rest of Ahsoka's story hasn't been told), doesn't embrace the dark side. Dooku, Krell, and Offee, all self-radicalized political idealists who found fault with the Order's political choices, embrace principles and actions antithetical to the Jedi path: terrorism, a wanton disregard for life, and the inducement of pain and suffering. Second, Ahsoka's choice to walk away without great fanfare, anger at the Council for turning her over to the military tribunal, or promises of retribution indicates a reasoned decision to find a different path. Her message is clear: she no longer has faith the Jedi Order is on the right path. Confused, disappointed, and disheartened, Ahsoka tells Anakin—who, in his defense, never doubted Ahsoka's innocence and argued vehemently against expelling her from the Order and turning her over to a military tribunal—that she needs to come to terms with her experience in her own way, away from the guidance of an institution that would not come to her defense. A disillusioned Ahsoka, as well as the criticism leveled by Letta and Offee, offers viewers the opportunity to question their own support for military policy and actions in the post–9/11 era. Do U.S. American policies regarding everything from detention, to the Iraq invasion, to the war in Afghanistan, to continued counterterrorism efforts in such nations as Libya, Pakistan, Somalia and Yemen adhere to the criteria of *jus ad bellum* and *jus ad bello*? Just as Ahsoka, Letta, and Offee question whether the Jedi continue to adhere to their core principles, the core narrative of season five's concluding arc encourages an interrogation of whether or not continued U.S. American military efforts undermine the nation's core principles.

For all the mistakes he makes throughout the prequel trilogy and *The Clone Wars* series, Yoda eventually comes to the same conclusion. Called by the Force to explore the mysteries of the afterlife, Master Yoda finds himself faced with a number of spiritual challenges. The challenges he faces, however, are mystical in nature and the viewer is never certain whether the unfolding events take place in the physical universe or some kind of landscape of the imagination. At one point in his mystical journey, Yoda finds himself wrestling with a dark duplicate of himself. Yoda's shadow shelf, depicted as a smoky mirror image with red glowing eyes, accuses the wise Jedi Master of having too much hubris, of having too much confidence in his ability to immerse himself in violence and not succumb to the lure of the dark side.

YODA: I choose not to give you power.
SHADOW: And yet you spend your days in the decadence of war. And with that I grow inside you. Know your true self. Face me now or I will devour you.[62]

Initially, Yoda refuses to acknowledge any relationship to the dark figure. The doppelganger or dark double trope is a common theme in science fiction texts. Robert Louis Stevenson's nineteenth-century classic, *Dr. Jekyll and Mr. Hyde*, is commonly recognized as a literary exploration of the possibility for good and evil that reside within each and every human. Classic science fiction film also utilizes the dark double trope. Dr. Morbius, the unintentional antagonist of *Forbidden Planet*, inadvertently unleashes a "hyperreal monster," an "image of his darker self," to rid Altair IV of those who might jeopardize his ongoing research into the advanced technology of the collapsed Krel civilization.[63] And as Lincoln Geraghty suggests in his comparison of myths in twentieth-century science fiction, *Star Trek* has a long history of utilizing a mirror universe of dark doubles to interrogate questions of human morality.[64] Given the pervasive history of the trope, it should come as no surprise that Master Yoda is forced to engage his dark counterpart physically and, over the course of the battle, comes to recognize the figure as his own dark side. Despite being one of the wisest, most admired Jedi in the history of the Order, an accomplished Master who thought he had his dark side well in hand, Yoda discovers the insidious nature of immersing oneself in violence. With this newfound knowledge in hand, Yoda comes to understand that winning the Clone Wars is unachievable, that his belief in war as a means to an end is misguided; the only way to bring balance back to the galaxy is through sacrificing everything, even the Galactic Republic and the Jedi Order.

When Yoda returns from his spiritual quest, he offers little to his Jedi colleagues regarding the ambiguous nature of his experiences. What is not ambiguous is the concrete lesson Yoda seems to have taken from his experiences, illusionary or otherwise. In the final *Clone Wars* episode, Master Yoda expresses his newfound perspective on war explicitly. When asked if his quest provided any answers on how to win the war with the Separatists, Yoda responded definitively: "No longer certain that one ever does win a war, I am. For in fighting the battles, the bloodshed, already lost we have."[65] This commentary on war is in direct contrast to Yoda's apparent position earlier in the series. The first televised episode, for example, portrays Master Yoda as a great warrior capable of decimating waves of battle droids and assault tanks while also inspiring the clone troopers under his immediate command. He engages in combat as part of a wager with the Force wielding Separatist assassin, Asajj Ventriss. Thus, the first and last episodes of the series provide disparate representations of Yoda and his views concerning the efficacy of war. In the first episode of the series Yoda is seen participating in the war effort directly. Not unlike President Obama, Yoda adopts the position that wars are sometimes worth fighting. The final episode shows the Jedi Master coming to see his previous assumptions as deeply flawed. A wise warrior who once deemed war a necessary part of the universe questions the ability to win a war at all. For in fighting a war, no matter how just it may appear, have those involved already lost?

Obama, Obi-Wan and the Possibility of Just War

Perpetual warfare is the new normal of the post–9/11 era. Given this state of affairs, it should come as no surprise that both President Obama's oratory and *The Clone Wars* might comment on the necessity of war as well as the necessity of conducting war in particular ways. As I've illustrated throughout the course of this chapter, the parallels between President Obama's Nobel Peace Prize lecture and the representations presented in *The Clone Wars* are significant. In both cases, peacekeeping traditions come into direct conflict with the never ceasing drumbeats of war. As a political candidate and eventual world leader, Obama's foundational principles stem from Martin Luther King's legacy, a legacy built on King's efforts to combat oppression and inequality with the nonviolent resistance. Pundits, political constituencies, and the Nobel Peace Prize committee situated Obama as a peacekeeper by default. When he ascended to the position of Commander in Chief, Obama surprised many when he grounded his foreign policy in Just War Theory rather than King's call to forge a new global community through soul force. In a real sense, Obama declared King's nonviolent approach inadequate for the post–9/11 world climate. Intentional or not, the writers, directors, and animators of *The Clone Wars* explored similar concerns within the Jedi Knights of the Galactic Republic. Defining themselves as peacekeepers and protectors, the Jedi find themselves thrust in the role of military generals in an expansive civil war. In a direct parallel to President Obama, the Jedi Knights set aside their core principles and entered into the murky waters of intergalactic warfare and politics. Rather than maintaining their position as protectors of the people, protectors not allied with any government or political faction, the Jedi Knights take up arms in defense of one side and not the other. And while *The Clone Wars* series focused far more on questions of conduct in war than just reasons for going to war, the Jedi Knights also turned to Just War Theory to legitimize their actions.

Obama's lecture positioned war and peace as intricately intertwined and brings the two seemingly contrary notions into sharper definition through dialogic contrast. Exploring the tensions between the two concepts, Obama posits that the way a nation thinks about and engages in war shapes how the same nation thinks about and engages in peace. Conversely, how one conceptualizes the realities of peace also shapes how one conceptualizes the realities of war. Keeping the dialogic relationship between the two in mind, Obama makes the curious move of declaring war as a part of "the world as it is" describing it as a force of nature with which humanity has contended since the beginning of human history. For Obama, a world without war is a fantasy land. While the never quite achievable vision of peace provides a transcendent value toward which humanity should strive, the reality is that the pursuit of peace might be able to guide the global community toward improved relations but will never emerge as the normal state of global affairs. There is a great contradiction in Obama's charge that sometimes his so-called "wagers of peace" will require the use of military action in the pursuit of international justice and amity. While the warp and woof of international debates and U.S. American policy decisions might centralize malleable definitions of war and peace, one thing should be quite clear from Obama's remarks. Standing before the Nobel Peace Prize committee, Obama declares peace an impossibility. In the Bakhtinian sense, Obama's lecture finalizes the discussion concerning war and peace. If war is inevitable and peace an impossibility, the only dialogue left to be had centers on how political entities justify war as well as conduct themselves within war. The foreclosure of the debate concerning the possibility of lasting peace requires Obama's turn toward Just War Theory.

Dialogically speaking, *The Clone Wars* covers much of the same territory as Obama's lecture. Early in the series, *The Clone Wars* appears to make an argument similar to Obama's. As peacekeepers and diplomats living in a galaxy consumed by war, the Jedi stress the need for peaceful negotiations and resolutions whenever and wherever possible. And while the authors of *The Clone Wars* never let audiences forget that Jedi Knights prefer diplomacy to violence, most conflict resolution in the *Star Wars* universe involves some kind form of armed confrontation. Similar to the way in which Obama enforces his notion of international justice through "wagers of peace," the Jedi maintain galactic justice and equanimity at the tip of a lightsaber. In the case of Obama and Obi-Wan, practical peace is maintained through pragmatic violence. Representations of the Jedi also position moral conduct in war as an ethical imperative. Tying the concept of *jus in bello* to individual and communal identity, adhering to a particular ethical code of conduct separates the Jedi, and U.S. military, from those who adopt a win at all costs mentality. When a person or nation becomes so focused on victory that sacrificing core values becomes acceptable or commonplace, the person or nation cedes a part of their identity.

This question of the ability to maintain one's identity in the midst of the violence and tragedy of war becomes the point of contention between President Obama and *The Clone Wars*. For all the hours spent portraying the Jedi Knights as heroic leaders of *The Clone Wars*, the series' authors ultimately argue a culture cannot remain unchanged when immersed in perpetual conflict. The inhabitants of the Galactic Republic come to this conclusion much quicker than the supposedly wise Jedi Knights. In choosing to fight as generals of the Grand Army of the Republic, the Jedi Order abdicates its role as peacekeepers. Master Yoda, however, comes to the same conclusion and makes this message clear in the closing lines of the series: when a government goes to war the people have already lost. This argument is in direct contradiction to that of Obama's lecture. When Obama finalizes the dialogue regarding war and peace, he contradicts what Paul F. McDonald identifies as the as one of the central themes in the *Star Wars* megatext. He writes, "One of the primal lessons of *Star Wars* is that the moment one picks up a weapon they are in danger of becoming the very thing they're fighting."[66] While Obama makes his case for the impossibility of peace and the necessity of justly conducted war, *Star Wars: The Clone Wars* suggests peace is the only way forward.

FIVE

Guardians of Peace

"Women have been the guardians of life—not because we are better or purer or more innately nurturing than men, but because the men have busied themselves making war."[1]—Starhawk

"Hasn't this war gone on long enough?"[2]—Senator Padmé Amidala

Organized in November 2002, Code Pink called for a four month vigil outside the White House as a statement against the Bush administration's prolonged build up toward war in Iraq. Months before television viewers experienced the shock and awe tactics of a U.S. bombing campaign, Code Pink protesters—the name parodies the Department of Homeland Security's terrorist alert system: red, orange, yellow, blue, and green—called on the U.S. government to explore nonviolent alternatives. In an October 21, 2002, essay titled "Code Pink: Women's Pre-Emptive Strike for Peace Call to Action," Starhawk—a Code Pink founding member—urged all women to take a principled stand against the looming Iraq invasion. She wrote, "Women have been the guardians of life—not because we are better or purer or more innately nurturing than men, but because the men have busied themselves making war."[3] As noted in a March 9, 2003, *New York Times* article titled "With Passion and a Dash of Pink, Women Gather to Protest War," the fledgling organization's culminating action, planned to coincide with International Women's Day, brought thousands of protesters to the streets of the U.S. capitol and into the national consciousness. While the protests did not halt the Bush administration's march toward war, Code Pink's antiwar rallying cry called U.S. Americans to at least consider the idea that warmaking is ill suited to solving international conflict, thus entrenching the group within the American peace movement tradition. More specifically, Code Pink's obvious nod to the gendered politics intertwined with war situates the antiwar group within the history of feminist protest.

Women's antiwar protest has a long and storied tradition in the United States. From the Women's International League for Peace and Freedom, to the National Committee on the Cause and Cure of War, to Women Strike for Peace, to Code Pink the presence of the feminist antiwar movement provided a counterpoint to aggressive foreign policy. No matter the era, several commonalities connect the various organizations associated with the feminist peace movement. First and foremost, participants in the feminist antiwar movement find themselves united in their denunciation of violence against women. As Harriet Alonso Hyman observes, "Women's rights peace activists have protested not only the physical abuse of women, but also their psychological, economic, and political oppression."[4] A second thematic revolves around motherhood. In her exploration of maternal thinking, Sara Ruddick speculates that maternal thinking provides unique opportunities related to peacemaking. She rejects the essentializing characterization of men as inherently violent and women as inherently peaceful; the tendency to equate masculinity with militaristic action and femininity with nonviolent action, she suggests, stems from long entrenched cultural scripts. A warrior or peacemaker "is not born, but rather becomes."[5] The mythic idealization of mother, with its culturally bound discourses concerning creation, protection, and responsibility to the other, offers values toward which peacemakers, both women and men, can strive. Finally, feminist peace activists champion the notion of women as dedicated political actors attempting to ensure U.S. American egalitarianism. Whether the individuals involved consider themselves abolitionists, suffragettes, prohibitionists, civil rights activists, or antiwar protestors, the various incarnations of the women's rights movement displays a commitment to a more just and ethical political state.

One of the women frequently associated with the twentieth-century feminist peace movement is two-time congressional representative and unrepentant pacifist, Jeannette Rankin. As the first woman elected to the U.S. House of Representatives (1917–1919), Rankin rose to national notoriety when she cast a "no" vote against entry into World War I; nearly a quarter century later, during her second term as a representative for Montana (1941–1943), she cast the sole congressional vote against World War II. Remembered historically as the only congressional voice to make a consistent call for peace, Rankin devoted her entire life to fighting for women's rights and opposing violent conflict. A "suffrage campaigner, progressive politician, and national peace lobbyist," Rankin worked tirelessly to promote the anti-war movement's principles.[6] Like the founders of Code Pink, Rankin considered women well-suited to speak out against the nation's militaristic foreign policy and robust support for an expansive military-industrial complex. She maintained, throughout her lengthy career as activist, "peace is woman's job."[7]

With Rankin's peace activism in mind, I contend *The Clone Wars* also articulates a gendered call for peace. Despite the reference to armed conflict in the title of the franchise, George Lucas identifies the criticism of violence as a central theme of *Star Wars*. When discussing the meaning of his mega-text with Charlie Rose, Lucas states succinctly, "Basically, don't kill people. And be compassionate and love people. And so that's basically all *Star Wars* is."[8] Luke Skywalker's spiritual journey in the original *Star Wars* trilogy, asserts John C. McDowell, lends credence to Lucas' claim. Throughout the first two films, Luke turns to violence as his primary means of striking back against the galactic Empire: he mounts an armed rescue mission, joins a starfighter assault on the Death Star, and rushes headlong into a trap laid by Darth Vader. When Yoda and a ghostly Obi-Wan advise against a potential confrontation with Darth Vader (*The Empire Strikes Back*), Luke rejects their collective counsel with nearly disastrous results. He fails to save his friend, Han Solo, and suffers horrific physical and psychological injury during his failed rescue attempt. In *Return of the Jedi*, a wiser, more contemplative Luke Skywalker displays a deeper understanding of Yoda's exhortation that "wars not make one great" as he once again faces his father, Darth Vader. Although Emperor Palpatine initially goads Luke into a lightsaber duel with Vader, Luke eventually embraces the path of nonviolence, throws down his weapon, and refuses to fight. As Roy M. Anker observes, the refusal to execute Vader and complete a rage induced journey to the dark side marks a moment of triumph for Skywalker; rather than making himself powerful through hate, anger and aggression, he makes a "gesture of faith, love, and sacrifice."[9] Luke turns to peaceful resistance, treats his fallen father with compassion, and rejects the Emperor's seductive dark side ministrations. The fact Emperor Palpatine stands ready to execute the young Jedi makes Luke's sacrifice even more meaningful. Luke's choice to reject the dark side, even in the face of death, has profound consequences as Darth Vader, inspired by his son's actions, turns back to the light side of the Force, rebels against his master, and liberates the galaxy from tyrannical rule. In a broader context, Luke's awakening to the futility of pitting violence against violence symbolizes the potentiality of nonviolent action as a viable path toward lasting peace.

Luke's actions in *Return of the Jedi* do, indeed, offer a powerful message regarding nonviolent resistance. As I suggested in the previous chapter, Yoda also comes to the conclusion that winning a war is impossible, that the only way to win a war is to never fight the war at all. The epiphanies of Luke and Yoda aside, a broader look at the entire *Star Wars* franchise suggests Jeannette Rankin's observations regarding peace hold true: peace, particularly in *The Clone Wars*, is primarily a woman's job. In stark contrast to their characterization as peaceful guardians, typically in word but not deed, Jedi Knights resolve almost every conflict with violence. The only regularly occurring characters consistently portrayed as valuing peace not only through talk but action are Senator Padmé Amidala and Duchess Satine Kryze. Padmé Amidala is the only *Clone Wars* character depicted as a true diplomat, moving both within the legislative avenues of the Republic Senate and through back channel, covert diplomatic missions intended to negotiate an end to the war. While Amidala follows a pragmatic path, preferring a negotiated settlement rather than armed conflict, she also utilizes armed conflict when all other options fail. At the other end of the nonviolence spectrum is Duchess Satine Kryze, the principled pacifist committed to leading her historically violent people into an era of peace. For Duchess Satine, nonviolence is both an ends and a means.

In the rest of this chapter, I turn my attention to how *The Clone Wars* evinces many of the values associated with the women's antiwar movement and contributes to ongoing cultural dialogues regarding peace and nonviolence. First, I begin with a discussion of the relationship between the women's antiwar movement and representations of war and peace in popular culture. In what ways do the arguments and positions of the feminist antiwar movement manifest in popular culture? How do various popular culture texts, particularly science fiction and fantasy texts, advocate for both pragmatic and principled approaches to peace? Next, I illustrate how Jeannette Rankin emerged as one of the preeminent women associated with the women's antiwar peace movement in the twentieth century. Her gendered understanding of peace, particularly in respect to women taking the lead in antiwar advocacy, continues to hold contemporary resonance. Specifically, I situate Padmé Amidala and Satine Kryze—two important characters within *The Clone Wars* storyline—as contemporary voices in the feminist antiwar tradition. Finally, I bring the dialogic intersections of Rankin, Amidala, and Kryze into sharp relief and situate all three individuals as an important counterbalance to continued calls for war.

Popular Culture and the Paths to Peace

In "Feminism and Peace: Seeing Connections," Karen J. Warren and Duane L. Cady ask a question that is particularly relevant for my current project: "Where do women fit in to concerns for peace?"[10] Gendered discourse has long been part of the U.S. American conversation concerning international relations, suggests Cohn, particular those conversations pertaining to matters of war and peace. Her reading of national security conversations makes it clear that while she does not equate tendencies toward war and peace as inherently masculine or feminine, she does note that emotions traditionally labeled masculine–"aggression, competition, macho pride, and swagger"–are celebrated while those traditionally associated with femininity—compassion, empathy, collaboration—are denounced.[11] This pattern of acclamation and censure in relation to gendered discourses limits the ways national security advisors and intellectuals discuss present and future policies : "It sets fixed boundaries, and in so doing, it skews what is discussed and how it is thought about."[12] Arguments regarding war and peace take place within these constrained discursive formations.

One tradition within feminism, a tradition of which Jeanette Rankin is part, articulates strong opposition to war as conflict resolution strategy. Describing themselves as antiwar feminists, Carol Cohn and Sara Ruddick write:

> We have an abiding suspicion of the use of violence, even in the best of causes. The ability of violence to achieve its stated aims is routinely overestimated, while the complexity of its costs is overlooked. Our opposition also stems from the perception that the practice of war entails far more than the killing and destroying of armed combat itself. It requires the creation of a 'war system,' which entails arming, training, and organizing for possible wars, allocating the resources these preparations require, creating a culture in which wars are seen as morally legitimate, even alluring; and shaping and fostering the masculinities and femininities that undergird men's and women's acquiescence to war.[13]

While many feminists adopt a principled commitment to nonviolence in all situations, Cohn and Ruddick acknowledge some antiwar feminists do support the use of violence as last recourse. Such an acknowledgment, however, does not legitimate the inevitability of war as much as it accepts the premise "that war may be morally justified in certain circumstances."[14] In their article addressing nonviolence and post–Cold War peacebuilding, Rebecca Spence and Jason McLeod describe both approaches, principled nonviolence and pragmatic nonviolence, as important means of enacting radical or incremental change in everything from social institutions to political policy.[15] Important to note here is that both positions—principled nonviolence as an ethical imperative and pragmatic nonviolence as a strategic means to an end—oppose war as a method of conflict resolution.

With an understanding of the feminist peace movement in hand, I now turn my attention to representations of war and peace in popular culture. Popular culture depictions of war are an important voice in ongoing cultural discourses regarding foreign policy and international relations, providing an opportunity to probe the dialogic interactions at the heart of responsive understanding and cultural meaning-making . Mediated texts, suggests Thomas A. Horne, present one avenue for wrestling with ideas of peace and war. As he observes in his critique of the 2007 remake of *3:10 to Yuma*, films "carry the meaning of our national destiny " and provide "a model for national action."[16] Unlike traditional Westerns, films frequently reinforcing the U.S. American cultural-political myth of redemptive violence, the *3:10 to Yuma* remake judges the cost of violent retribution—a path Horne argues mirrors the U.S. American mission in Iraq—as untenable. Horne's critique does not suggest war should be avoided at all costs. Rather, he bases his argument in pragmatic nonviolence, calling for critical public reflection before engaging in violent international conflict and urging a move toward a more peaceful and diplomatic foreign policy. Like Horne, Mark J. Lacy's discussion of *Apocalypse Now, Black Hawk Down*, and *Three Kings* as recent representations of contemporary geopolitics explores the way war cinema often works to distance viewers from historical events, thereby mediating moral anxieties associated with wartime actions and ramifications (e.g., civilian casualties, the psychological damage done to soldiers). While *Black Hawk Down* works as a "political technology" supportive of violent U.S. American security measures, thus reassuring viewers of the necessity of U.S. military efforts to bring peace and security at the end of a weapon, *Apocalypse Now* and *Three Kings* offer moral challenges to the cinematic normalization of military violence.[17] Rather than functioning as a curative to wartime moral anxieties, the latter two films induce moral anxieties and encourage national critical reflection.

The speculative nature of science fiction seems particularly well suited for the interrogation of historically situated discourses concerning international relations and the resulting cultural anxieties. Science fiction media frequently offers an allegorical critique of a contemporary state of affairs and follows that critique with a forward looking vision of the way things ought to be. Through the tension between the here and now, the there and then, "science fiction films can be seen to some extent as measures of the hopes and fears of the cultures in which the films are produced and consumed."[18] This is particularly true of the Cold War science fiction of the 1950s. As M. Keith Booker contends, many books and films produced during the 1950s offer subtle criticism of governmental practices, cultural anxieties, and individual jitters. These authors and film makers, recognizing the "Aesopian potential in setting their political commentary in other times or other galaxies," offer critical appraisals of the xenophobia arising from anticommunist hysteria and raise questions about nuclear proliferation, warning that scientists, military personnel and political leaders do not always understand the forces with which they play.[19] *Invasion of the Body Snatchers* (1956), for example, belittled governmental communist witch hunts as well as neighborhood paranoia over Soviet sleeper cells. In a similar vein, the mutated ants running amok in *Them* (1954) call on audiences to consider the potential consequences of continued nuclear testing. Although the Cold War had cooled significantly by the 1970s, film makers turned their attention to concerns raised by the burgeoning environmental movement and posed significant questions regarding green policy, or the lack thereof, through such mediated vehicles as *Silent Running* (1972), *Soylent Green* (1973), and *Logan's Run* (1976).

Criticism of communist xenophobia and environmental policy are only two of the international relations concerns engaged by science fiction media. Particularly relevant for this chapter are those texts contributing to public dialogues addressing war and peace. The 1951 science fiction classic, *The Day the Earth Stood*, is an example of "science fiction with a message" that interrogates "contemporary political issues in a mature and courageous way."[20] Lauding the film for its "advocacy of peace and international cooperation," the film takes a bold stand against the widely accepted militaristic ideologies of the 1950s.[21] Discussing the significance of *The Day the Earth Stood Still* for contemporary audiences, Joshua Pardon claims many of the arguments presented during the 1951 film are still relevant today. The film's critical depiction of anti-communist paranoia, for example, calls viewers to reflect on contemporary post–9/11 Islamophobia. Additionally, an anti-militarist thematic questions the U.S. American tendency to rely on physical force rather than diplomacy in times of international (or in this case, intergalactic) crisis. When Klaatu lands his spacecraft in Washington, D.C., and attempts to speak to the leaders of the world, the military misinterprets a peace offering as a hostile act and opens fire. He survives this initial encounter but finds himself on the run from all levels of law enforcement throughout the rest of the film. A second shooting, a shooting Klaatu does not survive, reinforces the critical assessment of the military's tendency to shoot first and ask questions later. As Pardon observes, "the portrayals of a preemptive ... brand of militarism are certainly relevant in a global political climate concerned with determining the appropriate response to terrorism and atomic proliferation."[22] At the same time, a temporarily resurrected Klaatu gives Earth governments an ultimatum: use atomic energy responsibly or be eliminated. Examined from a contemporary perspective, Klaatu's threat to destroy the Earth if global governments continue to pursue weapons of mass destruction is eerily similar to statements the Bush administration directed toward Iraq.

One of the most well-known antiwar science fiction texts is the constellation of television episodes, films, books, and comic books comprising the *Star Trek* franchise. The franchise, often hailed for its hopeful portrayal of a future where many of the twentieth and twenty-first century's sociopolitical challenges have been overcome, depicts humanity as a united race focused on exploring scientific exploration and maintaining interstellar détente. In his work addressing the *Star Trek: Deep Space Nine* television series, Michael Pounds describes the franchise as a progressive text willing to evoke provocative cultural tensions and dialogues through narratives involving complex social, political, and philosophical concerns: "race, species, religion, politics, physicality/non-corporeality, gender, space-time, and war and peace."[23] It is the last of these, war and peace, on which I wish to focus. From its inception during the tumultuous era of 1960s Vietnam War era, *Star Trek* has been lauded for its pro-peace and anti-war message. Premiering in an era of prolonged war (World War II, the Korean War, and the Vietnam War), civil rights protest, and social change (the emerging women's rights movement), the original *Star Trek* series sets a "generally peaceful" tone that plays throughout subsequent incarnations.[24] In his work titled "The Troubled Pacifism of *Star Trek*," Gary Westfahl makes a similar observation about Starfleet's portrayal as a military organization committed to violence as a last resort. *Star Trek*'s pacifistic idealism, he suggests, often gets overshadowed by the naval style starship battles, phaser firefights, and close quarters fisticuffs that make for compelling, ratings-garnering science fiction television and film. Although violent exchanges do not occur every episode, and the characters typically exhaust all options or find themselves in a situation where they have no other choice than to resort to violence, they occur frequently enough that a tension emerges between pacifism and militarism. This tension, suggests Westfahl, is best described as "a covert celebration of violence overlaid with an overt message of pacifism."[25]

Common to each of the previous examples is a dialogue centered around the military and the potential for peace. This tension between military action and non-violent resistance, argues Neta Crawford, is a hallmark of feminist science fiction and fantasy.[26] Referencing such well known feminist authors as Sally Miller Gearhart, Ursula K. Le Guin, and Octavia Butler, she enumerates how feminist science fiction and fantasy uncovers discourses that "constrain and dispose political actors" and "illustrates how other elements of culture and belief, especially ethno-centrism, militarism, and pacifism, constrain and dispose societies toward war or peace."[27] Feminist themes, she argues, are not limited to feminist writers and thread throughout speculative fiction. *Ender's Game* and its sequels, for example, unpack the horrors of ethnocentrism and genocide as Ender Wiggins matures from deceived military leader to interspecies peacemaker. Although not mentioned by Crawford, Tolkien's *Lord of the Rings* trilogy also grapples with matters of war and peace. Isolated from the tumultuous racial politics of Middle-earth, the elves of Rivendell and Lothlórien display an idealistic commitment to peace and nonviolent conflict resolution. Turning away from the ways of war, Elrond, Galadriel, and the elven nations represent the cultural potential possible when a people direct their collective attention to knowledge and healing.[28] Tolkien's epic fantasy provides another example of peace in practice with the hobbits of The Shire. Hobbits, explain Abigail E. Ruane and Patrick James, "live in a world of peaceful cooperation" and show no tendencies for warlike behavior at all.[29] The television series *Xena: Warrior Princess* also espouses a call for pragmatic peace. The central narrative arc features Xena, a former warlord responsible for tens of thousands of deaths, as she travels a path toward redemption. Although never able to fully turn away from violence as her primary means of resolving disputes she, not unlike the characters of *Star Trek* and *Lord of the Rings*, finds herself in the regrettable position of utilizing violent action to pursue the "values of peace and justice."[30]

While the vast majority of science fiction texts focus on pragmatic peace, there are those articulating a more principled approach to nonviolent resistance. The *Mobile Suit Gundam 00* series, for example, puts the tensions between armed conflict, pragmatic peace, and principled peace at the center of a multiple season storyline. The anime series' central plot revolves around the attempts of a secret, non state affiliated paramilitary organization to "end war and terrorism by deploying its four Gundam combat machines … against any bloc, nation, or group that attempts aggression."[31] While the paramilitary organization, Celestial Being, fails to bring peace through force, one of the Gundam jocks encounters a character committed to principled peace founded on dialogically enacted understanding. The Gundam pilot, Setsuna, finds himself transformed by his engagement with Princess Marina's position and embraces the "logic of peace through understanding."[32] Reading close parallels between the series and the global events of the early twenty-first century (e.g., terrorism, invasion of Iraq and Afghanistan), William Ashbaugh and Mizushima Shintarou interpret *Mobile Suit*

Gundam 00 as a scathing critique of aggressive U.S. American foreign policy. By series end, Setsuna's newfound commitment to principled peace brings a cessation to hostilities, an ending that calls viewers to consider peace through dialogue as a viable alternative to war.

Another text exploring the tension between military conflict and peaceful resistant is Starhawk's *The Fifth Sacred Thing*. Given her participation in Code Pink's early antiwar actions, Starhawk's 1993 near future science fiction novel offers a speculative glimpse into how an established community might resist armed invasion and occupation. The story depicts an egalitarian community organized around communal respect and responsibility for the four sacred things: earth, air, fire, and water. A society centered on the four sacred things liberates human spirit, the fifth sacred thing, and invites inhabitants to embrace an ethic of care: care for the Earth, care for the environment, care for others, and care for the self. An important dimension of this care is a principled approach to nonviolence. When an invading army descends on the utopian community and murders several inhabitants, community members struggle to resist the urge to counter violence with more violence. After a passionate debate the community resists the temptation to answer in kind, haunts the soldiers with stories of those killed, and even extends the hand of hospitality to soldiers who will lay down their arms and embrace the path of nonviolence. Starhawks portrayal of non-violence emphasizes that pacifism should not be confused with inaction. A turn to nonviolent resistance, her novel suggests, is not a concession, an indication of weakness, or an expression of apathy. Nonviolent resistance is a calculated action designed to confront and disrupt traditional power structures, structures all too familiar with violent resistance. When one encounters an alternative consciousness and experiences "the power of shifting perspective rather than getting trapped in habitual descriptions and positions," a potential transformation arises.[33] As Joan Haran suggests, the attempt to foster peace, justice, and social transformation by way of nonviolent resistance requires constant self-reflection, critical discernment, public dialogue, and principled action.[34]

The rest of this chapter examines how the writings of Jeannette Rankin, as well as the popular culture portrayals of Padmé Amidala and Satine Kryze, encourage personal self-reflection and issue a call for public deliberation over questions of war and peace. As all three individuals make either pragmatic or principled calls for peace, several questions come to mind. How is peace, as Rankin suggests, a woman's job? In what ways do their respective calls for peace encourage audiences to evaluate and assess historical and contemporary war efforts? How is war situated as a social and geopolitical problematic? How is peace offered as a solution? How is peace situated as a women's job? What is the *telos* of peace? How does each articulate her call for peace? Who is responsible for giving voice to new ways of conceptualizing peace? In the next section of this chapter, I turn my attention to those characters—both historical and science fictional— who offer the possibility for transformational thinking.

"Peace is woman's job"

On April 6, 1917, Jeanette Rankin joined 49 colleagues in the U.S. House of Representatives and cast a "no" vote on the question of U.S. American entry into World War I; 24 years later, after a long absence from Congress, Rankin cast the sole "No" on the question of war with Japan. Given the historical framing of both World War I and World War II, one might deem Rankin's votes the work of an out-of-touch contrarian, a radical, or even a traitor. She was, of course, denounced as all of these by her many detractors over the years. The arc of her life work, however, suggests she could not have voted otherwise. Reflecting on her first "no" vote she said, "I wanted to stand by my country, but I could note vote for war. I look back with satisfaction on that momentous occasion."[35] Grounded by the Montana ranch land where she was born and raised, fired by the political activism of the suffrage movement, and infused with the engaged pacifism of the peace movement, Rankin displayed the pioneering work ethic, stubborn ideological commitment, and penchant for public service necessary for congressional campaigns and social advocacy. As Joan Hoff Wilson documents, Rankin became enamored with women's suffrage in her early thirties and campaigned for the right to vote in both Washington state and her home state of Montana. Six years later, she channeled her political energy into her 1916 congressional campaign, a campaign which she won. Although she left the House of Representatives after a single term (1917–1919)–Rankin asserts her "no" vote made it impossible to run for an immediate second term—she returned to the nation's capital after a successful election in 1940 (1940–1942).[36] The interim twenty years provided Rankin ample opportunity to hone her pacifist arguments as a member of several peace organizations: "the National Committee on the Cause and Cure of War, the Women's Peace Union, the Women's International League for Peace and Freedom (WILPF), and finally the National Council for the Prevention of War (NCPW)."[37] James J. Lopach and Jean A. Luckowski suggest Rankin's intense involvement in various peace organizations cemented her position as "an absolute pacifist" whose second congressional campaign "would be seen as a vote on war."[38] Reflecting on her opposition to U.S. involvement in World War II, Rankin described the inevitability of her vote:

> This time I stood alone. It was a good deal more difficult than it had been the time before. Yet I think the men in Congress all sensed that I would vote "No" again. If I had done otherwise, I do not think I could have faced the remaining days in Congress. Even the men who were most convinced that we had to get into the war would have lost respect for me if I had betrayed my convictions.[39]

Her second high profile antiwar vote cast, Rankin established her credentials as one of the United States' most committed peace activists, credentials she continued to display after she left office.

Rankin retired from politics in 1942–she felt her war vote once again ended any chance of reelection—but continued to work for "the permanent abolition of war."[40] She remained uncharacteristically quiet during the Korean conflict, observes Joan Hoff Wilson, but she never lost faith in the cause of peace.[41] She attended conferences, traveled to India several times to study passive resistance as articulated by Gandhi, argued for election reform (e.g., direct presidential elections rather than the electoral college), emerged as a public opponent of the Vietnam war during the late 60s and early 70s, and continued to champion the antiwar cause until her death on May 18, 1973. In the four decades since her death, Rankin's voice continues to reverberate through the feminist antiwar movement as evidenced by a 2001 A. J. Muste Institute publication collecting key manuscripts from the arc of her activist career.

The essays collected in the Muste Institute pamphlet capture Rankin's lifelong rhetorical efforts to denounce war and promote peace. Throughout her rhetoric, Rankin was unequivocal and unwavering in her criticism: war is a "stupid and futile" practice supported by "dull and unimaginative" individuals incapable of grasping the threat systematic violence poses to civilization.[42] Many individuals, particularly those in Washington, D.C., failed to grasp the "stupidity, waste, and futility of war." Rankin rejected the inevitability of war and positioned armed struggle as only one of several conflict resolution techniques available to the global community. Describing war as "a method, a method of attempting to settle disputes," is important to her advocacy for peace as it suggested all people and nations might choose other methods to solve problems.[43] She made it clear that warfare is a flawed method, one that should be rejected outright rather than embraced unconditionally. She wrote, "the use of violence and force is an abnormal method which must be abolished from human affairs."[44] Her description of war as "abnormal" deserves extended attention. The term "abnormal" situates armed struggle as atypical or irregular, a practice outside the norm. While her rhetoric acknowledged that warfare has long been considered a viable means of mediating international conflict—she made numerous references to such historical conflicts as the American Revolution, World War I, World War II, and Vietnam—she also denounced war as an unnatural human state. In other words, despite humanity's history of armed conflict, war is neither inevitable or unavoidable. War is the aberration rather than the norm. Rankin avoided grandiose claims about a utopian existence free of conflict, differences of opinion, or even international disputes. She, like Bakhtin, considered conflict a normal part of human social life. While conflict is normal, war is not.

If war is a destructive deviation from the human norm, why is war accepted as a common practice in international relations? Turning to history for an explanation, Rankin referred to the contemporary propensity for armed conflict as a war habit, an involuntary, conditioned response occurring with little or no conscious thought. In one essay she compared the U.S. American war habit to driving a car: just as an accomplished driver gives little thought to the complicated responses required at the moment of an emergency—letting up on the accelerator, depressing the brake, steering around an obstacle—political leaders utilize the weapons of war without thinking. And while such habits might benefit one on the road, a reflexive response to an international crisis might lead to significant consequences. She attributed the habitual nature of war to both past and current influences when she wrote:

> The war habit comes to us through long traditions and history and teaching. We are unconscious of how many war habits we have and our method of perpetuating them. All our history and our music and our art and literature and family traditions and loyalties are tied up in war.[45]

Immersed in a culture valorizing armed conflict, she characterized her colleagues in the House of Representatives who voted for war as embracing tradition in a time of international anxiety. Unfortunately, Rankin argued, these uncritical reactions only reinforced the misguided choice to utilize violence in an effort to stem violence. She pointed out the historical ineffectiveness of war when she described violence as "disappointing for those who follow the will-o-wisp of using war for idealistic purposes. The last 'war to end war' should have taught us that we can't end war that way. Wars pave the way for more war."[46] The compounding nature of war, she suggested, contributes to a pervasive U.S. American war system.

The systemic nature of war extends beyond actual battlefields; the economic, social, and political consequences wend and wind throughout culture influencing communities, family, and national identity. From "laudatory monuments" to "compulsory military training" to "appropriations of the people's money to pay for these activities that make for war," every member of the electorate finds himself or herself ensnared within the insidious war system.[47] Rankin raised concerns about the extensive military industrial complex, "scattered all over the United States," springing forth as a result of preparing for, and waging, two world wars.[48] She called attention to widespread congressional arguments regarding the need for military bases, munitions factories, and the ideological desire to make the world safe for democracy. She criticized "peacetime expenditures for war" as an obvious precursor to war itself and chastised "war profiteers" for pushing the country toward armed conflict.[49] Her argument here is clear: a person with a weapon will eventually use it.

Another point Rankin made abundantly clear was that war and the war system were not just a habit but a masculine habit. In other words, Rankin held men responsible for warfare and the related war system. Her election to the House of Representatives marked the first time a woman's voice joined the formal conversation regarding a declaration of war. Her presence in Congress, she asserted, offered women the opportunity to counterbalance the war habit so intertwined with the masculine propensity for violence. She argued men "have a deeply rooted belief that ultimately the only way to get something is to take it away from somebody else. They are temperamentally competitive."[50] Reflecting on her vote against entry into World War I, Rankin tied the aforementioned war habit to masculine enculturation. When it came time to vote, many men in Congress fell back on their culturally and historically reinforced predispositions toward competitiveness, aggression, and violence. Rankin brought the distinction between the masculine and feminine approaches to conflict resolution into sharp contrast when she attributed her own vote against war to the peace habits she cultivated during her involvement with the suffrage movement. She wrote, "Those Congressman who voted for war in 1917 were reacting to their war habits. I, on the other hand, through my previous experiences and study had never formed the war habit and had developed peace habits…"[51]

Thus, Rankin draws a clear distinction between the habits of men and women in relation to peace. Men, she argued, display a tendency toward war; women, on the other hand, display a proclivity for peace. The difference between the predilection of men and women toward war and peace surfaces in a story she admitted to sharing frequently with Montanan high school students. Rankin recounted the supposedly true story of one of her school classmates who, as an infant, traveled to Montana "in a covered wagon across territory in which hostile Indians still roamed."[52] When the wagon train encountered a group of Native Americans, "The white men in the caravan ran for their guns."[53] While the men armed themselves and prepared for a violent conflict, the mother of Rankin's classmate took the infant boy out to meet the approaching group. According the Rankin, the Native Americans took this encounter with the infant boy and his mother as a "sign of trust and friendship" and "went on their way."[54] Whether the story relates an actual event or not, the important element is the way Rankin portrays the reactions of the men as opposed to the women. The men, sensing a potential dispute or conflict, embraced their war habit and prepared for armed conflict. The mother, protected from the ways of war as was socially typical for women in the late nineteenth century, mediated the encounter with the peaceful skills at her disposal. Rankin reinforced this claim about the gendered habits of contemporary men and women when she asserted that "Half the human race does not fight, and has never fought."[55] Her observations about women and war, however, should not be construed as support for immutable gendered behavior. Her rhetoric suggested an understanding of gendered norms that acknowledged the flexibility and fluidity of human behavior. Referencing historically celebrated women warriors like the Amazons and Joan of Arc, Rankin argued war is a learned behavior; women have proven they can embrace war culture as readily as men. As an advocate for peace, why would Rankin point out women's capability to embrace violence? That a woman might learn the ways of war, means the opposite must also be true: "If women could take on so thoroughly the behavior of the fighting male, why should not men learn something in their turn from the non-fighting female?"[56] Indeed, she credited 49 of her colleagues in the House of Representatives—all men— for displaying the ability to resist the war habit and vote against entry into World War I.

While Rankin lauded her like-minded compatriots for resisting the drumbeat of war in 1917, she also maintained the culturally ingrained war habit would be difficult to overcome without the assistance of women. For Rankin, one of the largest hurdles to overcome in the move toward to widespread peace and nonviolence was the historical masculine bias toward armed conflict. She recognized the wholesale adoption of peace as a tremendous transformation in U.S. American foreign policy, one requiring an unprecedented political paradigm shift in the way the nation approached global disputes. Despite the weight of history, she asserted humans display a remarkable ability to adapt behaviors and adjust prevailing social contracts toward more just ways of governing and living. She wrote,

> The idea that a world at peace has never yet existed need not deter us. Every day the world sees something come into existence which it never saw before. Correspondingly, our barbarous customs (and we must admit that we still have many surviving) are one by one outgrown and relegated to ancient days. There was a time when infanticide and parricide were not even against the law. This should hold encouragement for those who believe that war can likewise be overgrown.[57]

Rankin's mention of "barbarous customs" reveals a rhetor who understands war as an outdated practice inflicting significant physical harms on families and undermines the moral fabric of civil society. The national debate over war and peace, she argued, entailed more than a clash of differing philosophies, that the debate centered on the "welfare of my country."[58] With "the highly coordinated and intricately adjusted affair known as civilization" at stake, peace "is not merely a theory, a hope, a pious wish. It is a stern and bitter necessity."[59] The necessity for peace, and the obvious inability of male leaders to enact lasting peace, obligates women to take up the cause publicly. As Rankin asserted throughout a lifetime of advocacy, "Peace is woman's job."[60]

By virtue of their cultural position as creators and protectors of life, women possess the necessary temperament and experience to function as a consistent voice for peace and the betterment of society. Tasked with the "lifework of producing human beings," women exhibit a desire to nurture, educate, and protect the children they carry to term and mother throughout a lifetime. Her basic premise regarding the gendered expectations of women was clear: any to attempt to "deny life" is antithetical to those "who give life …"[61] Rankin observed, however, that this maternal behavior and thinking extends beyond a woman's own offspring and carries over into a care for the whole of society. She referenced the suffrage and temperance movements, movements populated largely by women and oriented toward addressing perceived social injustices and public health issues, as evidence for the culturally scripted maternal tendency to protect others. She made an explicit comparison between the dangers of consuming alcohol and the threat of war when she wrote:

> What shall we say then of the nation which intoxicates itself with war (for war is largely intoxication) and allows the children of the nation to go underfed and undereducated? No doubt the poor "drunk" thinks that his course of

conduct is inevitable, as the great nation is convinced that war is the only way even though it be a crime against childhood. The question is, how do women feel about it? Do they also feel that, with all apologies to suffering humanity, war is something that must still go on? Just as soon as they understand that war is something which belongs in the same class as a destroyer, they will find a way to make war less popular, to outlaw it, and eventually end it. As the strength of parental feeling grows in men, not merely as individuals but as citizens, they too will see the possibilities of a world without war.[62]

At the heart of the drunk on war metaphor is the possibility of healing and rehabilitation. Rankin's comparison between the impaired thinking of a drunkard and the impaired thinking of those who champion war rejected the perceived inescapability of each. Just as the overindulgent drinker might overcome his compulsion and find sobriety, the war hawk might overcome his addiction to violence and find lasting peace. In either case, women stand at the forefront of the cultural dialogue. If men are to rediscover their responsibility as active caretakers for both their families and the nation, women must show them the way.

As Rankin's rhetoric made clear, the responsibility for articulating a consistent message regarding the possibility of peace—the intentional cultivation of a peace habit—rested almost solely with women. She asserted women must be "willing to work for peace in the same spirit in which they have worked for a democratic franchise."[63] She questioned whether political leaders—a president, representative, or senator—possessed sufficient wisdom to make decisions in the best interest of 'the people." Recounting a high school speaking tour in 1939, a period during which she laid the groundwork for her second congressional campaign for the House of Representatives, Rankin spoke with students and pointed out the "futility of the war method as a means of settling disputes between nations."[64] She encouraged these students to talk with their parents, to discuss her ideas about war, and write President Roosevelt directly. Rankin called students to embrace their civic identity as active members of a deliberating public and resist the temptation to allow a national leader the sole voice in embracing peace or leading a nation to war. Indeed, Rankin's rhetoric suggests the leaders of her era were so enamored with armed conflict that they could not see another way forward.

As such, she called women to share their experience, to educate others about the ways of peace, and start the long and difficult process of peaceful transformation. In a piece titled "Peace Through Political Action," she encouraged readers to keep working toward the inevitable adoption of peace: "We must never forget peace is coming—not through political leaders, but through the voter. The great value of political action lies in its power to educate the masses."[65] This brief passage captures the prophetic spirit infused into Rankin's rhetoric. Rankin's prognostic writings predict change will come to pass provided the people to whom she's speaking—mainly women—make the choice to stand against the cultural tendency toward war and proselytize for peace. If the cultural war system continues as status quo, the nation's survival is at risk. A surety resonated through her words when she predicted peace would come to those willing to work tirelessly for that end. Predicated on the audiences' willingness to take up the cause, just as they had when fighting for the vote, Rankin called all women to educate the voting public, to reach out to children, to other women, and to men, to do everything in their political power "to get to the people, the grass roots as the saying goes."[66] The cultivation of a peace habit is "not made by voting on election day, but by continuous action three hundred and sixty-five days in the year."[67] Put simply, Rankin urged women to educate others about the possibilities for peace. If national leaders and legislators lacked the political will and the practical wherewithal to break the war habit and embrace new ways of thinking and acting about international conflict, women must educate the general public and "encourage a spiritual awakening that will make it possible to see another way out."[68]

Thus, while Rankin called women to take the lead in agitating for peace, a convincing peace movement must arise from the will of the general electorate and manifest as pervasive public opinion. Women cannot be the only voice speaking against war: "Peace must come as expressed desire in the hearts and minds of the masses of the people everywhere."[69] Engrossed by the war habit, the people of the United States must be taught (1) the peace habit and (2) the ways to articulate that peace habit to public leaders. When the electorate gives voice to "enlightened public opinion," displays "devotion to the true ideals of democracy," and participates in the crucial political task of self-governance, peace will become a viable alternative to war.[70] And if "governments derive their just power from the consent of the people," leaders must listen to the cohesive voice of the people.[71] In this spirit, Rankin instructed constituents to write their respective Representatives and Senators and engage him or her in an active conversation about matters of war and peace. She also stressed the importance of articulating public opinion through the ballot box. To make the voices of peace heard, citizens must vote as if "every vote cast is a vote for or against peace ..."[72] If the people speak persuasively, leaders must listen.

Calls for Peace in the Middle of The Clone Wars

As a character, Padmé Amidala has received a fair amount of scrutiny. According to Jeanne Cavelos, the prequel trilogy offers an inconsistent portrayal of character who is simultaneously "action hero and passive victim."[73] Starting out as the action oriented Queen Amidala who readily adopts the role of freedom fighter to liberate her homeworld, she slowly transforms over the course of the prequel trilogy. The woman who once ruled a planet as Queen, fought alongside Jedi Knights in the gladiatorial arena of Geonosis, and debated galactic policy as a respected Senator, concludes her theatrical story arc as an acquiescent, ineffectual character who "loses her voice, her self, and her life."[74] Despite Padmé's shortcomings, Ray Merlock and Kathy Merlock Jackson point out it wasn't all that long ago when finding a woman with any agency whatsoever was a rarity on the large screen. Despite her flaws, as well as the flaws of her on screen daughter Princess Leia Organa, Padmé helps make the *Star Wars* franchise a "better, safer, and a more tolerant, aware, and focused place."[75] In fact, McDowell posits Senator Amidala's call for diplomacy and cautious approach to increased militarism may be the most important voice in the prequel trilogy. He writes, "Hers is the voice of reason, of diplomacy, and that voice which the revelations in ROTS eventually suggest is not only the most insightful into what is transpiring politically but also perhaps the wisest."[76] Senator Amidala's wisdom is on full display in *The Clone Wars*.

Like Representative Jeannette Rankin and her two votes against war, Senator Amidala remains firmly committed to the pursuit of peace and diplomacy throughout the entirety of *The Clone Wars* series. Indeed, of all the characters represented, Padmé Amidala's is the one who consistently works toward a peaceful resolution to the galaxy spanning conflict by calling for substantive political deliberations, increased interplanetary statecraft, and meaningful peace talks. For example, during a conference addressing the growing refugee crises resulting from the war Senator Amidala calls on attendees to "open channels of diplomacy so that we can end this war."[77] In another episode, "Water War," Senator Amidala serves as a neutral political observer in a disagreement over a planetary transfer of leadership. When negotiations between the Mon Calamari and Quarren reach a point of impasse and threaten to plunge to the two peoples into a planetary civil war, Senator Amidala attempts to de-escalate the conflict: "Please, we're here to find a compromise. What can the Republic do to help keep the peace?"[78] Senator Amidala is no less ardent in her calls for peace when debating within the legislative arena of the Republic Senate. Deliberating a massive defense appropriations bill, a bill written with the intention of expanding the scope of the war by procuring another five million clone troopers, she rebukes her fellow senators for succumbing to a galactic version of Jeannette Rankin's "war habit" and reminds them diplomacy might offer another path to the war's conclusion.

> PADMÉ: Members of the Senate. Do you hear yourselves? More money. More clones. More war. Say nothing of fiscal responsibility, what about moral responsibility? Hasn't this war gone on long enough?
> SENATOR: Senator Amidala, are you suggesting we surrender to the Separatists?
> PADMÉ: Of course not. But negotiation might be a better course of action.[79]

Amidala's exchange in the Senate is an excellent example of her philosophy toward peace, war, and diplomacy. She implores her fellow senators to take a moment of self-reflection, examine the monologic tone of a debate centered around the all too similar outcomes of limited war or expanded war, and consider the possibility that they are so blinded by war that they cannot see alternatives to violence (e.g., statecraft). Also implicated in her comment regarding "moral responsibility" and the length of the war is a denouncement of war itself. No matter how just or righteous a war might seem, the destructive nature of war demands a responsible government do everything in its power—including diplomacy—to bring the conflict to a swift close. Reading Amidala's character as an advocate for pragmatic peace, as someone who abhors war but understands there may be historical moments when armed conflict cannot be avoided, she rejects an expanded conflict and questions whether continued military action alone will achieve the Republic's reunification. Her admonishment of the Senate reminds the viewer that reasoned discourse, applied at the right time and in the right context, may prove more effective than trying to overwhelm the enemy with insurmountable numbers of clones or outmaneuver Separatist vulture droids with the latest starfighters. As a pragmatic peace activist who participated in the military liberation of her homeworld, fought in the Battle of Geonosis (the first battle of the Clone Wars), and married a Jedi general, Senator Amidala is no stranger to armed conflict. She wields a blaster as deftly as a pen. Her ability to hold her own in a firefight aside, she positions peace as something toward which one should strive and attempts to address the political and material consequences of the galactic civil war wherever and whenever she can. She may not be able to achieve long lasting intergalactic peace but she can bring relief to a starving child, provide a safe home for a displaced refugee, or speak as the voice of the loyal opposition in the Senate.

In this sense, Senator Amidala displays a maternal responsibility for the people of the Republic, the Confederacy of Independent Systems, the Outer Rim, and beyond. In numerous episodes exploring intergalactic politics, Senator Amidala works toward resolving some of the socio-political problems facing the war-torn galaxy. From refugee crises, to planetary food shortages, to black market corruption, Senator Amidala's character sheds light on the war's ever increasing public impact. For example, after a terrorist attack on the Republic's capital fast tracks the aforementioned war expenditure bill, a bill Senator Amidala managed to postpone while peace talks got underway, she once again faces her colleagues and attempts to redirect the conversation toward the impact on the Republic's citizens. She reminds the Republic Senate to keep their attention focused on the people they serve, many of whom are experiencing great hardships because of the war. To drive this point home she tells a brief story about Senatorial aid Teckla Minnau and her family, a family who, as a result of limited governmental resources, experiences regular disruptions to basic services like energy and water. The senator criticizes her fellow legislators for preparing to divert even more money to the war effort, and away from the people, when she remarks,

> The Republic always funded these basic services but now there are those who would divert the money to the war with no thought for what the people need to survive. If not for people like Teckla and her children who are we fighting for? My people, your people, all of our people, this war is meant to save them from suffering, not increase it…. It is our duty, and our responsibility, to preserve the lives of those around us by defeating this bill.[80]

A public servant defined by her ethic of care, the Senator brings the tangible suffering experienced by those on the periphery of war into sharp focus. She serves as a touchstone for the inescapable tragedy of war that lurks in the background of epic space battles and dazzling lightsaber duels. Unlike Representative Rankin, who argued for peace as both an end and a means to that end, *The Clone Wars* renders Amidala as someone who hopes for peace but fixes her attention on addressing immediate public concerns. She advocates for peace pragmatically; she entreats both sides of the conflict to search for a peaceful resolution but appears more concerned with alleviating the suffering of those caught in the political, economic, and military crossfire of a galaxy at war.

Senator Amidala is not the only character who adheres to Jeannette Rankin's reminder that "peace is woman's job." While Senator Amidala represents a commitment to pragmatic peace, Duchess Satine Kryze represents a principled commitment to peace. Unlike Padmé Amidala, a character who has received her fair share of attention by media critics and *Star Wars* scholars alike, Duchess Satine's character remains largely unexplored. Duchess Satine Kryze, a pacifist head-of-state who aspires to lead her people, the Mandalorians, away from their warmongering past and toward a peaceful future, works with her council of ministers to rule the Mandalorian system democratically and justly. Declaring war "intolerable" and "an affront to life itself," she refuses to participate in the Clone Wars, withholds support for either the Republic or the Confederacy of Independent Systems, and organizes and leads the Council of Neutral States, a loose conglomeration of nonpartisan systems.[81] Her principled commitment to nonviolence, a position that manifested after her people suffered devastating casualties during a Mandalorian civil war, informs nearly every one of her appearances. Accused of idealism when she reasserts Mandalore's neutrality before the Galactic Senate, the Duchess characterizes herself as "a pacifist" and the Mandalorians as "a people who have chosen nonviolent action."[82] When Duchess Satine Kryze makes an entrance, a debate regarding the morality of peace and war is soon to follow. Her support for nonviolence is inflexible and unquestionable; peace is always the way forward. Diverging from Senator Amidala, a character who espouses pragmatic peace, Satine advances peace as both a means and an end. In Satine's first appearance on *The Clone Wars*, Mandalorian Prime Minister Almec describes the Duchess as a leader who "values peace more than her own life."[83] And, in fact, she lives up to Almec's assertion when she is kidnaped by a turncoat senator who threatens to blow up a starliner should anyone interfere with the abduction. Fearing a rescue attempt might pressure her kidnapper into detonating the bomb, thereby injuring or killing everyone on the starship, Satine tells her would be saviors to let the kidnapper's plan unfold without interference. Although the attempted kidnaping ultimately fails, Satine's willingness to sacrifice herself for the sake of others illustrates her commitment to maximizing the possibility of a peaceful resolution through peaceful resistance.

The most compelling aspect of the Duchess's pacifism, however, is the unquestioning confidence she holds for the will of her people. Satine is portrayed as a leader who understands that her desire for peace, a desire springing from her commitment to the Mandalorian people, must be supported by public opinion. While she might be the figurehead for the Mandalorian peace movement, the real peace movement resides in the hearts and voices of the people. Mandalorian Deputy Minster Jerec says as much when he calls on his people to follow Satine's lead and resist the temptation to invite the Jedi Knights to resolve an internal conflict: "We must have the temerity to stand strong in the name of peace.... We must listen to the Duchess Satine. If we do not, we will ultimately cause our defeat."[84]

The Duchess makes a similar argument when criticizing a Republic plan to intervene in Mandalorian politics despite protests against such action. Concerned that Republic intervention and occupation will make Mandalore a target for Separatist attack, thus dismissing the Mandalorian desire for neutrality, Satine castigates the Galactic Senate for circumventing her people's "right to self-determination" and "attempting to force its will upon innocent people."[85] In an argument with Obi-Wan Kenobi regarding the Republic's propensity to involve itself wherever and whenever it pleases, Satine affirms the people's right to self-determination, particularly in the face of military occupation, and wishes more citizens would "speak up when the Republic tramples on their rights."[86] In other words, for principled peace to achieve its transformative potential, the people must internalize, articulate, and practice nonviolence in all facets of their lives. The people must not rely solely on their political leaders but must "speak up," give voice to their political will, and participate in dialogues centered around matters of public consequence. A philosophical commitment to peace— the Mandalorian story arcs suggest the people of the system desire a change—requires the engaged political will of the entire *polis*. The people must not only heed the call of the government but must also check the government when it fails to stay true to guiding principles. For Mandalore to avoid a return to its violence past, the people must express a similar, principled commitment to peace. Duchess Satine's character arc also points out the fragility of relying on the people to maintain a commitment to peace.

When the Mandalorian people find themselves besieged by the criminal Black Sun syndicate, Duchess Satine tries to rally her frightened people behind the banner of nonviolent resistance. She loses the will of the people when Pre Vizsla, a descendent of a prominent warrior clan from Mandalore's violent past, appears on the scene and promises to eliminate the criminals by force. Pre Vizsla and his Death Watch troops eliminate the criminal threat, the people reject the pacifist teachings of the Duchess, and offer enthusiastic support for a return to Mandalore's war system.[87] In spite of Pre Vizsla's carefully orchestrated coup (the Black Sun attacks were part of Pre Vizsla's plan), Duchess Satine continues to follow the path of nonviolence, acknowledges the will of her people, and steps down as Mandalore's leader. Pre Vizsla's rule is short lived, however, as he is deposed by yet another military coup and the Mandalorian people find themselves immersed in yet another violent civil war. The words of Deputy Minister

Jerec true: the people's inability to remain faithful to the cause of nonviolence brings a peaceful Mandalorian renaissance to a bloody end.

In his January 26, 2013, *The Clone Wars* season five, episode 15 ("Shades of Reason") review, well known and respected TheForce.net new media journalist Eric Geller offers a scathing assessment of Duchess Satine's pacifistic political philosophy and governmental rule. Critical of her government's inability to respond to the threat posed by the Black Sun syndicate, as well as the political manipulations of Pre Vizsla and Death Watch, Geller asserts, "The irony of Satine's situation could not have been lost on her: her pacifism had led to a weak police force and poorly-trained security guards." He denounces her commitment to nonviolence as a "naive, impotent political philosophy" and accuses her of lacking the "courage to abandon her ideology when it really counted." The blame for Mandalore's fall rests almost entirely on the Duchess's inability to respond militarily. While Geller's literal interpretation is one way to understand Satine's broader character act, I want to offer an alternative, allegorical reading. Given the continual emphasis on Satine's respect for the will of the people, Mandalore's return to violent militarism rests firmly on the shoulders of the people. Satine's numerous depictions as the voice of the Mandalorian people makes this abundantly clear. Rather than a literal indictment of Duchess Satine and pacifism as a political philosophy, Mandalore's descent into civil war is an allegorical commentary on the U.S. American public's failure to maintain their composure and resolve when confronted with pain, hardship, and fear. It strikes me that a parallel exists between the animated narrative of the Mandalorian people and the real-life, post–9/11 U.S. American response. Horrified by attacks on the World Trade Center towers, as well as the Pentagon, an enraged U.S. American people went all in on President Bush's plan to "hunt down and punish those responsible for these cowardly acts."[88] Few Americans protested as the Bush administration and a compliant Congress curtailed personal liberties through the Patriot Act, adopted a "with us or against us" approach to diplomacy, and opened up wars on two fronts. Experiencing anger and fear, U.S. Americans waived their flags as the government engaged in policies and actions many citizens eventually questioned. Righteous indignation fueled the desire for violent retribution and revenge, drowning out the more subtle and nuanced calls for a measured response grounded in diplomacy and even nonviolence. And while I would never assert that peace politics had any hope of gaining serious traction in the post–9/11 environment, I would suggest that the voice of peace as articulated by individuals like Representative Barbara Lee (CA)– the only person to vote against an authorization of force bill in the aftermath of the terrorist attacks—and groups like Code Pink, had they been taken more seriously in the broader dialogue, could have tempered the U.S. American military response.

Practitioners of Galactic Motherhood

On December 7, 2001, NPR's All Things Considered ran a segment comparing the events of September 11, 2001, and December 7, 1941. While both days live in infamy in the U.S. American public imaginary, the segment turned away from the tragic attacks themselves and focused, instead, on the courageous votes of Jeannette Rankin and Barbara Lee. Jeannette Rankin, as I explained earlier, emerged as the sole voice against U.S involvement in World War II; Barbara Lee, situated by NPR as Rankin's kindred spirit in the antiwar movement, voted against granting President George W. Bush nearly unlimited war making powers post–9/11. Although their acts remain separated by roughly sixty years, NPR brought the actions of these two women to the attention of the public square, thereby bringing their voices into dialogue with one another and also the public at large. Barbara Levy Simon, a professor of social work, made a similar association between the two women and their acts on the floor of Congress. She suggested both women,

> had nourished themselves for years on a yeasty potion of feminist values, democratic fervor, and social work commitment. Although they were women of different generations and life circumstances, they nonetheless came to treasure and enact similarly the responsibilities of independent thought, vigorous debate, social reform, and spirited resistance to jingoism.[89]

What I want to point out here is the way in which both NPR and Levy Simon bring a historical figure, and a contemporary political actor, into an active dialogue oriented toward the broader public square. In this same sense, the rhetorics of peace articulated by Jeannette Rankin and the characters of *The Clone Wars,* namely Senator Padmé Amidala and Duchess Satine Kryze, also intersect some sixty years later and invite audiences to contemplate peace, diplomacy, and contemporary U.S. foreign policy. My contention here is that when one encounters the Senator Amidala's arguments for pragmatic peace, or Duchess Satine's principled commitment to neutrality, one also enters a dialogue with Jeanette Rankin's antiwar advocacy.

As illustrated throughout this chapter, Rankin's powerful antiwar message—articulated in both deed and word—wends its way through the decades and finds itself rearticulated within the characters of Senator Amidala and Duchess Satine. For Jeannette Rankin, as for *The Clone Wars*, "peace is woman's job." All three women make clear their disdain for the widely accepted war system; war and the intertwined social, economic, and political institutions that normalize the practice are morally reprehensible, abnormal, and intolerable. Rankin and Satine complement one another particularly well with their principled approach to peace: peace is an ethical tenet, a means of accomplishing as well as that which must be accomplished. The two adopt an uncompromising position and make no allowance whatsoever for the prospect of a constructive war within a thriving, civilized *polis*. And while they invoke the war system they're trying to overcome, their respective messages in the early to mid-twentieth century, as well as a long time ago in a galaxy far, far away, foreclose the possibility of any choice other than peace. Their monologic claim—there is no allowance for differing opinions—insinuates that a rejection of peace dooms a civilization to failure. Rankin's warning regarding the downfall of a civilization that does not adopt a full commitment to principled peace has yet to materialize. The storyline concerning Duchess Satine draws the opposite conclusion. Lacking the resolve to maintain a commitment to nonviolent resistance in times of crisis, the Mandalorian people turn away from peace and plunge themselves back into a familiar cycle of death and destruction. Similar to Rankin's cautionary words throughout the twentieth century, *The Clone Wars* offers a clear indictment of the ease with which U.S. American lawmakers and citizens accept armed conflict as a reasonable tool in international relations.

The Clone Wars also offers another way of thinking about peace and diplomacy. Once again challenging the charge of black and white thinking and morality in the *Star Wars* galaxy, *The Clone Wars'* Senator Padmé Amidala provides a pragmatic counterbalance to the historical and contemporary voices of principled peace. That is not to say the Senator rejects the notion of peace. On the contrary, she argues passionately for peaceful resolutions to various crises. Senator Amidala takes an approach to peace more in line with President Obama (see Chapter Four) than Representative Rankin when she acknowledges the Grand Army of the Republic is fighting for the good of the common citizen. She articulates her disdain for armed conflict and positions all war as morally problematic. At the same time, her rhetoric suggests there are times when war may be unavoidable, even necessary. In essence, Senator Amidala expresses more concern for the immediate welfare of those threatened by, or dramatically impacted, by war while Duchess Satine, who also expresses concern for her people, plays at a much longer game: the transformation of Mandalore's war culture. The tension between Amidala's pragmatic peace and Satine's principled peace illustrates the dialogic complexity arising from *The Clone Wars*. Unlike Rankin's rhetoric, which puts forth a contention grounded in absolute certainty, the narrative arcs of *The Clone Wars* offer contrasting positions grounded in multivocality. The dialogic intersection of the two characters and their related understandings of peace, asks audiences to consider the positions and come to their own conclusions. That is not to say, however, that all arguments regarding peace and war recognize the spirit of self-determination on the viewers' part.

As part of a broader cultural dialogue, Rankin's historical rhetoric and *The Clone Wars* contemporary discourse criticize the war system which pervades both real and fictional political landscapes. Whether its Rankin's observation regarding the adulation of war and the sprawling U.S. American military industrial complex, or Amidala's criticism of the Galactic Senate's inability to consider negotiation as a reasonable course of action during a war appropriations debate, or Satine's objection to the Senate's rejection of Mandalorian neutrality—and thus the Mandalorian people's right to enact a nonviolent solution to an internal problem—and the subsequent unilateral decision to invade and occupy the system, all three leaders reprimand their respective legislative bodies for engaging in a monologic debate. The one sidedness of each debate, a debate Amidala describes as revolving almost solely around "More money.... More war," excludes a peaceful resolution before even considered. While Rankin's arguments addressed the monologic deliberations around the conflicts of her historical era–World War I, World War II, and the Vietnam War–Amidala and Satine offer allegorical critiques of contemporary U.S. American conflicts. In both historical and contemporary circumstances, antiwar rhetoric challenges the ease with which the nation's resolve and resources are committed to war. When a nation's people embrace a war habit, acquiesce to the monologic call to arms, and fail to engage in robust, multivocal debate, they give tacit consent to such potentially costly foreign policy decisions as invasion and occupation in the name of national security and nation building (e.g., Afghanistan and Iraq). Often overlooked in these limited debates–Rankin, Amidala, and Satine articulate a concerted message on this point—are the significant harms to those responsible for fighting the wars and those victimized by the wars. Soldiers die or suffer significant injury (as do their friends and families), drained economies result in fewer services for citizens, and people find their personal rights curtailed. Such injuries and inconveniences demand action from the people.

Given the monologic nature of the debates concerning war and peace, both Rankin and *The Clone Wars* turn away from the transformative potential of political leaders and legislators and argues any real shift in policy begins with the people. Particularly important for this chapter are the explicit and implicit arguments positioning women as potential peacemakers. Rankin's message spells out the deliberative role for women directly. Unable to trust male leaders mired in a destructive war habit, Rankin appeals to women to take up their place as advocates for a national peace habit. Transforming national foreign policy from one grounded in violence to nonviolence requires women from all societal ranks to serve as educators. Rankin solicits all those with a vested interest in avoiding armed conflict—which would include everyone in civilized society—to raise their voices and (1) help the general population understand peace as a viable, and desirable, alternative to war and (2) teach the people how to share their will with political leaders. Only when public opinion reverberates with support for peace will leaders be moved to abandon their war habits.

While *The Clone Wars* does not differentiate between the war habit and peace habit of men and women as explicitly as Rankin, the representations of Senator Amidala and Duchess Satine as peacemakers do suggest a similar distinction. Senator Amidala and Duchess Satine receive significant attention in terms of the number of episodes in which they appear and the screen time within those episodes. Compared to the masculine characters with whom they interact—politicians and Jedi Knights who, for the most, are men—these two women spend a disproportionate amount of time advocating for a peaceful end to *The Clone Wars*. Though one takes a pragmatic approach and the other a principled approach, both Senator Amidala and Duchess Satine make repeated efforts to interject peaceful, diplomatic efforts into the public dialogue. No matter their approach, the two characters attempt to protect their people from the ravages of war. They insist on vigorous debate within the Galactic Senate, create alternative political organizations intended to promote peaceful dialogue and maintain neutrality, defend the rights and services of the people, and encourage the people to engage in similar practices.

The gendered nature of the positions articulated by Rankin and *The Clone Wars* calls to mind the principles associated with republican motherhood. Not to be confused with the conservative political ideology of the Republican party, the ideology of republic motherhood sprang forth from Enlightenment ideals concerning women and their evolving role in the political community. Never afforded the "possibility of political equality" in the contemporary sense, American women of the eighteenth, nineteenth, and early twentieth centuries inhabited an "important role as protectors of society's morals and manners."[90] The political landscape denied women the right to vote, a denial Jeannette Rankin worked furiously to change, but also expected women to act as moral conscience to their husbands and teacher of civic virtue to their children (particularly young men). Thus, while American women did not achieve the right to vote until August 18, 1920, American women presumably exerted considerable influence on political thought and action. In their examination of the rhetoric of American first ladies, Shawn J. Parry-Giles and Diane M. Blair observe vestiges of republican motherhood continue to resonate throughout the contemporary public square. As evidence the authors point to the political ideology on display as various first ladies "championed such commitments as volunteerism, moral citizenship, beautification, health, and education"[91] Their rhetoric and representations infused with an ethic of care, I want to suggest the dialogic rhetoric between Rankin and *The Clone Wars* gives rise to a galactic motherhood. Harkening back to Ruddick's maternal thinking as a potential path toward peace, Rankin, Amidala, and Satine participate in the rhetorical accomplishing of values fundamental to peacemaking. Despite the differing philosophical positions, as well as the rhetorical minutiae and historical distance separating the rhetors, Rankin and *The Clone Wars* interacting dialogically, calling viewers to consider the possibility of peace in times of war. In "fomenting suspicion of violence and inventing nonviolent action," the two texts work independently and collaboratively and urge listeners to adopt their rightful role as political arbiters and agitators.[92] The galactic mothers appeal to a sense of communal care and responsibility as they encourage the people to adopt a peace habit, challenge political leaders to temper the predisposition toward war with purposeful diplomatic pursuits, and actively defend the rights of themselves and others. Although the peaceful rhetoric of Rankin and *The Clone Wars* did not lead to the cessation of hostilities, and probably won't anytime soon, the reminder that the war habit is not the only way of seeing and acting in the world points toward a hopeful horizon where humanity values creation rather than destruction, advancement rather than stagnation, and peace rather than war.

Six

Attack of the Drones!

@starwars As if this video didn't make it perfectly clear, there is no First Law of Robotics in Star Wars. #chopper #StarWarsRebels[1]
—Leeland Chee (@HolocronKeeper)

"Machines lack morality and mortality, and should as a result not have life and death powers over humans."[2]—International Human Rights Clinic at Harvard Law School, *Shaking the Foundations Report*

The namesake clones aside, one science fiction element sets *The Clone Wars* apart from other installments in the *Star Wars* franchise: the ubiquity of droids. Travelers to any destination in a galaxy far, far away encounter the comforting presence of R2-D2 and C-3P0, two droids who serve as familiar signposts no matter the era. And while Artoo and Threepio do make their characteristic appearances in the prequel era series, *The Clone Wars* distinguishes itself from other *Star Wars* texts in that droids proliferate every corner of the animated galaxy. Droids, Lucas' term for highly autonomous robots, function as doctors, starship navigators and pilots, diplomatic interpreters, law enforcement officers, shopkeepers, chefs, and servers. Possessed of highly advanced artificial intelligence, droids interact flawlessly with sentient beings and assist in the completion of any number of menial or highly technical tasks. Not all droids, however, work toward the public good. *The Clone Wars*, more than any other text within the *Star Wars* galaxy, illustrates dangers associated with artificial intelligence and advanced robotics. For every droid serving in a beneficent capacity, there is also a cold-hearted, dangerous counterpart. For every astromech, protocol, or maintenance droid providing much needed service to the people of the Galactic Republic there is also a Separatist battle, interrogation, or assassin droid waiting to inflict harm. The conflicting representations—droids as

150

benign, helpful companions and droids as malicious killing machines—reveals an understanding of science fiction as cultural dialogue.

From *Forbidden Planet* (Robby the Robot) to *The Terminator* franchise (Arnold Schwarzenegger's memorable T-800 as both foe and friend), science fiction films present one avenue by which to equip audiences for the debates surrounding the increasing presence of artificial intelligence and robotics in everyday life. The dialogic positions articulated by such films, as well as television series like *The Clone Wars*, make indirect reference to debates in the public square. Some voices in the debate see the proliferation of robots as a boon to human endeavors. As Kevin Kelly writes in his December 24, 2012, Wired.com piece titled "Better Than Human: Why Robots Will—and Must—Take Our Jobs," the robots of today and tomorrow will liberate humanity from mundane tasks and "help us discover who we are. They will let us focus on becoming more human than we were." For Kelly, carefully researched and controlled robots provide an opportunity for humans to unshackle themselves from the day-to-day, menial tasks that require significant time and attention to pursue more meaningful undertakings. One might imagine a person sitting in their self-driving, robotic car, utilizing the hour long commute to compose the next great American novel rather than agonizing over time wasted as she or he negotiates mind-numbing stop and go traffic. In a similar vein, Mike Ramsey's April 17, 2015, *Wall Street Journal* piece explores how "Factory Workers Warm Up to the Mechanical Colleagues." Focusing on the automobile an industry, an industry that was ground zero in the robots versus workers debate during the mid to late twentieth century, Ramsey reports many twenty-first-century workers have come to appreciate the heavy lifting accomplished by their mechanical counterparts.

In her April 18, 2015, article titled "The Machines Are Coming" *New York Times* op-ed writer Zeynep Tufekci questions such an optimistic appraisal of the way in which artificial intelligence and robotics have become pervasive in the workplace. Although autonomous self-checkout lanes, customer service centers, surgical procedures, and fruit harvesting equipment may appear to benefit humanity in any number of ways, Tufekci expresses concern with what she describes as a kind of technological outsourcing that makes employees disposable and tips "the balance of power even more in favor of employers." On a more insidious level, numerous technology elites caution that there may be more at stake than jobs. As quoted in Matt McFarland's October 24, 2014, *Washington Post* article, Elon Musk described artificial intelligence "as summoning the demon." Early on in the process, the summoner is positive she or he can control the summoned creature; by the end of the story, the creature has typically taken control of the situation and dispensed with the person who did the summoning. Similarly, Rory Cellan-Jones' December 2, 2014, BBC article titled "Stephen Hawking Warns Artificial Intelligence Could End Mankind," quotes physicist Stephen Hawking as saying, "The development of full artificial intelligence could spell the end of the human race." Humanity, restricted by the slow pace of biological evolution, could eventually be surpassed by the rapid pace of technological evolution. Bill Gates—Microsoft co-founder, technology advocate, and philanthropist—articulated a similar sentiment in Eric Mack's January 28, 2015, article posted on Forbes.com. Gates stated, "I am in the camp that is concerned about super intelligence.... I agree with Elon Musk and some others on this and don't understand why some people are not concerned."

Despite what Bill Gates' might believe, there is one area in the public conversation regarding artificial intelligence and autonomous technology that has received significant attention: the recent development and prolific deployment of autonomous weapons systems. A July 30, 2011, article in *The Economist*, "Drones and the Man," spelled out a growing cultural uncomfortableness with the idea of deploying semi-autonomous drones—robots that fly autonomously for hours at a time but receive target and fire commands directly from a remote pilot—to kill enemy combatants. The piece points to future autonomous technology as it questions who would be responsible for a misguided attack resulting from a drone's inability to "distinguish between a tank and a school bus"? Such questions, the article argues, should be discussed openly and not behind the closed doors of government conference rooms. On November 1, 2012, *Washington Post* editorial board raised similar concerns. Citing increased public apprehension with "the antiseptic nature of U.S. personnel launching strikes that they watch on screens hundreds or thousands of miles from the action." The board called for increased accountability and transparency.

Concerns regarding robotic drones also surface in popular films. In his July 25, 2013, interview with i09.com's Meredith Woerner, *Robocop* (2014) remake director Jose Padilha admits his film explores contemporary anxieties over the rapid move toward intelligent machines. Addressing the proliferation of combat drones, as well as future killing machines implicated by the rapid advances in drone technology, Padilha identifies a number of emerging consequences:

> You can kill people from far away, without running any risks. And we're going to take a step beyond drones. Because we're eventually going to run into autonomous drones, which means drones don't even have people piloting

them—they're just complex software, running the machine. They're like, let's say, Terminator. And waging war or enacting law enforcement and when that happens everything changes because you no longer have accountability. If a cop pulls the trigger, because a cop is a human being you can question his choice. You can say "you made a mistake." When a drone pulls the trigger and makes a mistake, whose fault is it? Is it the drone's fault? Is it the guy who built the drone's fault? Is it the cops that put the drone out there? Is it the software designers? Accountability goes out of the window. And that opens a lot of questions. We should be worried about that. I am.

Amy Davidson raises similar questions in her May 20, 2013, *The New Yorker* review of *Star Trek: Into the Darkness*. Reading the film's plot as an allegory for contemporary drone warfare, Davidson connects the film with broader drone discourses concerning extrajudicial assassination, civilian casualties, governmental overreach, and national identity.

As Susan Sontag wrote, "But alongside the hopeful fantasy of moral simplification and international unity embodied in the science fiction films, lurk the deepest anxieties about contemporary existence."[3] Taking a cue from Susan Sontag, the rest of this chapter explores the contemporary debate over the anxieties associated with autonomous weapons systems. I begin the chapter by turning to J. P. Telotte's double-focused interpretation of robots as simultaneously celebrating and lamenting humanity's proclivity for rapid technological development. Having explored the dialogic tensions playing out in well known science fiction texts, I examine the real life apprehensions elucidated in the speculative non-fiction of several human rights reports condemning autonomous weapons. Next, I illustrate how *The Clone Wars* reinforces some of these concerns while challenging others. Finally, I argue the human rights reports reinforce a traditional human/machine schism while *The Clone Wars* collapses the same divide.

Science Fiction and Robotic Tensions

The tension between artificial intelligence as threat and artificial intelligence as celebrated technological advancement is a distinguishing feature of science fiction. In his analysis of the science fiction classic *Forbidden Planet*, Telotte describes the simultaneous celebration and denouncement of advanced technology as a mediated "double vision" springing forth from historically relevant cultural anxieties. Filmed and released in the early 1950s, an era when the atomic detonations at Nagasaki and Hiroshima still echoed throughout the global community and seemed all the more likely to reoccur in light of the burgeoning nuclear arms race between the United

States and Soviet Union, the film challenges audiences to consider the moral and material benefits and risks associated with technological development. The fascination with scientific discovery, advanced technology, and engineering marvels, brought to life via the spectacle of mediated images, discourse, and sounds, turns quickly to repulsion as those same wonders pose an ominous threat. Robby the Robot's "double focus" is particularly pertinent for this chapter. As Telotte explains, a doubling occurs when any humanoid robot appears in a book, movie, television show, or any other popular culture text. A robot stands as a representation of humanity's propensity for technological ingenuity and innovation, a mechanical twin capable of liberating its biological sibling from a variety of mundane tasks. At the same time, however, a robot's not-quite-humanness evokes unease, "suggests a subtle threat," and challenges its quite human counterpart to consider an unspoken question: is it possible technological advances might make humans unnecessary and insignificant?[4]

The film *Silent Running* explores this dialogic double focus. In a near future where a deforested Earth no longer supports plant life, Freeman Lowell tends a horticultural repository orbiting near Saturn, a kind of Noah's ark for the world's botanic legacy. When his Earth side superiors order Lowell and his colleagues to jettison the arboretum and return their spacecraft to commercial service, an obvious statement about capitalism's wanton neglect of the environment, Lowell preserves the oasis by killing his fellow scientists. As the sole human steward of Earth's lush past, Lowell works alongside three robots–Huey, Dewey, and Louie—as they care for arboretum's verdant cargo. Over time, Lowell comes to understand he cannot live in perpetual solitude—robotic companionship is no substitute for human interaction—and hands the care of the forest to Dewey thereby leaving the fate of the Earth's forests to a robot and "facilitates the unexpected alliance of technology and nature."[5] Huey, Dewey, and Louie waddle through the film as representations of Telotte's double focus. The three robots, argues Hughes, represent both the emancipatory potential of a highly mechanized future—robot companions can help humans care for the environment—and the depressing realization that the Earth's wilderness will never be free from technological influence.

Stephen T. Asma identifies *Wall-E* as another environmental film displaying a robotic double focus. Having fled an environmentally devastated Earth, humanity lives aboard a luxury space liner where robots address every need. In fact, "machines have made life entirely too comfortable for humans."[6] Floating about in hover chairs, interacting solely via holographic screens, and having every whim catered to by helpful robots—an obvious reference to much of humanity's increasingly technologized life—the film represents humans as the ultimate passive consumers. Immersed in their digital lap of luxury, inundated by mass media marketing and preferring to engage one another virtually rather than directly, *Wall-E*'s humans no longer possess the ability to move around on their own, think for themselves, or provide for their own needs. WALL-E, EVE, and handful of rebellious robots, robots capable of going beyond their original programming and acting with spontaneity and creativity, display a double vision wherein robots not only subjugate humans as mediated consumers unable to escape the stranglehold of technology but also point out the way to escape that subjugation. Through their rebellious actions, WALL-E and EVE set an example for other misfit robots and inspire humans to seize "the individual's right to pursue happiness and enjoy life."[7]

Examining *The Terminator* and *Terminator 2: Judgment Day* as allegory for the cultural anxieties arising from the conflict between U.S. auto workers and the shift in the automobile industry toward automated assembly lines, Robert F. Arnold argues fictional robots help viewers come to terms with "technology, subjectivity, and ideology."[8] Characterizing the conflict between the classic T-800 Terminator (a metallic body covered with flesh) and the advanced T-1000 (a robot comprised of metamorphic liquid metal) as a clash between "human and machine," static and malleable subjectivity, and "the modern (linear, hierarchic, industrial) and the postmodern (nonlinear, polymorphic, postindustrial)," Arnold identifies film as a site where cinema technologies (e.g., production techniques, distribution, image format) and narratives regarding technological anxieties intersect with broader communal dialogues, blurring the distinction between fiction and reality.[9] The *Terminator* films, he argues, speak with a double voicedness about the relationship between humans and robots in the workplace. The films suggest humans cannot ever be fully replaced by machines (Sarah Connor ultimately triumphs over the T-800) but also suggests humans might benefit from the protection afforded by machines (the T-800 protects Sarah and John Connor from the T-1000 in *Terminator 2*). The dialectic presented in the films, he argues, reflects the tension experienced by the 1980s autoworker. Anxious about the possibility of losing her job to automation, the worker also understands that robotic technologies free her from dangerous working conditions.

Science fiction's robotic double focus cannot always be read so optimistically. In her exploration of *Astro Boy*, an animated series involving a robotic, atomic powered boy created by Dr. Tenma as a replacement for his dead son, Alicia Gibson points out the double focused themes offered to audiences. Presented to its intended audience, children, as a human who is not human, a child who is not a child, and a peaceful creation who is not a peaceful creation, Astro Boy serves as an animated representation of a child's liminal state, calling her or him to reflect upon childhood's constant tension between wonder and constraint. At the same time, Astro Boy's atomic powered super abilities "become virtual representations of a universal power full of creative potential that, in actuality, is used for destruction on a mass scale."[10] As several scholars point out, nowhere is the technological tension between creation and destruction more apparent than in the *Terminator* films.

With a nod to Carl Jung, Janice Hocker Rushing and Thomas S. Frentz define the tendency of the human imaginary to dismiss, ignore, or hide our flawed dimensions as "the shadow." They write, "That which we hate, fear, and disown, and therefore repress into the personal/cultural unconscious, is the shadow."[11] In their book-length treatment of the shadow in popular film, the authors analyze *The Terminator* as a "technological shadow" representing humanity's misguided attempts to create and control technology's increasing pervasiveness and social influence.[12] Important to their argument is the fact that the Terminator, the relentless mechanized killing machine that hounds Sarah Connor throughout the film, is positioned as an external threat, as a technological Other far removed from humanity's biological Self. Devoid of emotion, unwilling to reason, and driven to fulfill its programming without deviation, the Terminator marches through the film as an alien presence intent on humanity's destruction. What Hocker and Rushing point out, however, is how this technological shadow arises as a result of human action: humans create the technology that eventually achieves self-awareness. The Terminator's alienness, otherness, and radical non-humanness creates an insurmountable rupture between the unstoppable killing machine (the technological shadow) and its human creators, thus absolving the creator of any responsibility for its creation. In its radical otherness, "the enemy remains outside ourselves, a disowned alter ego that must be battled to the death."[13] Likening the otherness of the Terminator to contemporary horror film serial killers Jason Vorhees and Michael Myers, Mark Jancovich describes the mechanized exterminator as "the thing with no consciousness."[14] As metaphors for humanity's shadow, a denied dark side brought to life in biological and robotic monsters, these filmic doppelgangers show little in the way of consciousness or conscience. At one level, the Terminator represents the dangers inherent in the never-ending pursuit of a highly technologized future; present technological advances will result in future catastrophes. At another level, the film suggests humans and the Terminator are two sides of the same coin. The relentless pursuit of an objective or ideological cause may result in people assuming the role of biological automatons acting without conscience, moving relentlessly toward their goal. This question of conscience emerges as a central issue in the debate over contemporary drone warfare and near future autonomous weapons technology.

Rise of the Drones

As has been well documented, the terrorist attacks of September 11, 2001, accelerated calls for the reformed military strategy advanced by the proponents of Donald Rumsfeld's "force transformation." Bill Keller's March 10, 2002, article appearing in the *New York Times Magazine* described this vision for a twenty-first-century fighting force as follows:

> They agree that threats to America have become less predictable, that the next war is likely to be very different from Vietnam or the gulf was and that the proper response entails incorporating new technology—vivid information-gathering sensors, fast computers, precision guidance, robotics— and new fighting dogma to make our forces more aware and more agile.

This increased awareness and agility came into sharp focus during February 2002 when, according to Jane Mayer's October 26, 2009, piece for *The New Yorker*, the CIA employed a Predator drone within Pakistani airspace to identify, target, and kill a man believed to be Osama bin Laden. Widely considered to be the first attempted targeted killing conducted by an unmanned aerial vehicle (UAV) outside an acknowledged war theater (drones were used regularly in both Iraq and Afghanistan), the attack marked a conscious move toward the aforementioned "new fighting dogma" whereby the United States would move swiftly and decisively to eliminate perceived threats anywhere in the world. As more information regarding this initial targeted killing surfaced, the flaws in the program became readily apparent. While the drone program proved cost effective in terms of both money and reduced American casualties, the initial strike killed three civilians rather than bin Laden. Despite the obvious risks involved with making the drone program a central feature of counterterrorism efforts, both the Bush and Obama administrations turned to the new weapon with increasing regularity. According to The Bureau of Investigative Journalism's online monthly drone war update dated February 2, 2015, the Bush administration authorized 52 strikes and the Obama administration 456.

Given Obama's presidential campaign commitment to draw down

troops and eventually end financially taxing combat operations in Iraq and Afghanistan, as well as the common understanding that drone warfare results in far fewer casualties than traditional invade and occupy combat operations, an increase in UAV strikes made strategic sense. In their October 1, 2011, *New York Times* article titled "Strike Reflects U.S. Shift to Drones in Terror Fight," Scott Shane and Thom Shanker reported, "Disillusioned by huge costs and uncertain outcomes in Iraq and Afghanistan, the Obama administration has decisively embraced the drone, along with small scale lightning raids like the one that killed Osama bin Laden ... as the future of the fight against terrorist networks." This shift in combat operations resulted in a sizable increase for the U.S. military drone inventory. As Spencer Ackerman and Noah Shachtman wrote in their January 9, 2012, piece for Wired.com, drone aircraft accounted for roughly 5 percent of the U.S. military aircraft arsenal in 2005; as of 2012 drones accounted for 40 percent. While most of these robotic UAVs serve as intelligence and surveillance platforms—from small 3-foot drones deployed by troops on the ground to 50-foot reconnaissance drones cruising at 60,000 feet—215 Predator and Reaper drones function primarily as attack aircraft for targeted, surgical strikes against identified enemy combatants.[15] These combat drones, as well as future, autonomous weapons systems, raise a number of concerns.

As Robert Sparrow attests in his article interrogating the ethical responsibilities inherent in utilizing killer robots, U.S. autonomous weapons platforms go far beyond drone technology. Whether in the air, at sea, or on land, the U.S. military deploys robots in an effort to reduce casualties and achieve military objectives. For example, cruise missiles, torpedoes, and anti-air defense weapons fitted with "Automatic Target Recognition capability" allow the weapons a small degree of autonomy in terms of target selection when it reaches a designated location.[16] While the Navy employs a variety of unmanned vehicles in anti-submarine and anti-mine operations, ground troops in Iraq and Afghanistan utilize remote controlled robots to detect and defuse Improvised Explosive Devices (IEDs) and survey suspicious locations for enemy activity. Ships, airbases, and forward operating bases alike are protected by the automated, radar guided ballistics of the Phalanx, a 20mm Gatling gun weapons system capable of shooting down incoming missiles, rockets, and mortar shells. My point in detailing the robotic capabilities of the U.S. military is not intended to give a comprehensive portrait of the systems at work throughout the world. Instead, I want to emphasize that the military landscape is being slowly but surely transformed by the rapid introduction of robots. Indeed, P.W. Singer points out that at the beginning of the Iraq war the United States deployed "zero robotic units on the ground.... By the end of 2008 it was projected to reach as high as 12,000."[17]

Although the droid armies of *The Clone Wars* exist only in the realm of science fiction, there is little doubt the U.S. military would deploy battle droids were they available. The use of robots in warfare would presumably reduce human combat casualties, be more cost effective (robots don't need a salary or food), and free humans from such "dull, dirty, or dangerous" jobs as clearing landmines, fighting fires, or navigating radioactive landscapes.[18] In light of these rapid transformations, and the presumed changes occurring in the near future, robot warfare presents a number of troubling questions. Can robotic engineers and programmers teach a robotic war machine the necessary critical discernment to act morally? Can intelligent war machines exercise human judgment? Will, as Adrianne Jeffries implies in her January 23, 2014, article for TheVerge.com, autonomous war machines always lack the nuanced observational skills needed to distinguish "between civilians and the terrorists and insurgents who live among them"? Does the remote physical distance between a drone controller and the semi-autonomous aircraft also create an emotional distance with those observed on a television screen? Is a drone controller more likely to pull the trigger on a target she or he encounters on a video screen rather than face to face? Human rights scholarship, advocacy, and legal justice organizations like the Center for Civilians in Conflict and Human Rights Clinic at Columbia Law School (CCC/HRC), The International Human Rights Clinic at Harvard Law School (IHRC), International Human Rights and Conflict Resolution Clinic at Stanford Law School (IHRCRC), and Global Justice Clinic at NYU School of Law (GJC) share these concerns.

Fearing the Reaper

As the Bush and Obama administrations relied increasingly on robotic technology in global counterterrorism efforts, particularly in Pakistan, Afghanistan, and Yemen, human rights organizations articulated an important counter-narrative. Rather than focusing on cost effectiveness (money and lives of military personnel) or operational success, two benefits difficult to refute, the various organizations questioned whether military and security benefits outweigh costs to civilians. These arguments, presented in several official reports, weave a cautionary tale regarding the proliferation of not only drone technology but also the autonomous weapons systems likely to join the battlefield in the near future. For the purposes of this chapter, I examine those reports addressing the civilian impact of current drone technology and those technologies representing what the International Human Rights Clinic at Harvard Law School (IHRC) described as a "step beyond current remote controlled drones" and includes "everything from remote-controlled drones to weapons with complete autonomy."[19] Not unlike the speculative nature of the science fiction genre, these reports ground various observations in the real-world impact of drone technology on contemporary civilian populations and contemplate how future robotic technology might duplicate, and even exacerbate, these repercussions. Taken as a kind of speculative non-fiction, the arguments treat drones as a precursor to fully autonomous weapons systems. "Drones," the IHRC warned ominously, "are seen as just the beginning of a technological revolution."[20] The cautions concerning drones and future autonomous weapons systems revolve around three important issues: distinction, dispassion, and disruption.

One of the most frequently cited objections to drones and future autonomous weapons concerns the matter of distinction, both physical and emotional. To what degree are semi-autonomous and autonomous systems capable of differentiating between military targets and civilian populations? In a physical sense, the prolific use of Predator and Reaper drones shift combat operations toward the new normal inherent in robotic warfare: "the distancing of human soldiers from their targets."[21] Drone pilots and surveillance analysts sit in command centers hundreds, and sometimes thousands, of miles away from the combat theater and, by nature of the technology, make life and death decisions based on a digital video feed. Limited video resolution, obscured lines of sight, and latency, the "delay between movement on the ground and the arrival of the video image via satellite to the drone pilot," complicate the process and make it difficult to assure civilian safety at all times.[22] For example, the Center for Civilians in Conflict and Human Rights Clinic at Columbia Law School recounted a 2012 drone strike attack on Al Qaeda linked militants that actually turned out to be a meeting of local stakeholders trying to negotiate a mining conflict.[23] The attack killed four Taliban—the Taliban are stakeholders in the region—and 38 civilians. The civilian casualties, suggests the report, illustrates the difficulties inherent in conducting strikes on potential targets moving among local populations.

The evaluative criteria for conducting strikes becomes even more complicated when considering the move toward fully autonomous weapons systems. Just as drone operators struggle to make a clear distinction between an enemy combatant and a child, a physical distinction if there ever was one, will fully autonomous weapons systems ever be capable of making close calls? The IHRC report, *Losing Humanity*, argued such complex evaluative processes will be far beyond the robotics capabilities of the near future. Deciding whether or not to open fire on an a target requires an appraisal and interpretation of a person's or group's physical movements and actions, as well as an assessment of intention. Is the potential threat a viable target or an innocent bystander?[24] Based on physical demeanor, what is she or he trying to accomplish? What is this group hoping to achieve? Is it reasonable to think that an armed machine, a killing machine guided by an artificial intelligence, might achieve the interpretive fluency needed to decipher physical behaviors? Considering the discomfort many feel about the semi-autonomous drone attacks, how comfortable will the public be when a fully autonomous weapons system makes such distinctions?

Concern over emotional distinction obscures matters even further. The ability to disconnect emotionally during combat is, of course, an important part of a soldier's training; to kill another human being requires a soldier to disassociate from her or his target, to dehumanize the other. One can only imagine the amount of internal torment a soldier might experience if she or he envisioned an enemy combatant as someone's parent, sibling, or friend every time she or he pulled the trigger. The geographical distance central to drone warfare keeps military personnel physically safe and assists in the emotional distance needed to do one's job effectively. That said, does the inability to clearly distinguish individuals on images collected from aerial surveillance encourage a greater degree of affective disengagement? When bombing potential militants looks more like killing pixels in a video game than people on the ground, to what degree might drone pilots disconnect from a scene emotionally? At the same time, however, a pilot's humanity always remains in the background, waiting to issue a call to conscience. The emotional affinity between humans might motivate a drone pilot to reassess a target that puts civilians at undue risk or encourage a boots-on-the-ground soldier to disobey an unlawful order to shoot a child. What happens when a human's capacity for emotional intelligence—the ability to distinguish between emotions and to use those distinctions to adjust behavior accordingly—is removed from the combat equation completely? Until a major technological breakthrough in artificial intelligence allows for such emotional aptitude, near future autonomous "weapons would lack compassion and empathy, important inhibitors to killing people needlessly."[25] Robotic soldiers, continued the IHRC *Shaking Foundations* report, "comprehend neither the value of individual life nor the significance of its loss."[26] Similarly, another report identified "human empathy" as "an important check on killing" and "one of the best safeguards against killing civilians."[27] Would a programmed robot, for instance, possess the emotional wherewithal to hold its fire against a grieving parent who acts erratically, perhaps in a manner that appears threatening? Could an autonomous weapons system evaluate whether a child, playing with a toy gun, poses a serious threat? Without fully developed and integrated emotional intelligence, a combat robot remains restricted to hard-wired operational logarithms; a robot, unlike a soldier, cannot respond to the call of conscience.

Stemming from concerns related to distinction, the human rights reports also issue a caution regarding a rising dispassion tied to autonomous weapons system. As all of the humanitarian reports acknowledge, drone technology (and future autonomous weapons systems) benefits both the military and the general public by removing troops from combat operations. In other words, Predator and Reaper drones "enable the US to kill from afar without immediate risk to American lives."[28] With fewer troops engaged in combat operations, casualties drop thereby lessening the possibility that a family, friendship group, and broader community might suffer a significant, heart-wrenching loss. The shift toward semi-autonomous weapons systems, speculated *The Civilian Impact of Drones* report, helped precipitate apathy toward combat operations abroad. As the actions in Afghanistan and Iraq wound down and fewer troops remained active in combat theaters, the U.S. American public directed their attention elsewhere. A section of the report read:

> US use of drones outside traditional combat zones has had the unforeseen consequence of reducing political and public interest in demanding alternatives to lethal targeting, or steps to mitigate civilian harm. In the absence of an outcry—indeed, with broad public and political support—drone strikes have become the policy norm and displaced alternative approaches that could be more protective of civilian life, in both the short- and long-term.[29]

Similar to the physical and emotional distance experienced by soldiers, the U.S. public experienced a disconnect between themselves, the people in whose name the government wages war, and the costs incurred by war. As the tangible consequences of war faded into the recesses of U.S. American public memory, people paid less attention to the remaining ongoing conflicts (e.g., Pakistan, Yemen, Somalia). With little public protest or outcry over a lack of transparency or the impact on civilians (a topic I'll address momentarily), the drone program continued unquestioned. When a mission's relevance—the direct, perceivable impact on a person or community—proves difficult to uncover, it fades from the public dialogue and consciousness. As war becomes increasingly automated will the people become even more apathetic?

Even more concerning than public dispassion is potential apathy toward armed conflict on the part of the government. The benefit of reducing military deaths on the battlefield may result in a hidden, long-term cost: "Unmanned systems may lessen the terrible costs of war, but in so doing, they will make it easier for leaders to go to war."[30] Few question the premise that "military fatalities" stand as "one of the greatest deterrents to combat" and cause governments to weigh military action thoroughly before committing human resources.[31] With human troop costs replaced by the material costs of autonomous weapons marching to war, will government dispassion lead to an increased propensity for problem solving via armed conflict? Will replacing human soldiers with killer robots make armed conflict more palatable? The IHRC's *Mind the Gap* report, a report focused on accountability and responsibility in the manufacture and deployment of autonomous weapons, raised concerns regarding the proliferation of killer robots to "irresponsible states" effectively "giving them machines that could be programmed to kill their own civilians or enemy populations."[32] Another report voiced a similar concern: "Abusive autocrats … could deploy these weapons to suppress protesters with a level of violence against which human security forces might rebel."[33] The same report predicted the development of autonomous weapons systems presages a new arms race wherein global local players strive to shore up their own reputations and legitimacy by pursuing the latest in military technology.

Such developments bring the final concern, disruption, into the proverbial crosshairs. I turn to the term "disruption" to describe the far reaching civilian impact resulting from the proliferation of present and future killer robots. All five reports examined for this chapter cite the impact on civilian populations, present and future, as the primary reason for opposing the development or deployment of semi-autonomous and autonomous weapons systems. Citing civilian protection as a guiding principle of contemporary warfare, the reports articulated two major objections to current drone practices. First, the reports suggested an increased reliance on "signature strikes" results in a higher risk of civilian death. While a personality strike targets a known, specific person (or persons) via carefully collected and analyzed intelligence data, a signature strike targets anonymous individuals who act suspiciously. Pre-planned personality strikes allow for the careful assessment and review of geographical location, civilian population, and a related "collateral damage estimation" thereby minimizing injury to noncombatants.[34] A signature strike, often ordered as a result of observations made mid-mission, relies largely on the previously mentioned video surveillance collected and analyzed at great physical distance. Lacking the detailed intelligence of a personality strike, the signature strike identifies and executes attack objectives by singling out individuals or groups displaying behaviors associated with militants. For instance, a group of people engaged in some kind of observable weapons training in a location known to harbor militant training camps could be reconnoitered, targeted, and attacked by a drone. As a report authored by the Center for Civilians in Conflict and Human Rights Clinic at Columbia Law School (CCC/HRC) pointed out, signature strikes increase the likelihood of civilian casualties in that drone operators might mistake innocent behaviors for those of someone intending to do harm.[35] The second major practice criticized by the reports pertains to whether an operation utilizes pre-planned or dynamic targeting. Pre-planned targeting occurs when U.S. personnel receive reliable intelligence regarding a target's location and, as the name suggests, create a detailed plan for striking at that person. This kind of planning suggested the CCC/HRC report on civilian impact, minimizes errors and allows for the best assessment of potential civilian casualties. Dynamic targeting, on the other hand, occurs when a drone is redirected mid-flight or even stumbles across potential militants during a scheduled reconnaissance flight. As one might imagine, dynamic targeting—which relies on assessing a militant's movements and behavior—results in the occasional case of mistaken identity. As NBCNews.com reporters Richard Engel and Robert Windrem suggested in their June 5, 2013, independent investigation of CIA documents, "The CIA did not always know who it was targeting and killing in drone strikes in Pakistan."

Regardless of the type of attack or the planning involved, drone attacks cause significant pain and suffering in civilian populations. Drawing on estimates offered by the Pakistan Institute for Peace Studies, Bureau of Investigative Journalism, Long War Journal, and New America Foundation, the CCC/HRC report *The Civilian Impact of Drones* estimated that targeted killings in Somalia, Yemen, and Pakistan resulted in between 551 and 1035 civilian casualties through 2012.[36] While the U.S. government acknowledges the regrettable fact that drone strikes do incur civilian casualties, the continued program suggests that officials see these losses as acceptable. The raw numbers, however, offer a sanitized version of the civilian casualty story and fail to acknowledge the long lasting consequences for families and communities. In addition to painful emotional absence resulting from the death of a loved one, some families contend with significant financial difficulties. "The death of one member can create long-lasting instability," contended the CCC/HRC, "particularly if a breadwinner is killed."[37] According to the *Living Under Drones* report, those "who live with the daily presence of lethal drones in their skies and with the constant threat of drone strikes in their communities," experience a near constant state of disruption.[38] From fitful sleep, to socializing with neighbors, to focusing on one's school work, to attending a funeral, to shopping in a market, the knowledge that drones hover overhead—watching, assessing, attacking—impacts almost every dimension of Pakistani life. In an interview conducted by the Center for Civilian Conflict, one Pakistani civilian reported, "We fear that drones will strike us again.... We are depressed, anxious, and constantly remembering our deceased family members ... it often compels me to leave this place."[39] Another civilian remarked, "Everyone is scared all the time. When you're sitting together in a meeting, we're scared there might be strike. When you can hear the drone circling in the sky, you think it might strike you. We're always scared. We always have this fear in our head."[40] The pervasive fear isolates individuals and families even within their own communities; afraid of being in the right place at the wrong time, people withhold aid to those wounded by attacks. This is, in large part, of result of U.S. "double tap" attacks, the practice of hitting a target and then launching a second strike when presumed militants arrive on the scene to offer medical assistance or sort through the wreckage for valuables. In light of this tactic, the *Living Under Drones* report alleged some humanitarian aid organizations enforce a strict six hour delay before arriving at strike locations.

Obviously, the degree to which fully autonomous weapons systems might disrupt civilian populations remains speculative. The various reports, however, envision a future where the expanded deployment of killer robots inflicts harms similar to those associated with contemporary drone warfare. Just as drone operators mistake civilian behaviors for those of militants, fail to accurately assess the possibility of collateral damage, and misinterpret intelligence data, robots also face unique challenges in responding to conditions in the field. Lacking human experience, emotion, and intuition, "it is highly unlikely that a robot could be pre-programmed to handle the infinite number of scenarios it might face so it would have to interpret a situation in real time."[41] How would a robotic soldier respond to a crowd of bereaved community members expressing their anger and frustration through riotous behavior? Is a surrendering soldier a noncombatant or a threat? Furthermore, the idea that a robot analyzes signature data as well as a person, suggested the various reports, is pure science fiction. Killer robots "would find it more difficult to recognize and interpret subtle behavioral clues whose meaning depends on context and culture."[42] A robot's emotional distance, its inability to comprehend complex human emotions and actions, puts civilian populations in harm's way. Additionally, the propensity for advanced technology to experience "communication interruptions, programming errors, or mechanical malfunctions" at one point or another increases the possibility of civilian injury.[43] Ultimately, when autonomous weapons systems march, fly, or swim into battle, the responsibility for reducing and avoiding unnecessary property damage, personal injury, or death, a responsibility traditionally shouldered by human combatants, falls to civilians. As the *Mind the Gap* report argued, the removal of humans from the battlefield inherently shifts "the burden of armed conflict from combatants to civilians."[44] Whereas human soldiers possess the wherewithal to assess a situation and choose to rethink an objective, respond with an appropriate level of force (or non-force), or call off an operation completely, a programmed autonomous weapon does not. An encounter with a pre-programmed autonomous weapon attempting to follow orders and complete a military objective places the burden of avoiding injury or death falls entirely on noncombatant shoulders. The burden is even more onerous if a maligned leader unleashes killer robots on her or his own people. Whereas human soldiers might turn against their leader when ordered to engage in a massacre, an autonomous weapon does not possess the capacity to question a leader's choice to "use weapons in intentional or indiscriminate attacks against their own people or civilians in other countries with horrific consequences."[45] Whether from an inability to judge a particular situation, some kind of technical failure, or programmed to pursue an objective at all costs, fully autonomous weapons will likely result in the same kinds of disruptions—physical, psychological, social—as contemporary drone warfare.

The various human rights reports centralize, as one would expect, the welfare of civilians. Turning to the available qualitative and quantitative data regarding contemporary drone warfare, the organizations warn the coming shift from semi-autonomous armed robots to fully autonomous weapons systems jeopardizes the safety of civilian populations around the globe. Given the already complicated concerns involved with targeted killing at a distance—distinction, dispassion, and disruption—the reports utilize a predictive logic to speculate about continued civilian maltreatment. Arguing the past is prologue, that present drone warfare foreshadows an ominous future for robotic warfare, all five reports acknowledge automated warfare's continued cost to civilians outweighs any benefits in terms of potential expediency and cost effectiveness. As such, the five reports call for "greater government disclosure to inform public debate" about current drone operations and encourage the global community to work toward banning "the development, production, and use of fully autonomous weapons through an international legally binding instrument."[46] Each report contrasts the human ability to experience mercy, compassion, and care when facing the other—combatant and noncombatant—with a robot's amoral indifference, an obvious inadequacy that positions autonomous systems as unfit for military service. Rhetorically speaking, the language constitutes the familiar impenetrable human/machine dichotomy wherein biology and machinery frequently come to cross purposes. Given the errors that already occur when a human has her or his finger on a Reaper drone's trigger, the prognostic, anti-robot rhetoric points toward a bleak future. The rhetoric of the reports draw a single conclusion: "Machines lack morality and mortality, and should as a result not have life and death powers over humans."[47] The reports never devolve into an apocalyptic rhetoric akin to *The Terminator*, but the imminent transformation to war fought primarily with automated weapons promises continued pain and suffering for civilian populations.

Attack of the Drones

From battle droids to protocol droids, from vulture droids to astromech droids, from interrogator droids to medical droids, *The Clone Wars* depicts scores of different types of droids supporting the respective war efforts of the Galatctic Republic and the Confederacy of Independent Systems. In fact, the pervasiveness of droids in a wartime setting allows *The Clone Wars* writers and creators an opportunity to offer allegorical readings of contemporary, real life autonomous weapons systems. These readings present several insights into the previously articulated concerns related to distinction, dispassion, and disruption. When it comes to the depiction of droids, the distinction concern permeates the entire series. Unlike the humanitarian reports, the distinction concern pertains more to emotional then physical distance; droids of all types distinguish between combatants and civilians with relative ease. Separatist battle droids patrol the streets of occupied cities, marching among civilians, and only turn their weapons on freedom fighters who pose an obvious threat. The bigger issue in the *Star Wars* universe pertains to emotional distinction. Unlike the emotionally distanced weapons systems predicted by the humans rights reports, *The Clone Wars* droids display a broad range of emotions. It seems fitting that Separatist droids, droids engaged primarily in combat situations, exhibit such wide ranging emotions as fear, antipathy, malice, and cruelty. While traditional battle droids show little emotion as they march forward relentlessly, shoulder to shoulder, destroying everything that stands between them and a military objective, other Separatist droids relish causing pain and suffering in others. For example, in the episode "Weapons Factory" a tactical droid laughs as it prepares to unleash a new superweapon on approaching Republic forces: "Ha, ha, ha, ha! The supertank is impervious to all weapons."[48] Similarly, in the episode "Grievous Intrigue" a tactical droid tortures a prisoner while would be rescuers Anakin Skywalker and Adi Gallia look onward. The droid electrocutes the captive Jedi repeatedly and taunts the onlookers with a cold, metallic voice: "One more step and your friend will die. Ha. Ha. Ha."[49] At other times super battle droids, droids of few words, grumble and growl as they express disappointment and frustration. During an argument with a biological being, a super tactical droid steps forward and attempts to physically intimidate its interlocutor.

On the other hand, some *Star Wars* droids establish interpersonal relationships with both mechanical and biological beings, possess a high degree of emotional intelligence, and make ethical decisions grounded in compassion. In his discussion of droids in the *Star Wars* films, Robert Arp observes,

> Droids communicate, have the capacity for reason, and can be involved in complex social relationships. More importantly, they express feelings of disillusion, contempt, pain, and suffering, as well as joy, satisfaction, and contentment. A being that has these traits appears to have mental states, and such a being is arguably a person, regardless of having been created by persons.[50]

Many droids, particularly those depicted as being allied with the Republic, develop friendships, demonstrate a capacity for creativity and ingenuity in times of crisis, and experience grief at the loss of a comrade. Droids chirp, whistle, bleep, and buzz as they communicate glee and melancholy, confidence and apprehension, acrimony and civility. Nowhere is a droid's affective personhood more apparent than in R2-D2's relationships with others; from his lifelong companionship with C-3P0 to his deep friendship with Anakin, R2-D2 blurs the emotional distance between droid and biological being. The potential for friendship between a human and droid emerges early in the form of R2-D2 and Anakin's relationship as a dynamic starpilot and astromech team. When Artoo goes missing in action, Anakin goes to great lengths to track down his droid companion declaring, "Artoo is more than a droid, he's a friend."[51] Later in the series, when Anakin finds himself at the mercy of a bounty hunter's trap, Artoo reaffirms their friendship as he dodges assassins, battles a gundark, survives a starfighter dogfight, and races off to the Jedi Temple to bring help. At the end of the episode Jedi Master Mace Windu, a character who criticized Anakin's close relationship with R2-D2, offered the faithful droid his praise: "I can see why your master trusts you little one. Good job."[52]

While R2-D2's friendship with Anakin blurs the emotional line between droid and biological being, a story arc in the latter part of season five completely collapses the distinction. When the possibility arises to purloin a Separatist encryption code that would allow the Galactic Republic to translate secret transmissions, the Jedi call on D–Squad to infiltrate an enemy ship and procure the war changing cipher. Comprised of five droids (CT-KT, M5-BZ, R2-D2, U9-C4, and WAC-47) and one biological humanoid (Colonel Meeber Gascon, a foot tall alien who looks like a biped frog with eye stalks), D–Squad sneaks aboard the enemy dreadnaught, outsmarts scores of enemy droids, procures the encryption code, and also manages to thwart a major Separatist attack on a Republic war strategy conference. Most intriguing about this narrative arc, however, is the interactions between the droids and Colonel Gascon. From the outset of the mission Colonel Gascon treats the droids as inferiors, a practice most evident in his use of dismissive epithets like "moron," "cyclops," "blockhead," and "ragtag collection of droids."[53] WAC-47, the droid who receives more abuse than others, gives as good as he gets by engaging the colonel in an ongoing verbal tit for tat. WAC intentionally irritates Gascon by referring to the colonel, and Galactic Republic assigned leader of D–Squad, as "corporal" or "captain." At one point during the mission, WAC confronts the colonel directly: "First of all, my name is WAC. Second of all, we will execute your plan but you have to stop calling us stupid names. Shorty." Shortly thereafter, the mission a complete success, Colonel Gascon and WAC call an end to hostilities; Gascon refers to the droids by their proper designations and WAC refers to their leader as "Colonel."

While the ongoing hostilities between these two characters (WAC speaks for the other four droids as they communicate in beeps and whistles) injects some humor into a tense episode, there is a serious side to these conversations. WAC, as an interpreter for the other four droids, defends their identity as living beings. Through their actions in the four episode arc the five droids exemplify duty to the Galactic Republic, innovative problem solving, initiative, comradery, and selflessness. By the end of the narrative arc, Colonel Gascon recognizes the humanness of his mechanical compatriots. When one of the droids sacrifices himself to save the others, a grieving D–Squad asks the colonel to say a few words. He complies.

When this D squad started our mission I had doubts, grave doubts, that we would survive let alone succeed. But we worked together, we didn't give up hope. We showed courage in the face of death. It shocks me to say this, but we make an excellent team. Now, we've lost one of our members, BZ. But we must remember, BZ sacrificed himself for us. That's what a good soldier does sometimes.[54]

This pathos filled moment marks more than the passing of a supporting character. As a narrative device the contemplative moment calls the audience to reflect on Gascon's transformation from emotionally distanced commander to an emotionally connected comrade. The brief commemorative moment reinforces each droid's affective personhood as Colonel Gascon humanizes the feeling, thinking, and acting soldiers of D–Squad.

Despite the affective personhood evinced by R2-D2 and D–Squad, *The Clone Wars* also articulates a contradictory concern regarding the dispassion arising from automated weapons systems. A war fought largely by manufactured units, whether constructed in a weapons factory or grown in a cloning facility, *The Clone Wars* depicts a conflict where the public bears little burden in relation to direct combat. The public, on both sides of the conflict, remains largely removed from direct combat fatalities; droids and clone troopers do the heavy lifting in that regard. When massive casualties put the war effort at risk, the Confederacy of Independent Systems manufactures more droids or the Galactic Republic grows more clones. Representations of the two capital cities, Raxus and Coruscant, suggest that the average citizen is able to go about her or his day-to-day business without much concern for the ongoing conflict. In the episode "Heroes on Both Sides," when Padmé Amidala and Ahsoka Tano visit the Separatist capital for covert peace negotiations, they stroll through beautiful gardens and enjoy casual drinks with old friends. And while Padmé treats with Separatist Senator Mira Bontera and discusses the possibility of peace, the actual conflict remains far removed from everyday life.[55] In fact, the civilian populations on both sides of the war appear largely apathetic until an episode late in season five where, after a terrorist attack on the Jedi Temple, a handful of Coruscant citizens protest the war.[56]

Similar to the dispassion expressed in relation to the proliferation of drone warfare, and the potential widespread use of autonomous weapons systems in international problem solving, the deployment of battle droids illuminates the consequences of the right weapon falling into the wrong hands. Given their representation in *The Clone Wars*, there is no doubt Count Dooku, Separatist political leader and secret apprentice to Darth Sidious, and General Grievous, the field leader and military tactician for the Separatist droid army, parallel the abusive leaders mentioned in the various humanitarian reports. Utilizing the droid armies with an amoral ruthlessness, the leaders' obvious disregard for civilian populations is readily apparent. Lok Durd, a Separatist military general, attempts to test a new weapon "designed to destroy all organic matter while leaving mechanicals unharmed" on a peaceful civilian village.[57] The attack fails, the Jedi and clone troopers intervene, but the Separatist indifference toward civilian life remains. On the planet Ryloth the occupying droid army hopes to stave off an impending Republic assault by surrounding proton canon emplacements with Twi'lek civilians.[58] The most brutal portrayal of apathy toward civilians involves a secret Separatist plot to derail peace negotiations. Count Dooku works against the wishes of his own people—the Separatist legislative body votes to open peace talks with the Republic—and sends demolition droids to strike at the Galactic Republic's capital.[59] Demolition droids disguised as cleaning droids infiltrate a power station, gun down civilian utility workers, link together to form an explosive device, and destroy a power reactor. The terrorist attack plunges the Republic Senate into turmoil, derails the peace talk vote entirely, and precipitates an increase in military funding. Most disturbing about this plot point is the brutal depiction on screen. The image pans around the power station control room showing, with perfect clarity, the cold-blooded murder of several workers. Viewers watch as blaster bolts strike the workers, mowing them down with little or no resistance. All three of these examples illustrate a blatant disregard for civilian populations; if the death, or potential death, of noncombatants advances an objective, lives are forfeit. Similar to a U.S. drone attack targeting a high level militant leader attending a tribal meeting, or militants using a civilian population as a human shield, or a terrorist attack on a public target, Separatist leaders position human life as expendable, as a justifiable wartime cost.

The dispassion associated with the automated weapons systems deployed by the Separatists leads to familiar territory: the widespread disruption of civilian lives. Beyond the civilian lives lost the series illustrates, sometimes directly and sometimes indirectly, the widespread pain and suffering experienced by noncombatants. In some storylines the direct consequences to noncombatants takes center stage, compelling the main characters to try and remedy the situation. While food shortages on Rodia play a central role in "Bombad Jedi" and leads to a dangerous confrontation between Senator Amidala and Nute Gunray, a Trade Federation blockade of Pantora prompts Ahsoka Tano to help Senator Riyo Chuchi free her homeworld.[60] From financial institutions to the Mandalorian black market, the economic impact of the war results in fiscal hardships for citizens of Separatist, Republic, and neutral systems alike. The occupation of several other planets and systems, as well as the widespread devastation that accompanies warfare, precipitates a refugee conference to try and resolve the complications resulting from so many displaced civilians.[61]

In a rhetorical move diverging from the human rights reports, *The Clone Wars* also advances a notion of automated combat systems as helpful, compassionate, and humanitarian. Droids like R2-D2 and the aforementioned mechanical members of D–Squad, participate in combat operations and fulfill numerous functions beyond the battlefield context. Droids frequently navigate, repair, and copilot starfighters, interface with enemy security systems and computer databases during covert operations, and gather data via a sophisticated sensor package. At the same time, droids also work alongside Republic personnel as attendants, interpreters, communication specialists, and analysts. Interestingly enough, there are moments in *The Clone Wars* where droids appear more human than the biological beings with whom they interact. In "Mercy Mission," an episode that features R2-D2, C-3P0, and several clone troopers coordinating relief efforts in the aftermath of an earthquake, the two droids treat the traumatized Aleen people with attentiveness and kindness.[62] While R2-D2 and C-3P0 connect with the native population—each of the droids receives a hug at different points in the episode—the clone troopers maintain an almost robotic distance. Clone troopers, like commanding officer Commander Wolffe, appear irritated by the non-combat mission and treat the Aleen as an annoyance. Rather than listening to their urgent request for a specific kind of assistance, Commander Wolffe approaches the situation with a by the book inflexibility. He states directly, "Here's how it is: my orders are to deliver supplies, reestablish power and communication systems." When the Aleen object to Commander Wolffe's efforts to set up a makeshift medical facility, communal kitchen, and restore computer systems, he dismisses them entirely. The droids, on the other hand, listen to the local civilian population, discover a second, subterranean civilization that also needs assistance, and work to solve the problems of both Aleen cultures. All the while, the clones remain fixated on the obvious earthquake damage and oblivious to the true plight facing the Aleen peoples. The subsequent story in this two episode droid arc, "Nomad Droids," features Artoo and Threepio introducing democracy to the diminutive Patitites and liberating the Balnabs from an oppressive holographic dictator controlled by cruel droids.[63]

Both of these episodes offer insight into the way some droids provide a counterbalance to the negative disruptions enacted by Separatist battle droids. Although R2-D2 functions frequently as a combat droid, working with Anakin Skywalker to engage Separatist troops in the name of the Galactic Republic, he also demonstrates the ability to act benevolently. Displaying a humaneness that eludes his biological compatriots, particularly the clones, Artoo works with Threepio to try and bring an end to others' hardships and misfortunes. The two droids listen, treat the beings they encounter as equals, initiate a dialogic give and take (this is C-3PO's forte), and discover problems and possibilities unnoticed by others. Working with mechanical (e.g., Artoo's D–Squad arc) and biological beings alike, the two droids forge meaningful, emotional relationships across the robot/human divide. Indeed, the intercultural competence exhibited by Artoon and Threepio contrasts sharply with the clone troopers lack of respect for both the droids themselves and the aliens encountered. This representation of the clone troopers and their dismissive behaviors towards others brings the well-trod clash of civilizations narrative to mind, a narrative that positions a particular culture as more civilized and advanced than another. Media depictions of the U.S. and Afghanistan perpetuate this misguided neocolonial belief that Western cultures are inherently superior to those in the Middle East (e.g., Iraq, Afghanistan). The clone troopers, then, display a clear superiority to the Aleen people and wave off the local population's energetic communication style as a melodramatic annoyance. With all this in mind, the episodes present the inverse of what one typically expects: humans (clones) act like unemotional robots and robots act like emotional humans.

At first glance, *The Clone Wars* presents a conflicted dialogue regarding the proliferation of autonomous weapons in wartime. On the one hand, the series calls the public imagination to consider a future where sentient, emotionally aware droids exhibit complex decision-making potential enabling them to draw clear distinctions between civilians and military personnel. Indeed, droids on both sides of the conflict demonstrate affective personhood, revealing emotional motives for any number of actions. This ability to display emotional distinction also proves problematic, however. While some droids act out of concern, selflessness, and friendship, others act with a sense of malice, dismay, and resentment. Droids like R2-D2, C-3PO, and the mechanical members of D–Squad, develop meaningful relationships with biological beings, blurring the distinction between droid and human and making an initial case for recognizing droids as persons. Despite the obvious nod toward affective personhood, *The Clone Wars* raises serious concerns regarding dispassion. Removing the warfare's human element and turning to manufactured units—whether droid or clone—shelters the public from a conflict's most effective deterrent: the loss of a family member, friend, or neighbor. The series calls upon viewers to consider how motivated a nation might be to sue for peace when the civilian population experiences few consequences. More troubling, suggests the series, is the question regarding amoral leadership. What happens when a leader uses automated weapons systems for her or his own benefit and dismisses the public good? As Count Dooku's actions attest, a droid army directed by an unscrupulous commander-in-chief puts civilian populations at significant risk. The dispassion arising from the widespread deployment of robot armies increases a conflict's disruptive potential. Alternatively, the proliferation of robots also offers the potential for a more beneficent disruption in the form of increased humanitarian assistance. From these contradictory positions regarding distinction, dispassion, and disruption, *The Clone Wars* ultimately dismantles the human/robot divide. What I want to suggest here is that *The Clone Wars*, particularly with its portrayal of thinking, feeling droids capable of establishing intimate relationships, isn't so much a commentary about automated weapons systems but the humans behind those systems. From an allegorical perspective, *The Clone Wars* argues that the people who design, construct, and deploy automated weapons systems—including those who give their respective governments the permission to utilize such weapons—*are* the weapons.

I, Robot?

As I suggested earlier in this chapter, Telotte singles out the science fiction genre as a site where humanity encounters its mechanical doppelganger, that "singularly compelling image for our current notions of self, as well as an effective metaphor for that sense of 'otherness' which underlies all our recent discussions about gender, race, and sexual orientation."[64] Expanding Telotte's notion of the robotic metaphor, I also want to suggest the dialogues outlined in this chapter function as a "compelling image" for our current understandings of, and relationships with, automated weapons systems. Telotte's double focus describes the mediated encounter between an audience and a robotic representation—a Predator drone described in a report's "what if" scenario or fictional battle droid marching through the streets of Christophsis—as a communicative moment wherein a person experiences a simultaneous allure and repulsion toward automated weapons systems. A person who reads these reports or watches the television series encounters a compelling, double focused message. An automated weapon system provides protection at a distance, keeping soldiers and military personnel out of harm's way; this same system also rains death and destruction from above, inevitably resulting in civilian suffering. This friction between conflicting incongruous positions resonates with Bakhtin's notion of the utterance "as a contradiction-ridden, tension filled unity of two embattled tendencies in the life of language."[65] For Bakhin, the heteroglossic clash between language systems, ideologies, and voices—the varied utterances articulated by human rights reports and *The Clone Wars*, for instance— marks a demonstrative moment of dialogic discourse, a moment when human rights advocacy, foreign policy, and popular culture intersect. The intersection of these rhetorical texts, then, provides insight into the human relationship with robotic weapons and reveals who we want to be as well as "how we would like our world to look."[66]

The texts examined in this chapter, whether speculative non-fiction or speculative science fiction, situate civilian life as a crucial concern in the cultural dialogue around automated weapons systems. To be clear, all the texts analyzed offer an optimistic view of the way advances in robotic technologies might transform human life in such wide ranging areas as manufacturing, medicine, and transportation. With droids involved with almost every aspect of everyday life, *The Clone Wars* presents an overwhelmingly positive future. Droids not only free biological species from dirty or dangerous jobs, but also possess the emotional intelligence to participate in deeply meaningful friendships. The ability to engage in friendships, however, does not mean autonomous weapons systems present little risk to the civilian populations of the Galactic Republic or the Confederacy of Independent Systems. Indeed, the same emotional intelligence that enables R2-D2 to experience joy and friendship and helps a Separatist droid distinguish between combatants and non-combatants also grants an automaton the capacity to experience fear, militancy, and animosity. Much like a human soldier fighting in Iraq, Afghanistan, or Syria, a droid draws on emotional intelligence to make crucial battlefield decisions. There are times, however, when these affective tendencies induce a soldier, or a droid, to act with malice. The authors of the various human rights reports offer a far more pessimistic assessment for the future of battlefield droids. The problems associated with conducting war at a distance, both physically and emotionally, raises serious questions about whether automated weapons technology will ever be capable of imbuing a robot with anything close to resembling human emotion. Considering how frequently human soldiers find themselves confronted with rapidly developing battlefield conditions, robotic weapons systems—denied the emotional capacity that enables a human soldier to respond to a call of conscience—will make mistakes and civilians will pay the price.

Despite the disagreement over whether artificial intelligence will ever transcend the human/robot divide, human rights advocates and the authors of *The Clone Wars* agree that robotic warfare leads to apathy on the part of the general public and leaders. The ability to mitigate a war's impact on a population by taking flesh and blood soldiers out of the line of fire, compels support for autonomous weapons programs. Keeping daughters and sons, mothers and fathers, friends and neighbors off the battlefield removes military fatalities and injuries from the war calculus and provides less motivation for the general populace to object to armed conflict. With lowered stakes in terms of human resources, will leaders be more likely to utilize robots to resolve international disagreements? *The Clone Wars* answers this important human rights question with a resounding "yes." As numerous episodes illustrate, a war conducted through manufactured troops lessens the impact on civilian populations appreciably. When a nation's people go about their day-to-day business unencumbered by thoughts of war, and the leaders maintain the freedom to stroll gardens and sip drinks as they engage in peace talks, the motivation to end a conflict diminishes. The conflict continues and civilian populations suffer. The same holds true when a ruthless leader like Count Dooku puts his own political interests before those of the people and sends droids to attack civilian populations.

Another point of agreement in the dialogue concerning autonomous weapons systems deals with the question of apathy. While Predator drones and battle droids might reduce the cost of war for some, others always pay the price. This price to noncombatant, civilian populations drives the advocacy efforts of the human rights groups as well as robotic representations in *The Clone Wars*. No matter the text or audience, a central question comes to the fore: to what degree will civilian life be impacted by the proliferation of robotic weapons? U.S. combat fatalities benefitted, and continue to benefit, significantly from the Obama administration's turn toward semiautonomous warfare. Even though the cost to civilians is far less than the wholesale destruction incurred as a result of traditional warfare, drone warfare still disrupts the lives of many. The consistent use of both personality and signature strikes in Afghanistan, Pakistan, and Yemen results in innocent deaths and widespread psychological distress. Despite planning and precautions, mistakes do occur and these attacks destroy families, damage homes, and disturb the long-term economic and social stability of communities. Those living in the areas patrolled regularly by drones experience something akin to the double vision anxieties described by Telotte. Conscious of the semi-autonomous presence circling overhead, an inhabitant of the Pakistani tribal region might see a drone as potential freedom from oppressive militants. At the same time, she might also fear the drone's detached and dispassionate means of dispensing death. *The Clone Wars* expands this double focus approach to robotic warfare. The series addresses the various ways the Galactic civil war impacts civilian populations: food shortages, corruption, displaced refugees. Where *The Clone Wars* differs from the human rights advocates, however, is in the representation of droids as a potential source of humanitarian relief. In all fairness, the human rights reports focused specifically on concerns regarding automated weapons; extended speculation on the humanitarian benefits associated with robotics didn't contribute to the purpose of the reports. That said, *The Clone Wars* presents a more nuanced discussion of the role droids might play in wartime. Rather than positioning autonomous weapons systems as dealers of death and destruction, the series also suggests droids might function as a source of life and creation.

On the surface, the two speculative texts in this chapter—one a piece of speculative non-fiction and the other a more traditional work of speculative fiction—give voice to numerous concerns regarding the obvious dangers associated with autonomous weapons systems. As I conclude this chapter, however, I want to suggest that a deeper dialogue regarding the robot/human divide also occurs within and between the texts. Taking a more pragmatic approach, an approach that makes complete sense from an advocacy perspective, the human rights reports maintain a clear contrast between humans and their robotic counterparts. This is particularly apparent in the discussions concerning emotional distinction and the ability to utilize affective agency when faced with uncertain, unpredictable situations as well as morally complicated predicaments. Without fully developed emotional faculties, something the human rights reports attribute solely to humans, autonomous weapons systems will be more likely to make mistakes or participate in atrocities. The humans rights reports speculative logic denies affective personhood to robots and positions humans as the sole arbiters of morally complex quandaries. To a certain degree then, the reports situate autonomous weapons systems as unthinking, Terminator-esque killing machines that, once unleashed, stop at nothing to achieve an objective. Following its programming, an autonomous weapons system acts without compassion, remorse, or hesitation. The responsibility for atrocities rests solely with the human masters.

The Clone Wars, based as it is in a science fiction universe, takes a figurative, allegorical approach and obliterates the human/robot divide. While waves of Separatist battle droids marching lockstep makes an obvious nod to the unthinking automatons of previous science fiction texts, *The Clone Wars* simultaneously challenges this depiction by granting droids a highly advanced emotional intelligence. As I illustrated earlier in the chapter, droids act out joy and sadness, courage and fear, friendship and enmity leading viewers to consider the possibility that droids aren't machines but living, sentient beings. Asp makes similar observations about *Star Wars* droids and observes, "Droids also seem to have beliefs about themselves, others, and the world around them."[67] Blurring the robot/human divide by suggesting robots are human recasts the pain and suffering caused by Separatist droids in a new light. Rather than considering these droids as unthinking weapons employed by an unscrupulous leader, let me suggest Separatist droids represent the human capacity for horrendous atrocity during wartime. Like some soldiers who follow through with orders putting civilians at risk unnecessarily, or those who wage ideologically based war and have no regard for innocents, battle droids exemplifies human beings at their worst. Conversely, droids like R2-D2 and C-3PO represent the human capacity to transcend the horrors of war through acts of compassion and friendship. Two sides of the same coin, *The Clone Wars* grapples with what Telotte describes as the central question arising from representations of robots in film: What does it mean to be human?[68]

SEVEN

The Clone Wars, Dialogue and the Public Square

"In the actual life of speech, every concrete act of understanding is active."[1]—Mikhail Bakhtin

"Luke, you're going to find that many of the truths we cling to depend greatly on our own point of view."[2]—Ben Kenobi, *Return of the Jedi*

As I stated early on in this book, I felt called to write about, to critique and call attention to, the political themes echoing throughout *The Clone Wars* and illustrate the ways political dialogues emerge from all corners of the public square. When I started studying rhetoric some twenty odd years ago, I never imagined I'd turn my attention to an animated television series broadcast on a children's television network. My personal scholarly trajectory, however, illustrates one of the central arguments of this current manuscript: the conception of public dialogue, of rhetorical deliberations about matters of public consequence, includes far more than congressional debates, presidential oratory, newspaper editorials, pamphlets, and human rights reports. Instead, as Lisbet van Zoonen explains, the intersection of politics and entertainment provides a unique public space wherein popular culture artifacts such as television series, films, or pop songs "can function as resources for discussing, criticizing, and imagining politics for the performance of citizenship."[3] These discussions, critiques, and speculative musings, as one might imagine, have been an integral part of my life for the better part of three years. The casual encounter at a dinner party proves fertile ground for discussing the ethics of torture, a conversation typically kicked off by an innocent question: "What are you writing?" Once I reveal my subject of study, *The Clone Wars*, and articulate some of the political themes addressed by the series, the conversation turns to a discussion of the U.S. government's use of torture as a counterterrorism method and the appropriateness thereof. Similar dialogues regarding cloning, Just War Theory, peace, and drone warfare surface during classroom discussions, conference conversations, and even phone calls with my mother and father. I realize these anecdotal accounts don't constitute much in the way of empirical evidence, but I want to suggest such conversations do capture the everydayness of Bakthin's dialogic public square. From mundane encounters with friends and families, to reading and responding to tweets, to listening to podcasts, to liking a Facebook post, to writing a book length manuscript, audiences engage the ideas presented in popular culture and incorporate them into their own lived practices, their next distinctive utterances.

To be clear, Bakhtinian dialogics developed from an effort "to establish a philosophical basis for the understanding of how discourse in life relates to discourse in art."[4] Using an idealized version of the fluid, collaborative, and messy exchanges that constitute common discourse between everyday people, not unlike the fictional dialogue I alluded to in the previous paragraph, Bakhtin contemplated a form of artistic prose grounded in dialogic utterances. Such utterances—always responding to previous discursive utterances, deployed in the present historical moment, and oriented toward future responses—never exists in solitude, but traverses, converges, and collides with a multitude of other utterances. Bakhtin explained, "The word, breaking through to its own meaning and its own expression across an environment full of alien words and variously evaluating accents, harmonizing with some of the elements in this environment and striking a dissonance with others, is able, in this dialogized process, to shape its own stylistic profile and tone."[5] In his articulation of dialogic discourse in art, Bakhtin criticized rhetoric, as well as poetics, for lacking the constitutive quality he celebrated as indicative of lively and meaningful artistic discourse. He denounced rhetoric as a monologic communicative act whereby a rhetor crafts an utterance in isolation, cut off from the surrounding discursive texture of variable meanings, understanding, and value judgments. His denunciation of rhetoric and poetics led him to celebrate the novel as "a distinctive art of prose" that gives dialogue "its fullest and deepest expression."[6]

My own affinity for Bakhtin's conception of dialogics, as well as my understanding of rhetoric as a means by which to engage in meaningful public deliberations over ideas that matter, was part of the inspiration for this project. As I suggested in chapter one, I simply don't recognize the rhetoric Bakhtin describes as a monologic practice. There are, of course, those speeches and texts—e.g., a campaign speech, a protest march, a social justice documentary, even episodes of *The Clone Wars*—that articulate a single viewpoint and exclude all others. Such utterances, I'll concede, may speak with a monologic voice and argue for singular, uncompromising purpose. This is clearly the case with several of the political texts I engaged in this book. Obama's Nobel Peace Prize speech leaves little room for equivocation: although peace is desirable, war is inevitable. Similarly, the various human rights reports regarding drone warfare and the proliferation of future autonomous weapons systems make a clear call for investigating the humaneness of the drone program and a ban on autonomous weapons research. However, even texts that appear monologic operate within broader cultural conversations. Obama's speech, for example, emerged from the tensions between two different conflict resolution traditions: (1) Martin Luther King, Jr.'s legacy of nonviolent resistance and (2) Just War Theory. Obama's exhortation on the *telos* of war received little praise from the Nobel Peace Prize committee, surprised those who considered Obama an antiwar president, and received praise from others who support U.S. international military efforts grounded in Just War Theory. An utterance espousing a finalized position, particularly when examined as a singular speech act, takes on a different meaning when considered part of a broader political text. Whether Obama intended it or not, and given his stature as the president of the United States I'll posit he understood his speech would receive significant scrutiny, his words enter the public square and join the ongoing dialogue concerning war and peace. Despite the monologic utterance, the speech functions dialogically.

Our disagreement regarding rhetoric aside, I do agree with Bakhtin that there are some artistic enterprises that afford more opportunities to capture the boisterous, animated dialogue indicative of human life. So while Bakhtin turns to the multi-voiced discourse of the novel as an exemplar of social dialogue, a choice that makes sense given the historical moment at which he was writing, my work advances television, film, and other popular culture texts (e.g., comic books) as additional sites of Bakhtinian dialogics. As my analysis of *The Clone Wars* illustrates, science fiction's speculative outlook offers an excellent opportunity to examine how popular culture texts contribute to a wide variety of political, social, and ethical conversations. Displaying a high degree of intertextuality, a concept echoing with the sounds of Bakhtinian dialogics, *The Clone Wars* invites audiences to participate in collaborative interpretation and meaning-making . When a *Star Wars* fan encounters a Clone Wars era Anakin Skywalker, the series calls her to access what she knows about his past through previous *Star*

Wars texts like *Episode I: The Phantom Menace* and *Episode II: Attack of the Clones* (e.g., his position as The Chosen One, his destructive temper, his secret marriage to Padmé Amidala) as well as his future as represented in *Episode III: Revenge of the Sith* and the original *Star Wars* trilogy (e.g., his turn to the dark side, his transformation into Darth Vader, his ultimate redemption). Making connections with these external texts, a connection implicated by the authors of *The Clone Wars* but enacted by the viewers, brings Anakin to life in a way not possible through internal dialogics alone. Likewise, musical references to well-known theatrical themes as the Imperial March, visual nods to unique *Star Wars* designs, and even appearances by previously encountered *Star Wars* characters (e.g., Boba Fett, Chewbacca, Captain Wilhuff Tarkin) immerse audience members in a complex meaning-making experience. While *The Clone Wars* makes narrative sense without such intertextual references, a richer, more vivid text comes alive when the series, and the viewer, dialogue with other texts.

Of greater interest for my present work are the political dialogues at work in the series. To some degree, my work with the political rhetoric permeating the series responds to Carl Silvio and Tony M. Vinci's call to

> move away from myth-based criticism of *Star Wars* and adopt a cultural studies model that analyzes it as a culturally and historically specific phenomenon, that is, as a site of ideological investment that both reflects and shapes late twentieth and early twenty-first century global culture.[7]

Rather than grounding my work in cultural studies explicitly—a theoretical approach concerned with the institutionalized constitution and perpetuation of hierarchies associated with a wide range of social categories (e.g., class, race, sexuality)—I add my voice to *Star Wars* criticism by embracing rhetorical studies and elucidating how the television series calls viewers to engage ongoing political deliberations concerning a nation mired in prolonged war. While many of my colleagues in rhetorical studies produce excellent work under the banner of cultural studies, this book is more inspired by public policy and international relations. In responding to Silvio and Vinci's invitation, drawing on already existing *Star Wars* scholarship, and incorporating the work of public critics, my book dialogues with other popular culture scholars.

The focal point of my ongoing exchange with other scholars are the various political dialogues embedded throughout *The Clone Wars*. Revealing the congruent and incongruent positions expressed by newspaper editorialists and how those positions intersect with representations of Jedi Knights, for example, illustrates the way the complex moral debate over torture reaches beyond congressional hearings and cabinet meetings. Both the editorialists and the writers/creators for *The Clone Wars* answered an appeal arising from a broader cultural context. The revelation that the United States government sanctioned torture created a need for public discussion; the various perspectives put forth by editorialists and *The Clone Wars* responded to this exigence. As such, a dialogic encounter with either of these texts, or both, prompts an individual to consider the ethical implications of torture as a government sanctioned activity. The reader not only encounters the arguments in the written word, but also watches as an individual he characterizes as a hero–Obi-Wan Kenobi, for example—attempts to protect the public by acting inhumanely. The represented act and its clear parallel to actions undertaken in the name of the U.S. government urges the viewer to render judgment. The scene elicits a response.

I identified a similar call/response when discussing peace activism in chapter five. Exploring the historical arguments of Representative Jeannette Rankin re-articulated by fictional characters like Senator Padmé Amidala and Duchess Satine Kryze draws attention to voices for peace often muted during periods of war. While none of these contentions will likely result in replacing the war habit with a peace habit, the dialogic encounter raises a number of important questions for consideration. To what degree do national leaders explore peaceful solutions before turning to armed conflict? If Rankin and Kryze are correct and any peace movement requires the concerted will of the people, to what degree are the people responsible for living in a prolonged state of war? To what degree is my vote responsible for armed conflict? Like the conversations related to torture and peace, the dialogue between human rights reports and the portrayal of droids simultaneously responds to a perceived problem (present and future civilian casualties) and calls upon a viewer to engage questions concerning autonomous weapons technology and affective personhood. Although both texts issue a caution regarding robotic weapons, the human rights reports draw a clear distinction between human and machine and urge support for a ban on all weapons. *The Clone Wars*, on the other hand, takes a more philosophical approach and wrestles with what it means to be human. The series conflates the difference between human and autonomous weapons system: humans are the weapons systems they create. To be human is to be responsible for the proliferation of autonomous weapons systems and the resulting pain and suffering. When a reader or viewer encounters these utterances she might ask herself any number of the following questions. What constitutes an acceptable number of civilian casualties in counterterrorism efforts? As a citizen of the United States, does protecting my safety and security outweigh the safety and security of others? To what degree am I responsible for the weapons systems deployed by my government?

Bakhtin characterizes the acts of questioning, considering, and responding to texts as unavoidable elements of vibrant social dialogue. The way I respond to the peace advocacy of Jeannette Rankin, Padmé Amidala, and Satine Kryze seeps into future dialogues and influences whether or not I vote for a political candidate, send a critical email to a legislator, or even contribute financially to a specific cause. The actual response on the part of the active viewers, whether one accepts, rejects, or continues to wrestle with formulating a specific position, is crucial to Bakhtin's conception of responsive understanding. The dialogic constitution of everything from cultural values, to individual and communal identity, to public policy, occurs in the responsive interactions between utterances. Ken Hirschkop describes Bakhtin's commitment to the centrality of the communicative response as follows:

> In order to understand, one must therefore act: this general obligation, constitutive of language as such, then parallels the "oughtness" Bakhtin sought to restore to modern culture. For just as ethical responsibility entails acknowledging one's position and the need to act which flows from it, so communication understood in subjective terms, involves not abstractly entertaining the ideas of others but reacting to them by agreement or disagreement, doubt or conviction, with reciprocating passion or revulsion.[8]

The intentional articulation of a political contention—*The Clone Wars'* criticism of U.S. just war policy—requires an active, evaluative response. The spirited call and response brings Bakhtinian dialogics into alignment with contemporary rhetoric. Rhetoric, as intentional communication that contributes to the creation, negotiation, or transformation of individuals and communities, hinges on the collaborative response of the other. When a human rights activist or a writer for *The Clone Wars* crafts a message for public consumption, she anticipates an interaction with a reader or viewer; she composes a text knowing it will be read and evaluated.

Bakhtin's emphasis on responsive understanding captures the rhetorical relationship constituted between cultural dialogues, texts, and audiences and grounds human communication in an ethic of responsibility. An ethic of responsibility, or "oughtness" as Hirshchop suggests, demands more than indifferent engagement; it calls for genuine consideration of the Other and entreats interlocutors to recognize the obligation to meaningful, collaborative communication. The dialogic encounter posits a captivating, dynamic exchange wherein speaker and listener, author and reader, animator and viewer, listen thoughtfully, perceive actively, and respond critically. Baktin writes,

In the actual life of speech, every concrete act of understanding is active: it assimilates the word to be understood into its own conceptual system filled with specific objects and emotional expressions, and is indissolubly merged with the response, with a motivated agreement or disagreement.[9]

Meaning emerges in that energetic moment of communicative interaction where past utterance encounters the present response all while recognizing the potential for future responses. As he makes clear in the quoted passage, an ethic of responsibility does not hinge on an amicable exchange where people come together in courteous conformity. Harmonious consensus between author and reader may characterize a particular exchange but discordant disagreement is just as likely. *The Clone Wars'* disturbing representations of torture might repulse a viewer, causing him to shout "No!" as he watches a graphic scene play out. In the same way, a reader might feel the tug of her conscience as she agrees with Krauthammer's depiction of torture as a necessary evil and reiterates his arguments at a social gathering. Such utterances embody the inspired response associated with an ethic of responsibility. In a Bakhtinian sense, this responsibility to responsive understanding "ought" to be present in every instance of social dialogue. This is, of course, not the case. To participate with another responsibly—in opposition or accord—acknowledges that person, responds to his articulated understandings, and contributes to the rhetorical constitution of self, other, and community.

Bakhtin's public square provides the essential discursive space for the responsible encounter between such diverse speakers and responders as a current president, a fictional Jedi Knight, and an average citizen. Like the idealized medieval public square Bakhtin holds up as a model, the contemporary public resounds with a never-ending cacophony of colloquial and formal rhetorics interacting in perpetual dialogue. Ribald yet refined, mundane yet extraordinary, the discursive public square manifests as a deliberative space where communication from all social classes, cultures, geographical locations, and ideological positions intersect, collide, and intermingle. The proliferation of mass media, new media technologies, and mobile technologies facilitate interactions where the utterances of the president, a CEO, the supervising director of *The Clone Wars*, a talk show host, or newspaper columnist encounter the responses of a television viewer, radio listener, blogger, tweeter, podcaster, or YouTuber. In other words, these ubiquitous media, as well as more traditional forms of dialogic exchange like letter writing and conversation, provide access to limitless public dialogues for anyone who wishes to participate. Participants in the anything goes public square address such wide ranging topics as aesthetics, communal values, social problematics, cultural norms, national identity, international relations, and public policy. I want to reiterate, however, that access does not translate to equality. As I stated back in chapter one, Bakhtin made no claim to parity in the public square; the public square is celebrated for its pervasive and vigorous dialogue, not egalitarianism and levelheadedness. The citizen who engages another by way of newspaper editorial, tweet, street art, animated science fiction series, or conversation over a cup of coffee adds another voice to the noisy, uneven spectacle that is the contemporary public square.

To be certain, not every popular culture text contains the multiple, conflicting voices associated with a robust or even responsible political dialogue. Some texts, however, dare audiences to analyze and make sense of the way political conversations from the past intersect with the present and look toward the future. In an era when political apathy permeates the public square, the politically-relevant content of speculative science fiction provides an opportunity for "the people" to take up the dare and participate responsibly. Indicative of dynamic responsive understanding, science fiction reaches out to viewers and "establishes a series of complex interrelationships, consonances and dissonances" and creates a dialogic space where "various points of view, conceptual horizons, systems for providing expressive accents, various social 'languages' come to interact with one another."[10] The fantastic, futuristic settings of science fiction like *The Clone Wars* allow authors to contemplate alternate ways of addressing socio-problematics and reinforcing or challenging political policy. When *The Clone Wars* contemplates the agency of manufactured soldiers, the allegorical resemblance between interchangeable clone troopers and the uniformity displayed by real life military personnel exhorts viewers to consider the casualness and indifference with which a nation state deploys largely anonymous troops. Bakhtin's ethic of dialogic responsibility, the "oughtness" of human communication, enjoins a viewer to participate in the ongoing act of responsive understanding, to contemplate the plight of the clones and use that fictional depiction to make sense of her or his social world. The utterance of the other, in this case the writers and animators of *The Clone Wars*, demands responsive action. To not act, to not scrutinize the value judgments and positions articulated by the other, to dismiss *The Clone Wars* as "just entertainment," denies one's responsibility to the rhetorical accomplishing necessary for the life of the community. A person's refusal to enter into the animated social dialogue of the public square is a disavowal of her or his place in the tension-filled performance of historical becoming.

Historical becoming holds particular relevance for *The Clone Wars*, a text I read as a meditation on politics, communal responsibility, and public policy during a protracted war. As I've illustrated repeatedly, the discourse of *The Clone Wars* addresses already existing tensions within the public square and hails viewers to respond responsibly, to take up their role as active rhetorical agents. Bakhtin identifies discourse in art, particularly discourse in the novel, as an authentic internal dialogue resonating with multiple voices, aesthetic values, and historical viewpoints. Indeed, Bakhtin situates the interaction between author, text, and reader as constitutive of a historical moment.

> And finally, at any given moment, languages of various epochs and periods of socio-ideological life cohabit with one another. Even languages of the day exist: one could say that today's and yesterday's socio-ideological and political "day" do not, in a certain sense, share the same language; every day represents another socio-ideological semantic "state of affairs," another vocabulary, another accentual system, with its own slogans, its own ways of assigning blame and praise.[11]

In other words, to truly engage *The Clone Wars* with all its intertextual references to previous science fiction texts, to the broader *Star Wars* megatext, and contemporary political dialogues is to respond responsibly and participate in the rhetorical constitution of the historical present. The active rhetorical accomplishing inherent in historical becoming recognizes the dialogic potential for simultaneously reinforcing, rethinking, and reconfiguring the political viewpoints, cultural traditions, shared definitions, communal values, and commonly accepted social truths of a particular culture and time. Thus, *The Clone Wars* isn't simply an interrogation of life during wartime but a consideration of twenty-first-century life during an extended conflict with multiple enemies and ambiguous or non-existent fronts. Taken as a dynamic text in the rhetorical negotiation of historical becoming, *The Clone Wars* prompts an audience member to accept her or his responsibility as not only a practitioner of dialogue and an author of her or his own life, but also as an architect for the future of the community.

Chapter Notes

Introduction

1. Mikhail M. Bakhtin, *Speech Genres & Other Late Essays*, ed. Caryl Emerson and Michael Holquist, trans. Vern W. McGee (Austin: University of Texas Press, 1986), 93.

2. Bryan Young, "Why Aren't You Watching *The Clone Wars?*" The Huffington Post, March 30, 2011, http://www.huffingtonpost.com/bryan-young/why-arent-you-watching-th_b_841727.html.

3. Frederik Pohl, "The Politics of Prophecy," in *Political Science Fiction*, ed. Donald M. Hassler and Clyde Wilcox (Columbia: University of Carolina Press, 1997), 7.

4. Andrew Gordon, "Star Wars: A Myth for Our Time," *Literature Film Quarterly* 6, no. 4 (Fall 1978): 314–326.

5. Brian Ott and Eric Aoki, "Counter-Imagination as Interpretive Practice: Futuristic Fantasy and *The Fifth Element*," *Women's Studies in Communication* 27 (2004): 149–176; Brian Ott and Eric Aoki, "Popular Imagination and Identity Politics: Reading the Future in *Star Trek: The Next Generation*," *Western Journal of Communication* 65 (2001): 392–415.

6. *Star Wars: Episode V—The Empire Strikes Back*, dir. Irvin Kershner, 20th Century Fox, 1980.

7. Carl Silvio and Tony M. Vinci, *Culture, Identities and Technology in the Star Wars Films: Essays on the Two Trilogies* (Jefferson, NC: McFarland, 2007), 4.

8. Peter Kramer, "*Star Wars*," *History Today* 49, no. 3 (1999): 43.

9. David S. Meyer, "*Star Wars*, Star Wars, and American Political Culture," *The Jour-nal of Popular Culture* 26, no. 2 (September 1, 1992): 99–115.

10. Dan Rubey, "*Star Wars*: Not So Long Ago, Not So Far Away," *Jump Cut: A Review of Contemporary Media* 18 (August 1978): 10.

11. *Ibid.*, 9–14.

12. Michael Ryan and Douglass Kellner, *Camera Politica: The Politics and Ideology of Contemporary Hollywood Film* (Bloomington: Indiana University Press, 1988), 229–230.

13. *Ibid.*, 234.

14. Stephen P. McVeigh, "The Galactic Way of Warfare," in *Finding the Force of the Star Wars Franchise: Fans, Merchandise, & Critics*, ed. Matthew W. Kapell et al. (New York: Peter Lang, 2006), 35.

15. *Ibid.*, 45.

16. *Ibid.*, 46.

17. The question of whether or not clones are humans is considered, at length, in Chapter Three.

18. Anne Lancashire, "*Return of the Jedi*: Once More with Feeling," *Film Criticism* 8, no. 2 (1984): 61.

19. Anne Lancashire, "The Phantom Menace: Repetition, Variation, Integration," *Film Criticism* 24 (2000): 36.

20. Anne Lancashire, "*Attack of the Clones* and the Politics of *Star Wars*," *Dalhousie Review* 82, no. 2 (2002): 242.

21. *Ibid.*, 239.

22. "Weekend Journal," *Wall Street Journal*, May 20, 2005, W11.

23. Dana Milbank, "The Chamber Meets the Force," *Washington Post*, May 20, 2005, A5.

24. Scott Thill, "Rebooted Darth Maul Closes Down *The Clone Wars*," Wired: Underwire Blog, March 15, 2012, http://

www.wired.com/underwire/2012/03/clone-wars-darth-maul/.

25. Gerard A. Hauser and Chantal Benoit-Barne, "Reflections on Rhetoric, Deliberative Democracy, Civil Society, and Trust," *Rhetoric & Public Affairs* 5, no. 2 (Summer 2002): 264.

26. Scott Thill, "Rebooted Darth Maul Closes Down *The Clone Wars*," Wired: Underwire Blog, March 15, 2012, http://www.wired.com/underwire/2012/03/clone-wars-darth-maul/.

27. Bakhtin, *Speech Genres*, 93.

28. James Jasinski, "Heteroglossia, Polyphony, and the Federalist Papers," *Rhetoric Society Quarterly* 27, no. 1 (Winter 1997): 25.

29. John B. Hatch, "Dialogic Rhetoric in Letters Across the Divide: A Dance of (Good) Faith Toward Racial Reconciliation," *Rhetoric & Public Affairs* 12 (2009): 493.

30. Mikhail M. Bakhtin, *The Dialogic Imagination: Four Essays by M. M. Bakhtin*, ed. Michael Holquist, trans. Caryl Emerson and Michael Holquist (Austin: University of Texas Press, 1981), 254.

31. Brian L. Ott, "Set Your Cathode Rays to Stun(ning)," *Flow* 1, no. 1 (February 2005). Accessed August 14, 2012, http://flowtv.org/2005/02/set-your-cathode-rays-to-stunning/.

32. Derek R. Sweet, "More Than Goth: The Rhetorical Reclamation of the Subcultural Self," *Popular Communication* 3, no. 4 (2005): 241.

33. Michael Isikoff, "Bin Laden's Death Rekindles 'Enhanced' Interrogation Debate," NBCNews.com, May 2, 2011. Accessed October 28, 2011, http://www.msnbc.msn.com/id/42863247/ns/world_news-death_of_bin_laden/#.UD57idZlTYg.

34. Barack Obama, "Nobel Peace Prize Lecture," speech presented to the Norwegian Nobel Committee, Oslo, Norway, December 10, 2009, par. 19. Accessed November 1, 2011, http://www.nobelprize.org/ nobel_prizes/peace/laureates/2009/obama-lecture_en.html.

35. Howard Fineman, "Reaction to Obama's Nobel Speech," interview with Robert Siegel, National Public Radio: All Things Considered, December 10, 2009. http://www.npr.org/templates/story/story.php?storyId =121304855.

36. Obama, "Peace Prize Lecture," par. 24.

37. Jeannette Rankin, "Peace and the Disarmament Conference," Rankin Papers, Radcliffe College, quoted in Joan Hoff Wilson, "'Peace is a Woman's Job ...' Jeannette Rankin and the Origins American Foreign Policy: The Origins of Her Pacifism," *Montana: The Magazine of Western History* 30, no. 1 (Winter 1980): 35.

38. Norma Hoff, *Jeannette Rankin: America's Conscience* (Helena: Montana Historical Society Press, 2002), 114.

39. Noah Shachtman, "CIA Chief: Drones 'Only Game in Town' for Stopping Al Qaeda," Wired.com, May 19, 2009. http://www.wired.com/dangerroom/2009/05/cia-chief-drones-only-game-in-town-for- stopping-al-qaeda/.

40. *Return of the Jedi*, dir. Richard Marquand, 20th Century Fox, 1983.

41. Ken Hirschkop, *Mikhail Bakhtin: An Aesthetic for Democracy* (Oxford: Oxford University Press, 1999), 4.

Chapter One

1. Mikhail M. Bakhtin, *The Dialogic Imagination: Four Essays by M. M. Bakhtin*, ed. Michael Holquist, trans. Caryl Emerson and Michael Holquist (Austin: University of Texas Press, 1981), 279.

2. *Star Wars: Episode IV—A New Hope*, dir. George Lucas, 20th Century Fox, 1977.

3. Darko Suvin, "On the Poetics of the Science Fiction Genre," *College English* 34, no. 3 (December 1972): 377.

4. *Ibid.*, 379.

5. Patricia Kerslake, *Science Fiction and Empire* (Liverpool: Liverpool University Press, 2007), 1.

6. Jutta Weldes, *To Seek Out New Worlds: Exploring Links Between Science Fiction and World Politics* (New York: Palgrave Macmillan, 2003), 8.

7. Donald M. Hassler and Clyde Wilcox, eds., *Political Science Fiction* (Columbia: University of South Carolina Press, 1997), 6.

8. Calvin O. Schrag, *Resources of Rationality: A Response to the Postmodern Challenge* (Bloomington: Indiana University Press, 1992), 136.

9. *Ibid.*, 84.

10. Kenneth Burke, *The Philosophy of Literary Form: Studies in Symbolic Action*, 3d ed. (Berkeley: University of California Press, 1973), 293.

11. *Ibid.*, 296.
12. *Ibid.*, 298.
13. *Ibid.*, 304.
14. Barry Brummett, "Burke's Representative Anecdote as a Method in Media Criticism," *Critical Studies in Mass Communication* 1 (1984): 161.
15. Barry Brummett, "Electric Literature as Equipment for Living: Haunted House Films," *Critical Studies in Mass Communication* 2 (1985): 248.
16. *Ibid.*, 247.
17. *Ibid.*, 251.
18. Brummett, "Representative Anecdote," 174.
19. Brian L. Ott and Bett Bonnstetter, "'We're at Now, Now': *Spaceballs* as Parodic Tourism," *Southern Communication Journal* 72, no. 4 (October–December 2007): 312.
20. *Ibid.*, 322.
21. *Ibid.*, 313.
22. Michelle J. Kinnucan, "Pedagogy of (the) Force: The Myth of Redemptive Violence," in *Finding the Force of the Star Wars Franchise: Fans, Merchandise, & Critics*, ed. Matthew W. Kapell et al. (New York: Peter Lang, 2006), 59.
23. *Ibid.*, 65.
24. Joshua Atkinson and Bernadette Calafell, "Darth Vader Made Me Do It! Anakin Skywalker's Avoidance of Responsibility and the Gray Areas of Hegemonic Masculinity in the *Star Wars* Universe," *Communication, Culture & Critique* 2 (2009): 16.
25. Brian L. Ott and Carl R. Burgchardt, "On Critical-Rhetorical Pedagogy: Dialoging with Schindler's List," *Western Journal of Communication* 77, no. 1 (January–February 2013): 17.
26. *Ibid.*, 15.
27. Gary S. Morson and Caryl Emerson, *Mikhail Bakhtin: Creation of a Prosaics* (Stanford: Stanford University Press, 1990), 125.
28. Mikhail M. Bakhtin, *The Dialogic Imagination: Four Essays by M. M. Bakhtin*, ed. Michael Holquist, trans. Caryl Emerson and Michael Holquist (Austin: University of Texas Press, 1981), 284.
29. *Ibid.*, 281.
30. *Ibid.*, 291.
31. Mikhail M. Bakhtin, *Speech Genres & Other Late Essays*, ed. Caryl Emerson and Michael Holquist, trans. Vern W. McGee (Austin: University of Texas Press, 1986), 68.
32. *Ibid.*, 68.
33. *Ibid.*, 68–69.
34. *Ibid.*, 68.
35. Kay Halasek, "Starting the Dialogue: What Can We Do About Bakhtin's Ambivalence Toward Rhetorc?" *Rhetoric Society Quarterly* 22, no. 4 (Autumn 1992): 5.
36. Ken Hirschkop, *Mikhail Bakhtin: An Aesthetic for Democracy* (Oxford: Oxford University Press, 1999), 245.
37. Martin Flanagan, *Bakhtin and the Movies: New Ways of Understanding Hollywood Film* (New York: Palgrave Macmillan, 2009), 10.
38. Bakhtin, *The Dialogic Imagination*, 256.
39. *Ibid.*
40. *Ibid.*, 254.
41. Peter Lev, "Whose Future? 'Star Wars,' 'Alien,' and 'Blade Runner,'" *Literature Film Quarterly* 26, no. 1: 31.
42. Douglas Brode and Leah Deynaka, *Myth, Media, and Culture in Star Wars: An Anthology* (Lanham, MD: Scarecrow Press, 2012). In the introduction, Brode situates the *Star Wars* franchise within the space opera sub-genre of science fiction. In Chapter One, Brode positions the same franchise as an epic Western. One chapter later (Chapter Two), Arthur Berger describes the original *Star Wars* film as a fairy tale.
43. Flanagan, *Bakhtin and the Movies*, 8.
44. Julia Kristeva, "Word, Dialogue, and Novel," in *The Kristeva Reader*, ed. Toril Moi (New York: Columbia University Press, 1986), 37.
45. Anne Lancashire, "The Phantom Menace: Repetition, Variation, Integration," *Film Criticism* 24 (2000): 24.
46. *Ibid.*, 25.
47. Will Brooker, *Hunting the Dark Knight: Twenty-First Century Batman* (New York: Palgrave Macmillan, 2012), 47.
48. Jeffrey Bussolini, "Television Intertextuality After Buffy: Intertextuality of Casting and Constitutive Intertextuality," *Slayage: The Journal of the Whedon Studies Association* 10, no. 1 (Winter 2013). Accessed October 13, 2013. /http://slayageonline.com/Numbers/slayage35.htm.
49. Ken Hirschkop, "Is Dialogism for Real?" *Social Text* 30 (1992): 108.
50. Hirschkop, *Mikhail Bakhtin*, 245.
51. Mikhail M. Bakhtin, *Problems of Dostoevsky's Poetics*, trans. Caryl Emerson (Min-

neapolis: University of Minnesota Press, 1984), 110.

52. Bakhtin, *Speech Genres*, 150.

53. Bakhtin, *The Dialogic Imagination*, 325.

54. John M. Murphy, "Mikhail Bakhtin and the Rhetorical Tradition," *Quarterly Journal of Speech* 87, no. 3 (August 2001): 274.

55. *Ibid.*, 272.

56. Kay Halasek, "Starting the Dialogue: What Can We Do About Bakhtin's Ambivalence Toward Rhetoric?" *Rhetoric Society Quarterly* 22, no. 4 (Autumn 1992): 2.

57. Bakhtin, *The Dialogic Imagination*, 279.

58. James P. Zappen, *The Rebirth of Dialogue: Bakhtin, Socrates, and the Rhetorical Tradition* (Albany: State University of New York Press, 2004), 40–41.

59. Thomas B. Farrell, *Norms of Rhetorical Culture* (New Haven: Yale University Press, 1993), 238.

60. Calvin O. Schrag, "Rhetoric Situated at the End of Philosophy," *Quarterly Journal of Speech* 71, no. 2 (1985): 169.

61. James Jasinski, "Heteroglossia, Polyphony, and The Federalist Papers," *Rhetoric Society Quarterly* 27, no. 1 (Winter 1997): 25.

62. Calvin O. Schrag, *Doing Philosophy with Others: Conversations, Reminiscences, and Reflections* (West Lafayette: Purdue University Press, 2010), 56.

63. *Ibid.*, 57.

64. *Ibid.*

65. Calvin O. Schrag, *Philosophical Papers: Betwixt and Between* (Albany: State University of New York Press, 1994), 231.

66. *Ibid.*, 107.

67. Chris Pak, "The Dialogic Science Fiction Megatext: Vivisection in H. G. Wells's *The Island of Dr Moreau* and Genetic Engineering in Gene Wolfe's *The Woman Who Loved the Centaur Pholus*," *Green Letters: Studies in Ecocriticism* 12, no. 1 (October 2012): 27.

68. Flanagan, *Bakhtin and the Movies*, 8–9.

69. Bakhtin, *Speech Genres*, 69.

Chapter Two

1. George W. Bush, "President George W. Bush's Address on Stem Cell Research," CNN, August 9, 2001. Accessed May 28, 2015, http://edition.cnn.com/2001/ALL POLITICS/08/09/bush.transcript/.

2. "Carnage of Krell," *Star Wars: The Clone Wars*, dir. Kyle Dunlevy, writ. Matt Michnovetz, Cartoon Network, 18 November 2011.

3. Jason T. Eberl, "I, Clone: How Cloning Is (Mis)Portrayed in Contemporary Cinema," *Film & History* 40, no. 2 (2010): 28.

4. Gabriele Griffin, "Science and the Cultural Imaginary: The Case of Kazuo Ishiguro's *Never Let Me Go*," *Textual Practice* 23, no. 4 (2009): 657.

5. Sheryl N. Hamilton, "Science Fiction and the Media," *Science Fiction Studies* 30, no. 2 (July 2003): 267–282.

6. Patrick D. Hopkins, "Bad Copies: How Popular Media Represent Cloning as an Ethical Problem," *The Hastings Center Report* 28, no. 2 (March-April 1998): 6–13.

7. Gina Kolata, "Scientist Reports First Cloning Ever of Adult Mammal," *New York Times*, February 23, 1997, 1.

8. Hopkins, "Bad Copies," 6–13.

9. Gail H. Javitt, Kristen Suthers, and Kathy Hudson, *Cloning: A Policy Analysis* (Washington, D.C.: Genetics and Public Policy Center, 2005).

10. William J. Clinton, "Remarks Announcing the Prohibition on Federal Funding for Cloning of Human Beings," *The American Presidency Project*, March 4, 1997. Accessed October 8, 2012, http://www.presidency.ucsb.edu/ws/index.php?pid=53815.

11. National Bioethics Advisory Commission, *Cloning Human Beings* (Washington, D.C.: Government Printing Office, 1997), iv.

12. Gretchen Vogel, "Cloning: Could Humans Be Next?" *Science* 291, no. 5505 (February 2, 2001): 808. Academic Search Complete, EBSCOhost (accessed November 1, 2012).

13. George W. Bush, "Address on Stem Cell Research."

14. 144 Cong. Rec. S508 (daily ed. February 9, 1998) (statement of Sen. Harkin).

15. In an early House hearing Representative Upton remarked that the possibility of human cloning forces society to grapple with the idea of "what it means to be human." *Cloning: Legal, Medical, Ethical, and Social Issues. Hearing Before the Subcom-*

mittee on Health and Environment of the
Committee of Commerce, 105th Cong., 10
(February 12, 1998) (statement of Rep.
Upton). Three years later, Senator Brownback echoed the sentiment and suggested
that human cloning calls on congress and
the broader society to "debate first principles—most particularly, the meaning of
human life." *Human Cloning: Hearing Before
the Subcommittee on Science, Technology, and
Space of the Committee on Commerce, Science,
and Transportation*, 107th Cong., 1 (May 2,
2001) (statement of Sen. Brownback).

16. 144 Cong. Rec. S434 (daily ed. February 5, 1998) (statement of Sen. Kennedy).

17. National Bioethics Advisory Commission, *Cloning Human Beings*, 66.

18. 147 Cong. Rec. H4929 (daily ed. July
31, 2001) (statement of Rep. DeMint).

19. 144 Cong. Rec. S319 (daily ed. February 3, 1998) (statement of Sen. Bond).

20. *The Human Cloning Prohibition Act
of 2001 and the Cloning Prohibition Act of
2001: Hearing Before the Subcommittee on
Health of the Committee on Energy and Commerce*, 107th Cong., 9 (June 20, 2001).

21. *Cloning: Legal, Medical, Ethical, and
Social Issues. Hearing Before the Subcommittee
on Health and Environment of the Committee
of Commerce*, 105th Cong., 40 (February 12,
1998) (statement of Nigel M. de S.
Cameron).

22. *Issues Raised by Human Cloning
Research: Hearing Before the Subcommitte on
Oversight and Investigations of the Committee
on Energy and Commerce*, 107th Cong., 96
(March 28, 2001) (statement of Arthur
Caplan).

23. Joyce C. Havstad, "Human Reproductive Cloning: A Conflict of Liberties,"
Bioethics 24, no. 2 (2010): 77.

24. *Human Cloning: Hearing Before the
Subcommittee on Crime of the Committee on
the Judiciary*, 107th Cong., 10 (June 7, 2001)
(statement of Dr. Leon Kass).

25. 143 Cong. Rec. S1735 (daily ed. February 27, 1997) (statement of Sen. Bond).

26. *Ibid.*

27. *Issues Raised by Human Cloning
Research: Hearing Before the Subcommittee on
Oversight and Investigations of the Committee
on Energy and Commerce*, 107th Cong., 3
(March 28, 2001) (statement of Rep. Green-
wood).

28. National Bioethics Advisory Commission, *Cloning Human Beings*, 72.

29. 147 Cong. Rec. H4927 (daily ed. July
31, 2001) (statement of Rep. Tiahrt).

30. 147 Cong. Rec. S7851 (daily ed. July
18, 2001) (statement of Sen. Frist).

31. *Issues Raised by Human Cloning
Research: Hearing Before the Subcommittee on
Oversight and Investigations of the Committee
on Energy and Commerce*, 107th Cong., 9
(March 28, 2001) (statement of Rep.
Stearns).

32. *The Human Cloning Prohibition Act
of 2001 and the Cloning Prohibition Act of
2001: Hearing Before the Subcommittee on
Health of the Committee on Energy and Commerce*, 107th Cong., 68 (June 20, 2001)
(statement of Stuart A. Newman).

33. 149 Cong. Rec. H1400 (daily ed. February 27, 2003) (statement of Rep. Musgrave).

34. 147 Cong. Rec. H4921 (daily ed July
31, 2001) (statement of Rep. Pitts).

35. *Issues Raised by Human Cloning
Research: Hearing Before the Subcommittee on
Oversight and Investigations of the Committee
on Energy and Commerce*, 107th Cong., 101
(March 28, 2001) (statement of Professor
Pence).

36. *Science and Ethics of Human Cloning:
Hearings Before the Senate Committee on
Commerce, Science, and Transportation, Subcommittee on Science, Technology, and Space*,
108th Cong., 36 (January 29, 2003) (statement of Leon Kass).

37. *Human Cloning: Hearing Before the
Subcommittee on Science, Technology, and
Space of the Committee on Commerce, Science,
and Transportation*, 107th Cong., 5 (May 2,
2001) (statement of Sen. Weldon).

38. *Ibid.*, 33.

39. Jorge L. A. Garcia, "Human Cloning:
Never and Why Not," in *Human Cloning:
Science, Ethics, and Public Policy*, ed. Barbara
MacKinnon (Urbana: University of Illinois,
2000), 94.

40. "Ambush," *Star Wars: The Clone Wars*,
dir. Dave Bullock, writ. Steven Melching,
Cartoon Network, 3 October 2008.

41. "Carnage of Krell," *Star Wars: The
Clone Wars*.

42. "Fugitive," *Star Wars: The Clone Wars*,
dir. Danny Keller, writ. Katie Lucas, Netflix,
March 7, 2014.

43. "The Deserter," *Star Wars: The Clone
Wars*, dir. Robert Dalva, writ. Carl
Ellsworth, Cartoon Network, 1 January
2010.

44. "Plan of Dissent," *Star Wars: The Clone Wars,* dir. Kyle Dunlevy, writ. Matt Michnovetz, Cartoon Network, 11 November 2011.

45. "Carnage of Krell," *Star Wars: The Clone Wars.*

46. "The Hidden Enemy," *Star Wars: The Clone Wars,* dir. Steward Lee, writ. Drew Z. Greenberg, Cartoon Network, 6 February 2009.

47. "ARC Troopers," *Star Wars: The Clone Wars,* dir. Kyle Dunleavy, writ. Cameron Litvack, Cartoon Network, 17 September 2010.

48. "Clone Cadets," *Star Wars: The Clone Wars,* dir. Dave Filoni, writ. Cameron Litvack, Cartoon Network, 17 September 2010.

49. *Ibid.*

50. Brian Ott, "(Re)framing Fear: Equipment for Living in a Post–9/11 World," in *Cylons in America: Critical Studies in Battlestar Galactica,* ed. Tiffany Potter and C. W. Marshall (London: Continuum International, 2007), 19.

51. Mikhail M. Bakhtin, *The Dialogic Imagination: Four Essays by M. M. Bakhtin,* ed. Michael Holquist, trans. Caryl Emerson and Michael Holquist (Austin: University of Texas Press, 1981), 324.

Chapter Three

1. Dick Cheney, "The Vice President Appears on *Meet the Press* with Tim Russert," President George W. Bush White House Archives, September 16, 2001. Accessed August 20, 2013, http://georgewbush-whitehouse.archives.gov/ vicepresident/news-speeches/speeches/vp20010916.html.

2. "Cloak of Darkness," *Star Wars: The Clone Wars,* dir. Dave Filoni, writ. Paul Dini, Cartoon Network, 5 December 2008.

3. "Convention (III) Relative to the Treatment of Prisoners of War: Article III," International Committee of the Red Cross. Last modified May 14, 2012, http://www.icrc.org/applic/ihl/ihl.nsf/vwTreaties1949.xsp.

4. United Nations, Convention against Torture and Other Cruel, Inhuman or Degrading Treatment or Punishment, Treaty Series, vol. 1465 (December 10, 1984): 113–114.

5. Michael P. Vicaro, "A Liberal Use of 'Torture': Pain, Personhood, and Precedent in the U.S. Federal Definition of Torture," *Rhetoric & Public Affairs* 14, no. 3 (2011): 404.

6. Rebecca Leung, "60 Minutes II Has Exclusive Report on Alleged Mistreatment," CBSNews.com, April 27, 2004. Accessed April 10, 2013, http://www.cbsnews.com/news/abuse-of-iraqi-pows-by-gis-probed/.

7. Dana Milbank, "Bush Seeks to Reassure Nation on Iraq," *Washington Post,* May 25, 2004. Accessed April 10, 2013, http://www.washingtonpost.com/wp-dyn/articles/A52711-2004May24.html.

8. Bob Herbert, "It's Called Torture," *New York Times,* February 28, 2005. Accessed April 10, 2013, http://www.nytimes.com/2005/02/28/opinion/its-called-torture.html.

9. "About those Black Sites." *New York Times,* February 18, 2013, Late Edition (East Coast). http://search.proquest.com/docview/1288302259?accountid=27921.

10. Jeremy Scahill, "The CIA's Secret Sites in Somalia," *The Nation,* August 1, 2011, 11–16.

11. "Cloak of Darkness," *Star Wars: The Clone Wars.*

12. Bob Rehak, "Adapting *Watchmen* after 9/11," *Cinema Journal* 51, no. 1 (Fall 2011): 158.

13. Jeffrey C. Alexander, et al., *Cultural Trauma and Collective Identity* (Berkeley: University of California Press, 2004), 1.

14. Rehak, "Adapting *Watchmen,*" 157.

15. Claire Sisco King, "Rogue Waves, Remakes, and Resurrections: Allegorical Displacement and Screen Memory in Poseidon," *Quarterly Journal of Speech* 94, no. 4 (November 2008): 435.

16. *Ibid.,* 448.

17. Vincent M. Gaine, "Remember Everything, Absolve Nothing: Working Through Trauma in the *Bourne* Trilogy," *Cinema Journal* 51, no. 1 (Fall 2011): 159.

18. *Ibid.,* 163.

19. Anna Froula, "'9/11—What's That?' Trauma, Temporality, and Terminator: The Sarah Connor Chronicles," *Cinema Journal* 51, no. 1 (Fall 2011): 175.

20. Matthew B. Hill, "'I Am a Leaf on the Wind': Cultural Trauma and Mobility in Joss Whedon's *Firefly,*" *Exploitation* 50, no. 3 (2009): 485.

21. *Ibid.,* 503.

22. Aristotelis Nikolaidis, "Televising

Counter Terrorism: Torture, Denial, and Exception in the Case of 24," *Continuum: Journal of Media & Cultural Studies* 25, no. 2 (April 2011): 217.

23. Keren Tenenboim-Weinblatt, "'Where Is Jack Bauer When You Need Him?' The Uses of Television Drama in Mediated Political Discourse," *Political Communication* 26, no. 4 (2009): 368.

24. *Ibid.*, 381.

25. Karen Randell, "'Now the Gloves Come Off': The Problematic of 'Enhanced Interrogation Techniques' in *Battlestar Galactica*," *Cinema Journal* 51, no. 1 (Fall 2011): 169.

26. Ott, "(Re)Framing Fear," 19–20.

27. Randell, "'Now the Gloves Come Off,'" 173.

28. John Ip, "The Dark Knight's War on Terrorism," *Ohio State Journal of Criminal Law* 9, no. 1 (2011): 210.

29. *Star Wars: Episode V—The Empire Strikes Back,* dir. Kershner, 20th Century Fox, 1980.

30. Burton J. Lee, III, "The Stain of Torture," *Washington Post*, July 1, 2005, A25.

31. David Lubin, "Liberalism, Torture, and the Ticking Bomb," in *The Torture Debate in America*, ed. Karen J. Greenberg (New York: Cambridge University Press, 2006), 45.

32. Richard H. Dees, "Moral Ambiguity in a Black-and-White Universe," in *Star Wars and Philosophy: More Powerful Than You Can Possibly Imagine*, ed. Kevin S. Decker and Jason T. Eberl (New York: Barnes and Noble, 2009), 39.

33. "Mystery of a Thousand Moons," *Star Wars: The Clone Wars*, dir. Jesse Yeh, writ. Brian Larsen, Cartoon Network, 13 February 2009.

34. "Brain Invaders," *Star Wars: The Clone Wars*, dir. Steward Lee, writ. Andrew Kreisberg, Cartoon Network, 4 December 2009.

35. "The Wrong Jedi," *Star Wars: The Clone Wars*, dir. Dave Filoni, writ. Charles Murray, Cartoon Network, 2 March 2013.

36. "Cloak of Darkness," *Star Wars: The Clone Wars*.

37. *Ibid.*

38. "Lightsaber Lost," *Star Wars: The Clone Wars*, dir. Giancarlo Volpe, writ. Drew Z. Greenberg, Cartoon Network, 22 January 2010.

39. "Tera Sinube," *Star Wars: The Clone Wars Databank*. Accessed April 20, 2013, http://www.starwars.com/databank/tera-sinube.

40. "Overlords," *Star Wars: The Clone Wars*, dir. Steward Lee, writ. Christian Taylor, Cartoon Network, 28 January 2011.

41. "Children of the Force," *Star Wars: The Clone Wars*, dir. Brian Kalin O'Connell, writ. Henry Gilroy and Wendy Mericle, Cartoon Network, 9 October 2009.

42. *Star Wars: Episode I—The Phantom Menace*, dir. George Lucas, 20th Century Fox, 1999.

43. "Children of the Force," *Star Wars: The Clone Wars.*

44. *Ibid.*

45. "Grievous Intrigue," *Star Wars: The Clone Wars*, dir. Giancarlo Volpe, writ. Ben Edlund, Cartoon Network, 1 January 2010.

46. "Prisoners," *Star Wars: The Clone Wars*, dir. Danny Keller and written by Jose Molina, Cartoon Network, 23 September 2011.

47. Mikhail M. Bakhtin, *The Dialogic Imagination: Four Essays by M. M. Bakhtin*, ed. Michael Holquist, trans. Caryl Emerson and Michael Holquist (Austin: University of Texas Press, 1981), 280.

48. Seidman, 918.

49. Thomas A. Bass, "Counterinsurgency and Torture," *American Quarterly* 60, no. 2 (June 2008): 239.

50. Jason Dittmer, *Captain America and the National Superhero: Metaphors, Narratives, and Geopolitics* (Philadelphia: Temple University Press, 2013), 2–3.

Chapter Four

1. Barack Obama, "A Just and Lasting Peace," *Vital Speeches of the Day* 76, no. 2 (February 2010): 50.

2. "Sacrifice," *Star Wars: The Clone Wars*, dir. Steward Lee, writ. Christian Taylor, Netflix, 7 March 2014.

3. *Star Wars: Episode I—A Phantom Menace*, dir. George Lucas, 20th Century Fox, 1999.

4. "Sabotage," *Star Wars: The Clone Wars*, dir. Brian Kalin O' Connell, writ. Charles Murray, Cartoon Network, 9 February 2013.

5. Michael Walzer, "Coda: Can the Good Guys Win," *The European Journal of International Law* 24, no. 1 (2013): 434.

6. *Ibid.*

7. Barack Obama, "Obama's Speech

Against the Iraq War," npr.org, delivered October 2, 2002, last modified January 20, 2009. http://www.npr.org/templates/story/story.php?storyId=99591469.

8. Norwegian Nobel Committee, "The Nobel Peace Prize for 2009," Nobel prize.org, October 9, 2009. Accessed June 12, 2014, http://www.nobelprize.org/nobel_prizes/peace/laureates/2009/press.html.

9. Barack Obama, "Remarks by the President on Winning the Nobel Peace Prize," *whitehouse.gov*, delivered October 9, 2009. Accessed June 12, 2013, http://www.whitehouse.gov/the_press_office/Remarks-by-the-President-on-Winning-the-Nobel-Peace-Prize/.

10. Barack Obama, "Ebenezer Baptist Church Address," American Rhetoric Online Speech Bank, delivered January 20, 2008. Accessed May 21, 2015, http://www.americanrhetoric.com/speeches/barack obama/barackobamaebenezerbaptist.htm.

11. Martin Luther King, Jr., "Beyond Vietnam—A Time to Break Silence," American Rhetoric Online Speech Bank, delivered April 4, 1967. Accessed June 15, 2013, http://www.americanrhetoric.com/speeches/mlkatimetobreaksilence.htm.

12. Obama, "Lasting Peace," 50.

13. *Ibid.*

14. *Ibid.*, 51.

15. *Ibid.*

16. James T. Kloppenberg, *Reading Obama: Dreams, Hope, and the American Political Tradition* (Princeton: Princeton University Press, 2011), xii.

17. *Ibid.*, 775.

18. Obama, "Lasting Peace," 51.

19. *Ibid.*, 50.

20. *Ibid.*

21. *Ibid.*, 51.

22. *Ibid.*, 52.

23. *Ibid.*, 51, 53.

24. *Ibid.*, 52.

25. *Ibid.*, 53.

26. *Ibid.*, 52.

27. *Ibid.*, 53.

28. Michael Walzer, *Just and Unjust Wars: A Moral Argument with Historical Illustrations* (New York: Basic Books, 1977), 21.

29. Obama, "Lasting Peace," 52.

30. *Ibid.*

31. *Ibid.*, 51.

32. *Ibid.*

33. *Ibid.*

34. Roger Stahl, "Why We 'Support the

Troops": Rhetorical Evolutions," *Rhetoric & Public Affairs* 12, no. 4 (Winter 2009): 557.

35. Obama, "Lasting Peace," 51.

36. Robert Terrill, "An Uneasy Peace: Barack Obama's Nobel Peace Prize Lecture," *Rhetoric & Public Affairs* 14, no. 4 (2011): 772.

37. *Ibid.*, 776.

38. Joshua Reeves and Matthew S. May, "The Peace Rhetoric of a War President: Barack Obama and the Just War Legacy," *Public Affairs* 16, no. 4: 640.

39. *Ibid.*

40. Kelly Denton-Borhaug, "Beyond Iraq and Afghanistan: Religion and Politics in United States War-Culture," *Dialog: A Journal of Theology* 51, no. 2 (Summer 2012): 126.

41. *Star Wars: Episode IV–A New Hope*, dir. George Lucas, 20th Century Fox, 1977.

42. Nick Jamilla, "Defining the Jedi Order: *Star Wars'* Narrative and the Real World," in *Sex, Politics, and Religion in Star Wars: An Anthology*, ed. Douglas Brode and Leah Deyneka (Lanham, MD: Scarecrow Press, 2012), 155.

43. "Tresspass," *Star Wars: The Clone Wars*, dir. Brian Kalin O'Connell, writ. Steven Melching, Cartoon Network, 30 January 2009.

44. "Heroes on Both Sides," *Star Wars: The Clone Wars*, dir. Kyle Dunlevy, writ. Daniel Arkin, Cartoon Network, 19 November 2010.

45. "The Academy," *Star Wars: The Clone Wars*, dir. Giancarlo Volpe, writ. Cameron Litvack, Cartoon Network, 15 October 2010.

46. In the episode "Assassin," Senator Amidala attends a refugee relief conference on the planet Alderaan. Ahsoka Tano serves as a member of Senator Amidala's diplomatic security. "Assassin," *Star Wars: The Clone Wars*, dir. Kyle Dunlevy, writ. Katie Lucas, Cartoon Network, 22 October 2010.

47. The storyline runs for three consecutive episodes in Season Four: "Water War," *Star Wars: The Clone Wars*, dir. Duwayne Dunham, writ. Jose Molina, Cartoon Network, 16 September 2011; "Gungan Attack," *Star Wars: The Clone Wars*, dir. Brian Kalin O'Connell, writ. Jose Molina, Cartoon Network, 16 September 2011; and "Prisoners," "Water War," *Star Wars: The Clone Wars*, dir. Danny Keller, writ. Jose Molina, Cartoon Network, 23 September 2011.

48. "Shadow Warrior," *Star Wars: The Clone Wars*, dir. Brian Kalin O'Connell, writ. Daniel Arkin, Cartoon Network, 30 September 2011.

49. *Star Wars: The Clone Wars*, dir. Dave Filoni, Burbank, CA: Warner Bros. Pictures, 2008.

50. "A War on Two Fronts," *Star Wars: The Clone Wars*, dir. Dave Filoni, writ. Chris Collins, Cartoon Network, 6 October 2012.

51. *Ibid.*

52. *Ibid.*

53. "Lair of Grievous," *Star Wars: The Clone Wars*, dir. Atsushi Takeuchi, writ. Henry Gilroy, Cartoon Network, 12 December 2008.

54. "The Zillo Beast," *Star Wars: The Clone Wars*, dir. Giancarlo Volpe, writ. Craig Titley, Cartoon Network, 9 April 2010.

55. "Lair of Grievous," *Star Wars: The Clone Wars*.

56. "Jedi Crash," *Star Wars: The Clone Wars*, dir. Rob Coleman, writ. Katie Lucas, Cartoon Network, 16 January 2009.

57. "The Mandalore Plot," *Star Wars: The Clone Wars*, dir. Kyle Dunlevy, writ. Melinda Hsu, Cartoon Network, 29 January 2010.

58. "Sabotage," *Star Wars: The Clone Wars*.

59. Paul F. McDonald, *The Star Wars Heresies: Interpreting the Themes, Symbols, and Philosophies of Episodes I, II, and III* (Jefferson, NC: McFarland, 2013), 106.

60. "The Jedi Who Knew Too Much," *Star Wars: The Clone Wars*, dir. Danny Keller, writ. Charles Murray, Cartoon Network, 16 February 2013.

61. "The Wrong Jedi," *Star Wars: The Clone Wars*, dir. Dave Filoni, writ. Charles Murray, Cartoon Network, 2 March 2013.

62. "Destiny," *Star Wars: The Clone Wars*, dir. Kyle Dunlevy, writ. Christian Taylor, Netflix, 7 March 2014.

63. J. P. Telotte, "Science Fiction in Double Focus: Forbidden Planet," *Film Criticism* 13, no. 3 (Spring 1989): 31.

64. Lincoln Geraghty, "Creating and Comparing Myth in Twentieth Century Science Fiction: Star Trek and Star Wars." *Literature/Film Quarterly* 33 (2005): 194.

65. "Sacrifice," *Star Wars: The Clone Wars*.

66. McDonald, *The Star Wars Heresies*, 149.

Chapter Five

1. Starhawk, "Code Pink," Starhawk. org. Accessed May 27, 2015, http://starhawk. org/writing/ activism/iraq/.

2. "Heroes on Both Sides," *Star Wars: The Clone Wars*, dir. Kyle Dunlevy, writ. Daniel Arkin, Cartoon Network, 19 November 2010.

3. Starhawk, "Code Pink."

4. Harriet Hyman Alonso, *Peace as a Women's Issue: A History of the U.S. Movement for World Peace and Women's Rights* (Syracuse: Syracuse University Press, 1993), 8.

5. Sara Ruddick, *Maternal Thinking: Toward a Politics of Peace* (New York: Ballantine, 1990), 145.

6. Joan Hoff Wilson, "'Peace is a Woman's Job …' Jeannette Rankin and the Origins American Foreign Policy: The Origins of Her Pacifism," *Montana: The Magazine of Wester History* 30, no. 2 (Spring 1980): 40.

7. Jeannette Rankin, "Peace and the Disarmament Conference," in *"Two Votes Against War" and Other Writings on Peace* (New York: A. J. Muste Institute, 2001), 21.

8. Charlie Rose, "George Lucas on the Meaning of *Star Wars*," *YouTube* video, 3:33, from a live interview conducted during Chicago Ideas Week on October 17, 2014, posted by Charlie Rose, October 23, 2014, https://www.youtube.com/watch?v=-pbRGt WkHWg.

9. Roy M. Anker, *Catching Light: Looking for God in the Movies* (Grand Rapids: Wm. B. Eerdmans, 2004), 235.

10. Karen J. Warren and Duane L. Cady, "Feminism and Peace: Seeing Connections," *Hypatia* 9, no. 2 (Spring 1994): 4.

11. Carol Cohn, "Wars, Wimps, and Women: Talking Gender and Thinking War," in *Gendering War Talk*, ed. Miriam Cooke and Angela Woollacott (Princeton: Princeton University Press, 1993), 241.

12. *Ibid.*

13. Carol Cohn and Sara Ruddick, "A Feminist Ethical Perspective on Weapons of Mass Destruction," in *Ethics and Weapons of Mass Destruction: Religious and Secular Perspectives*, ed. Sohail Hashmi and Lee Steven (Cambridge: Cambridge University Press, 2004), 406.

14. Lucinda J. Peach, "An Alternative to Pacifism? Feminism and Just-War Theory,"

in *Bringing Peace Home: Feminism, Violence, and Nature*, ed. Karen J. Warren and Duane L. Cady (Bloomington: Indiana University Press, 1996),192.

15. Rebecca Spence and Jason McLeod, "Building the Road as We Walk It: Peacebuilding as Principled Revolutionary Nonviolent Praxis," *Social Alternatives* 21, no. 2 (Autumn 2002): 62.

16. Thomas A. Horne, "James Mangold's *3:10 to Yuma* and the Mission in Iraq," *Journal of Film and Video* 65 no. 3 (Fall 2013): 40.

17. Mark J. Lacy, "War, Cinema, and Moral Anxiety," *Alternatives* 28 (2003): 624.

18. Geoff King and Tanya Krzywinska, *Science Fiction Cinema: From Outerspace to Cyberspace* (London: Wallflower Press, 2000), 7.

19. M. Keith Booker, *Monsters, Mushroom Clouds, and the Cold War: American Science Fiction and the Roots of Postmodernism, 1946–1964* (Westport, CT: Greenwood Press, 2001), 3.

20. M. Keith Booker, *Alternate Americas: Science Fiction Film and American Culture* (Westport, CT: Praeger, 2006), 31.

21. *Ibid.*, 34.

22. *Ibid.*, 143.

23. Michael Charles Pounds, "'Explorers'–Star Trek: Deep Space Nine," *African Identities* 7, no. 2 (May 2009): 215.

24. Jules Weldes, "Going Cultural: Star Trek, State Action, and Popular Culture," *Millenium–Journal of International Studies* 28 (1999): 127.

25. Gary Westfahl, *Science Fiction, Children's Literature, and Popular Culture: Coming of Age in Fantasyland* (Westport, CT: Greenwood Press, 2000), 77.

26. Neta Crawford, "Feminist Futures: Science Fiction, Utopia, and the Art of Possibilities in World Politics," in *To Seek Out New Worlds: Exploring Links Between Science Fiction and World Politics*, ed. Jutta Weldes (New York: Palgrave Macmillan, 2003), 204.

27. *Ibid.*, 197–198.

28. Abigail E. Ruane and Patrick James, "The International Relations of Middle-earth: Learning from *The Lord of the Rings*," *International Studies Perspectives* 9 (2008): 380–381.

29. *Ibid.*, 383.

30. Wim Tigges, "Xena Rules: A Feminized Version of Antony and Cleopatra," *Feminist Media Studies* 10, no. 4 (2010): 452.

31. William Ashbaugh and Mizushima Shintarou, "'Peace Through Understanding': How Science-Fiction Anime *Mobile Suit Gundam 00* Criticizes U.S. Aggression and Japanese Passivity," *Asian Journal of Global Studies* 5, no. 2 (2012–2013): 110–111.

32. *Ibid.*, 114.

33. Anjana Mebane-Cruz and Margaret Wiener, "Imagining 'The Good Reality': Communities of Healing in Two Works of Utopian Fiction," *Contemporary Justice Review* 8, no. 3 (September 2005): 316.

34. Joan Haran, "Redefining Hope as Praxis," *Journal for Cultural Research* 14, no. 4 (October 2010): 393–408.

35. Jeanette Rankin, "Two Votes Against War," in *"Two Votes Against War" and Other Writings on Peace* (New York: A. J. Muste Institute, 2001), 5.

36. *Ibid.*, 8.

37. Joan Hoff-Wilson, "'Peace is a Woman's Job ...' Jeannette Rankin and the Origins American Foreign Policy: The Origins of Her Pacifism," *Montana: The Magazine of Western History* 30, no. 1 (Winter 1980): 39.

38. James J. Lopach and Jean A. Luckowski, *Jeannette Rankin: A Political Woman* (Boulder: University Press of Colorado, 2005), 181.

39. Rankin, "Two Votes Against War," 11.

40. Norma Smith, *Jeannette Rankin: America's Conscience* (Helena: Montana Historical Society Press, 2002), 201; Rankin, "Two Votes Against War," 8.

41. Hoff-Wilson, "Jeannette Rankin," 50.

42. Jeannette Rankin, "Mass Action and Its Effect on International Cooperation for World Peace," in *"Two Votes Against War" and Other Writings on Peace* (New York: A. J. Muste Institute, 2001), 30; Jeanette Rankin, "Peace Through Political Action," in *"Two Votes Against War" and Other Writings on Peace* (New York: A. J. Muste Institute, 2001), 16.

43. Rankin, "Mass Action," 30.

44. Jeannette Rankin, "Beware of Holy Wars!" in *"Two Votes Against War" and Other Writings on Peace* (New York: A. J. Muste Institute, 2001), 35.

45. Rankin, "Mass Action," 31.

46. Jeannette Rankin, "I Would Vote 'No' Again," in *"Two Votes Against War" and Other Writings on Peace* (New York: A. J. Muste Institute, 2001), 28.

47. Rankin, "Peace Through Political Action," 15.

48. Rankin, "Mass Action," 33.

49. *Ibid.*, 27, 29.

50. Jeannette Rankin, "Peace and the Disarmament Conference," 20–21.

51. Rankin, "Beware of Holy Wars!" 36–37.

52. Rankin, "Two Votes Against War," 10.

53. *Ibid.*

54. *Ibid.*

55. Rankin, "Peace and the Disarmament Conference," 20.

56. *Ibid.*

57. *Ibid.*, 23–24.

58. Rankin, "You Cannot Have Wars Without Women," in *"Two Votes Against War" and Other Writings on Peace* (New York: A. J. Muste Institute, 2001), 38.

59. *Ibid.*, 19.

60. Rankin, "Peace and the Disarmament Conference," 21.

61. Rankin, "You Cannot Have Wars Without Women," 38.

62. Rankin, "Peace and the Disarmament Conference," 23.

63. Rankin, "Disarmament Conference," 21.

64. Rankin, "Two Votes Against War," 10.

65. Rankin, "Peace Through Political Action," 15.

66. Rankin, "Two Votes Against War," 8.

67. Rankin, "Peace Through Political Action," 15.

68. *Ibid.*, 14.

69. *Ibid.*

70. *Ibid.*

71. Rankin, "Mass Action," 29.

72. Rankin, "Peace Through Political Action," 15.

73. Jeanne Cavelos, "Stop Her, She's got a Gun! How the Rebel Princess and the Virgin Queen Become Marginalized and Powerless in George Lucas's Fairy Tale," in *Star Wars on Trial: Science Fiction and Fantasy Writers Debate the Most Popular Science Fiction Films of All Time*, ed. David Brin and Matthew Woodring Stover (Dallas: Benbella, 2006), 318.

74. Diana Dominguez, "Feminism and the Force: Empowerment and Disillusionment in a Galaxy Far, Far Away," in *Culture, Identities and Technology in the Star Wars Films*, ed. Carl Silvio and Tony M. Vinci (Jefferson, NC: McFarland, 2006), 128.

75. Ray Merlock and Kathy Merlock Jackson, "Lightsabers, Political Arenas, and Marriages for Princess Leia and Queen Amidala," in *Sex, Politics, and Religion in Star Wars: An Anthology*, ed. Douglas Brode and Leah Deyneka (Lanham, MD: Scarecrow Press, 2012), 87.

76. John C. McDowell, "'Wars Not Make One Great': Redeeming the Star Wars Mythos from Redemptive Violence Without Amusing Ourselves to Death," *Journal of Religion and Popular Culture* 22, no. 1 (Spring 2010): 42.

77. "Assassin," *Star Wars: The Clone Wars*, dir. Kyle Dunlevy, writ. Katie Lucas, Cartoon Network, 22 October 2010.

78. "Water War," *Star Wars: The Clone Wars*, dir. Duwayne Dunham, writ. Jose Molina, Cartoon Network, 16 September 2011.

79. "Heroes on Both Sides," *Star Wars: The Clone Wars*.

80. "Pursuit of Peace," *Star Wars: The Clone Wars*, dir. Duwayne Dunham, writ. Daniel Arkin, Cartoon Network, 3 December 2010.

81. "Voyage of Temptation," *Star Wars: The Clone Wars*, dir. Brian Kalin O'Connell, writ. Paul Dini, Cartoon Network, 5 February 2010.

82. "Duchess of Mandalore," *Star Wars: The Clone Wars*, dir. Brian Kalin O'Connell, writ. Drew Z Greenberg, Cartoon Network, 12 February 2010.

83. "The Mandalore Plot," *Star Wars: The Clone Wars*, dir. Kyle Dunlevy, writ. Melinda Hsu, Cartoon Network, 29 January 2010.

84. *Ibid.*

85. "Duchess of Mandalore," *Star Wars: The Clone Wars*.

86. *Ibid.*

87. "Shades of Reason," *Star Wars: The Clone Wars*, dir. Bosco Ng, writ. Chris Collins, Cartoon Network, 26 January 2013.

88. George W. Bush, "9/11 Remarks at Barksdale Air Force Base," American Rhetoric Online Speech Bank, delivered September 11, 2001. Accessed May 22, 2015, http://www.americanrhetoric.com/speeches/gwbush911barksdale.htm.

89. Barbara Levy Simon, "Women of Conscience: Jeannette Rankin and Barbara Lee," *Affilia* 17, no. 3 (Fall 2002): 385.

90. Rosemarie Zagarri, "Morals, Manners, and the Republic Mother," *American Quarterly* 44, no. 2 (June 1992): 207.

91. Shawn J. Parry-Giles and Diane M. Blair, "The Rise of the Rhetorical First Lady: Politics, Gender, Ideology, and Women's Voice, 1789–2002," *Rhetoric and Public Affairs* 5, no. 4 (Winter 2002): 575.

92. Ruddick, *Maternal Thinking*, 220.

Chapter Six

1. Leland Chee, Twitter post, February 13, 2015, 12:45 a.m., https://twitter.com/holocronkeeper/.

2. International Human Rights Clinic at Harvard Law School, *Shaking the Foundations: The Human Rights Implications of Killer Robots* (New York: Human Rights Watch, 2014): 24.

3. Susan Sontag, "The Imagination of Disaster," *Commentary* 14 (October 1965): 47.

4. J. P. Telotte, "Science Fiction in Double Focus: Forbidden Planet," *Film Criticism* 13, no. 3 (Spring 1989): 28.

5. Rowland Hughes, "The Ends of the Earth: Nature, Narrative, and Identity in Dystopian Film," *Critical Survey* 25, no. 2 (2013): 27.

6. Stephen T. Asma, *On Monsters: An Unnatural History of Our Worst Fears* (Oxford: Oxford University Press, 2009), 258.

7. Eric Herhuth, "Life, Love, and Programming: The Culture and Politics of WALL-E and Pixar Computer Animation," *Cinema Journal* 53, no. 4 (Summer 2014): 60.

8. Robert F. Arnold, "Termination or Transformation: The Terminator Films and Recent Changes in the U.S. Auto Industry," *Film Quarterly* 52, no. 1 (Autumn 1998): 22.

9. *Ibid.*

10. Alicia Gibson, "Atomic Pop! Astro Boy, the *Dialectic of Enlightenment*, and the Machinic Modes of Being," *Cultural Critique* 80 (Winter 2012): 195–196.

11. Janice Hocker Rushing and Thomas S. Frenz, *Projecting the Shadow: The Cyborg Hero in American Film* (Chicago: University of Chicago Press, 1995), 39.

12. *Ibid.*, 178.

13. *Ibid.*, 179.

14. Mark Jancovich, "Modernity and Subjectivity in The Terminator: The Machine as Monster in Contemporary Culture," *The Velvet Light Trap* 30 (Fall 1992): 5.

15. Congressional Research Service, *U.S. Unmanned Aerial Systems*, by Jeremiah Gertler, R42136 (Washington, D.C.: Congressional Research Service, January 3, 2012), 8.

16. Robert Sparrow, "Killer Robots," *Journal of Applied Philosophy* 24, no. 1 (2007): 63.

17. P. W. Singer, "Robots at War: The New Battlefield," *The Wilson Quarterly* 33, no. 1 (Winter 2009): 31–32.

18. *Ibid.*, 36.

19. International Human Rights Clinic at Harvard Law School, *Mind the Gap: The Lack of Accountability for Killer Robots* (New York: Human Rights Watch, 2015), 6; International Human Rights Clinic at Harvard Law School, *Losing Humanity: The Case Against Killer Robots* (New York: Human Rights Watch, 2012), 2.

20. *Losing Humanity*, 6.

21. *Ibid.*

22. International Human Rights and Conflict Resolution Clinic at Stanford Law School and Global Justice Clinic at NYU School of Law, *Living Under Drones: Death, Injury, and Trauma to Civilians from U.S. Drone Practices in Pakistan* (Stanford: Stanford Law School, 2012).

23. Center for Civilians in Conflict and Human Rights Clinic at Columbia Law School, *The Civilian Impact of Drones: Unexamined Costs, Unanswered Questions* (New York: Columbia Law School, 2012): 34.

24. *Losing Humanity*, 30.

25. International Human Rights Clinic at Harvard Law School, *Shaking the Foundations: The Human Rights Implications of Killer Robots* (New York: Human Rights Watch, 2014), 6.

26. *Shaking Foundations*, 23.

27. *Losing Humanity*, 37.

28. *Living Under Drones*, 7.

29. *Civilian Impact*, 68.

30. P. W. Singer, *Wired for War: The Robotics Revolution and Conflict in the 21st Century* (New York: Penguin, 2009), 319.

31. *Losing Humanity*, 40.

32. *Mind the Gap*, 7.

33. *Shaking the Foundations*, 13.

34. *Civilian Impact*, 11.

35. *Ibid.*, 8.

36. *Ibid.*, 20.

37. *Ibid.*

38. *Living Under Drones*, 55.

39. *Civilian Impact*, 24.

40. *Living Under Drones*, 81.

41. *Losing Humanity*, 32.

42. *Shaking the Foundations*, 16.

43. *Mind the Gap*, 24.

44. *Ibid.*, 7.

45. *Mind the Gap*, 11.

46. *Civilian Impact*, 3; *Shaking the Foundations*, 4; *Losing Humanity*, 5.

47. *Shaking the Foundations*, 24.

48. "Weapons Factory," *Star Wars: The Clone Wars*, dir. Giancarlo Volpe, writ. Brian Larsen, Cartoon Network, 13 November 2009.

49. "Grievous Intrigue," *Star Wars: The Clone Wars*, dir. Giancarlo Volpe, writ. Ben Edlund, Cartoon Network, 1 January 2010.

50. Robert Arp, "'If Droids Could Think...': Droids as Slaves and Persons," in *Star Wars and Philosophy: More Powerful Than You Can Possibly Imagine*, ed. Kevin S. Decker and Jason T. Eberl (New York: Barnes and Noble, 2009), 130.

51. "Duel of the Droids," *Star Wars: The Clone Wars*, dir. Rob Coleman, writ. Kevin Campbell and Henry Gilroy, Cartoon Network, 12 November 2008.

52. "Artoo Come Home," *Star Wars: The Clone Wars*, dir. Giancarlo Volpe, writ. Eoghan Mahony, Cartoon Network, 30 April 2010.

53. "Secret Weapons," *Star Wars: The Clone Wars*, dir. Danny Keller, writ. Brent Friedman, Cartoon Network, 1 December 2012.

54. "Point of No Return," *Star Wars: The Clone Wars*, dir. Bosco Ng, writ. Brent Friedman, Cartoon Network, 12 January 2013.

55. "Heroes on Both Sides," *Star Wars: The Clone Wars*, dir. Kyle Dunleavy, writ. Daniel Arkin, Cartoon Network, 19 November 2010.

56. "Sabotage," *Star Wars: The Clone Wars*, dir. Brian Kalin O'Connell, writ. Charles Murray, Cartoon Network, 9 February 2013.

57. Jason Fry, *Star Wars: The Clone Wars Episode Guide* (New York: DK, 2013), 44.

58. "Innocents of Ryloth," *Star Wars: The Clone Wars*, dir. Justin Ridge, writ. Henry Gilroy, Cartoon Network, 6 March 2009.

59. "Heroes on Both Sides," *Star Wars: The Clone Wars*.

60. "Bombad Jedi," *Star Wars: The Clone Wars*, dir. Jesse Yeh, writ. Kevin Rubio, Henry Gilroy, and Steven Melching, Cartoon Network, 21 November 2008; "Sphere of Influence," *Star Wars: The Clone Wars*, dir. Kyle Dunlevy, writ. Katie Lucas and Steven Melching, Cartoon Network, 1 October 2010.

61. "Assassin," *Star Wars: The Clone Wars*, dir. Kyle Dunlevy, writ. Katie Lucas, Cartoon Network, 22 October 2010.

62. "Mercy Mission," *Star Wars: The Clone Wars*, dir. Danny Keller, writ. Bonnie Mark, Cartoon Network, 7 October 2011.

63. "Nomad Droids," *Star Wars: The Clone Wars*, dir. Steward Lee, writ. Steve Mitchell and Craig Van Sickle, Cartoon Network, 14 October 2011.

64. J. P. Tellote, *Replications: A Robotic History of the Science Fiction Film* (Urbana: University of Illinois Press, 1995), 7.

65. Mikhail M. Bakhtin, *The Dialogic Imagination: Four Essays by M. M. Bakhtin*, ed. Michael Holquist, trans. Caryl Emerson and Michael Holquist (Austin: University of Texas Press, 1981), 272.

66. Tellote, *Replications*, 23.

67. Asp, 128.

68. J. P. Tellote, "Human Artifice and the Science Fiction Film," *Film Quarterly* 36 no. 3 (Spring 1983): 44.

Chapter Seven

1. Mikhail M. Bakhtin, *The Dialogic Imagination: Four Essays by M. M. Bakhtin*, edited by Michael Holquist and translated by Caryl Emerson and Michael Holquist (Austin: University of Texas Press, 1981), 282.

2. *Star Wars: Episode VI—Return of the Jedi*, dir. Richard Marquand, CA: 20th Century Fox, 1983.

3. Lisbet van Zoonen, *Entertaining the Citizen: When Politics and Popular Culture Converge* (Lanham, MD: Rowman & Littlefield, 2005), 124.

4. Martin Flanagan, *Bakhtin and the Movies: New Ways of Understanding Hollywood Films* (London: Palgrave Macmillan, 2009), 6.

5. Bakhtin, *The Dialogic Imagination*, 277.

6. *Ibid.*, 275.

7. Carl Silvio and Tony M. Vinci, *Culture, Identities and Technology in the Star Wars Films: Essays on the Two Trilogies* (Jefferson, NC: McFarland, 2007), 3.

8. Ken Hirschkop, *Mikhail Bakhtin: An Aesthetic for Democracy* (Oxford: Oxford University Press, 1999), 184.

9. Bakhtin, *The Dialogic Imagination*, 282.

10. *Ibid.*

11. *Ibid.*, 291.

Works Cited

Alexander, Jeffrey C., Ron Eyerman, Bernard Giesen, Neil J. Smelser, and Piotr Sztompka. *Cultural Trauma and Collective Identity*. Berkeley: University of California Press, 2004. EBSCOhost eBook Academic Collection. Accessed February 6, 2014.

Alter, Jonathan. "Time to Think About Torture." *Newsweek*, November 4, 2001.

Anker, Roy M. *Catching Light: Looking for God in the Movies*. Grand Rapids: Wm. B. Eerdmans, 2004.

Arnold, Robert F. "Termination or Transformation: The Terminator Films and Recent Changes in the U.S. Auto Industry." *Film Quarterly* 52, no. 1 (Autumn 1998): 20–30.

Arp, Robert. "'If Droids Could Think': Droids as Slaves and Persons." In *Star Wars and Philosophy: More Powerful than You Can Possibly Imagine*, edited by Kevin S. Decker and Jason T. Eberl, 120–131. New York: Barnes and Noble, 2009.

Ashbaugh, William, and Mizushima Shintarou. "'Peace Through Understanding': How Science-Fiction Anime *Mobile Suit Gundam 00* Criticizes US Aggression and Japanese Passivity." *Asian Journal of Global Studies* 5, no. 2 (2012–13): 108–118.

Asma, Stephen T. *On Monsters: An Unnatural History of Our Worst Fears*: Oxford: Oxford University Press, 2009.

Atkinson, Joshua, and Bernadette Calafell. "Darth Vader Made Me Do It! Anakin Skywalker's Avoidance of Responsibility and the Gray Areas of Hegemonic Masculinity in the *Star Wars* Universe." *Communication, Culture & Critique* 2 (2009): 1–20.

Bakhtin, Mikhail M. *The Dialogic Imagination: Four Essays by M. M. Bakhtin*. Edited by Michael Holquist. Translated by Caryl Emerson and Michael Holquist. Austin: University of Texas Press, 1981.

_____. *Problems of Dostoevksy's Poetics*. Edited and translated by Caryl Emerson. Minneapolis: University of Minnesota Press, 1984.

_____. *Speech Genres and Other Late Essays*. Edited by Caryl Emerson and Michael Holmquist. Translated by Vern W. McGee. Austin: University of Texas Press, 1986.

Bergoffen, Debra B. "The Just War Tradition: Translating the Ethics of Human Dignity into Political Practices." *Hypatia* 23, no. 2 (Spring 2008): 72–94.

Booker, M. Keith. *Alternate Americas: Science Fiction Film and American Culture*. Westport, CT: Praeger, 2006.

_____. *Monsters, Mushroom Clouds, and the Cold War: American Science Fiction and the Roots of Postmodernism, 1946–1964*. Westport, CT: Greenwood Press, 2001.

Brode, Douglas, and Leah Deynaka, *Myth, Media, and Culture in Star Wars: An Anthology*. Lanham, MD: Scarecrow Press, 2012

Brooker, Will. *Hunting the Dark Knight: Twenty-First Century Batman.* New York: I. B. Tauris, 2012.

Brummett, Barry. "Burke's Representative Anecdote as Method in Media Criticism." *Critical Studies in Mass Communication* 1 (1984): 161–176.

_____. "Electric Literature as Equipment for Living: Haunted House Films." *Critical Studies in Mass Communication* 2 (1985): 247–261.

Burke, Kenneth. *The Philosophy of Literary Form,* 3d ed. Berkley: University of California Press, 1974.

Bush, George W. "9/11 Remarks at Barksdale Air Force Base." American Rhetoric Online Speech Bank, delivered September 11, 2201. Accessed May 22, 2015. http://www.americanrhetoric.com/speeches/gwbush911barksdale.htm.

Bussolini, Jeffrey. "Television Intertextuality After Buffy: Intertextuality of Casting and Constitutive Intertextuality." *Slayage: The Journal of the Whedon Studies Association* 10, no. 1 (Winter 2013). Accessed October 13, 2013. /http://slayageonline.com/Numbers/slayage35.htm.

Cavelos, Jeanne. "Stop Her, She's Got a Gun! How the Rebel Princess and the Virgin Queen Become Marginalized and Powerless in George Lucas's Fairy Tale." In *Star Wars on Trial: Science Fiction and Fantasy Writers Debate the Most Popular Science Fiction Films of All Time,* edited by David Brin and Matthew Woodring Stover, 305–322. Dallas: Benbella, 2006.

Cheney, Dick. "The Vice President Appears on *Meet the Press* with Tim Russert." *President George W. Bush White House Archives,* September 16, 2001. Accessed August 20, 2013. http://georgewbush-whitehouse.archives.gov/vicepresident/news-speeches/speeches/vp20010916.html.

Clinton, William J. "Remarks Announcing the Prohibition on Federal Funding for Cloning of Human Beings." *The American Presidency Project,* March 4, 1997. Accessed October 8, 2012. http://www.presidency.ucsb.edu/ws/index.php?pid=53815.

Cohen, Richard. "Using Torture to Fight Terror." *Washington Post,* March 6, 2003.

Cohn, Carol. "Wars, Wimps, and Women: Talking Gender and Thinking War." In *Gendering War Talk,* edited by Miriam Cooke and Angela Woollacott, 227–246. Princeton: Princeton University Press, 1993.

Cohn, Carol, and Sara Ruddick. "A Feminist Ethical Perspective on Weapons of Mass Destruction." In *Ethics and Weapons of Mass Destruction: Religious and Secular Perspectives,* edited by Sohail Hashmi and Lee Steven, 405–435. Cambridge: Cambridge University Press, 2004.

Crawford, Neta. "Feminist Futures: Science Fiction, Utopia, and the Art of Possibilities in World Politics." In *To Seek Out New Worlds: Exploring Links Between Science Fiction and World Politics,* edited by Jutta Weldes, 195–220. New York: Palgrave Macmillan, 2003.

Crawford, Neta. C. "Just War Theory and the U.S. Counterterror War." *Perspectives on Politics* 1, no. 1 (March 2003): 5–25.

Dees, Richard H. "Moral Ambiguity in a Black-And-White Universe." In *Star Wars and Philosophy: More Powerful than You Can Possibly Imagine,* edited by Kevin S. Decker and Jason T. Eberl, 39–53. New York: Barnes & Noble, 2005.

Denton-Borhaug, Kelly. "Beyond Iraq and Afghanistan: Religion and Politics in United States War-Culture." *Dialog: A Journal of Theology* 51, no. 2 (Summer 2012): 125–134.

Dittmer, Jason. *Captain America and the National Superhero: Metaphors, Narratives, and Geopolitics,* Philadelphia: Temple University Press, 2013.

Dominguez, Diana. "Feminism and the Force: Empowerment and Disillusionment in a Galaxy Far, Far Away." In *Culture, Identities and Technology in the Star Wars Films,* edited by Carl Silvio and Tony M. Vinci, 109–133. Jefferson, NC: McFarland, 2006.

Eberl, Jason T. "I, Clone: How Cloning Is (Mis)Portrayed in Contemporary Cinema." *Film & History* 40, no. 2 (2010): 27–44.

Farrell, Thomas B. *Norms of Rhetorical Culture*. New Haven: Yale University Press, 1993.

Fiala, Andrew G. "Citizenship, Epistemology, and the Just War Theory." *Logos: A Journal of Catholic Thought and Culture* 7, no. 2 (Spring 2004): 100–117.

Fineman, Howard. "Reaction to Obama's Nobel Speech." Interview with Robert Siegel. National Public Radio: All Things Considered, December 10, 2009. Accessed October 25, 2011. http://www.npr.org/templates/story /story.php?storyId.

Flanagan, Martin. *Bakhtin and the Movies: New Ways of Understanding Hollywood Film*. New York: Palgrave Macmillan, 2009.

Froula, Anna. "'9/11—What's That?' Trauma, Temporality, and Terminator: The Sarah Connor Chronicles." *Cinema Journal* 51, no. 1 (Fall 2011): 174–179.

Fry, Jason. *Star Wars: The Clone Wars Episode Guide*. New York: DK, 2013.

Gaine, Vincent M. "Remember Everything, Absolve Nothing: Working Through Trauma in the *Bourne* Trilogy." *Cinema Journal* 51, no. 1 (Fall 2011): 159–163.

Garcia, Jorge L. A. "Human Cloning: Never and Why Not." In *Human Cloning: Science, Ethics, and Public Policy*, edited by Barbara MacKinnon, 85–103. Urbana: University of Illinois, 2000.

Geraghty, Lincoln. "Creating and Comparing Myth in Twentieth Century Science Fiction: Star Trek and Star Wars." *Literature/Film Quarterly* 33 (2005): 191–200.

Gibson, Alicia. "Atomic Pop! Astro Boy, the *Dialectic of Enlightenment*, and the Machinic Modes of Being." *Cultural Critique* 80 (Winter 2012): 183–204.

Gordon, Andrew. "Star Wars: A Myth for Our Time." *Literature Film Quarterly* 6, no. 4 (Fall 1978): 314–326.

Griffin, Gabriele. "Science and the Cultural Imaginary: The Case of Kazuo Ishiguro's *Never Let Me Go*." *Textual Practice* 23, no. 4 (2009): 645–633.

Halasek, Kay. "Starting the Dialogue: What Can We Do About Bakhtin's Ambivalence Toward Rhetoric?" *Rhetoric Society Quarterly* 22, no. 4 (Autumn 1992): 1–9.

Hamilton, Sheryl N. "Science Fiction and the Media." *Science Fiction Studies* 30, no. 2 (July 2003): 267–282.

Haran, Joan. "Redefining Hope as Praxis." *Journal for Cultural Research* 14, no. 4 (October 2010): 393–408.

Hassler, David M., and Clyde Wilcox. *Political Science Fiction*. Columbia: University of South Carolina Press, 1997.

Hatch, John B. "Dialogic Rhetoric in Letters Across the Divide: A Dance of (Good) Faith Toward Racial Reconciliation." *Rhetoric & Public Affairs* 12 (2009): 485–532.

Havstad, Joyce C. "Human Reproductive Cloning: A Conflict of Liberties." *Bioethics* 24, no. 2 (2010): 71–77.

Herbert, Bob. "It's Called Torture." *New York Times*, February 28, 2005.

Herhuth, Eric. Life, Love, and Programming: The Culture and Politics of WALL-E and Pixar Computer Animation." *Cinema Journal* 53, no. 4 (Summer 2014): 653–675.

Hill, Matthew B. "'I Am a Leaf on the Wind': Cultural Trauma and Mobility in Joss Whedon's Firefly." *Exploitation* 50, no. 3 (2009): 484–511.

Hirschkop, Ken. "Is Dialogism for Real?" *Social Text* 30 (1992): 102–113.

_____. *Mikhail Bakhtin: An Aesthetic for Democracy*. Oxford: Oxford University Press, 1999.

_____. "Mikhail Bakhtin: Historical Becoming in Language, Literature, and Culture." In *The Cambridge History of Literary Criticism, Volume 9: Twentieth-Century Historical, Philosophical, and Psychological Perspectives*, edited by Christina Knellwolf and Christopher Norris, 145–154. Cambridge: Cambridge University Press, 2001.

Hoff, Norma. *Jeannette Rankin: America's Conscience*. Helena: Montana Historical Society Press, 2002.

Hoff-Wilson, Joan. "'Peace Is a Woman's Job...' Jeannette Rankin and the Origins American Foreign Policy: The Origins of Her Pacifism." *Montana: The Magazine of Western History* 30, no. 1 (Spring 1980): 38–53.

Hopkins, Patrick D. "Bad Copies: How Popular Media Represent Cloning as an Ethical Problem." *The Hastings Center Report* 28, no. 2 (March-April 1998): 6–13.

Horne, Thomas A. "James Mangold's *3:10 to Yuma* and the Mission in Iraq." *Journal of Film and Video* 65 no. 3 (Fall 2013): 40–48.

Hughes, Rowland. "The Ends of the Earth: Nature, Narrative, and Identity in Dystopian Film." *Critical Survey* 25, no. 2 (2013): 22–39.

Hyman Alonso, Harriet. *Peace as a Women's Issue: A History of the U.S. Movement for World Peace and Women's Rights*. Syracuse: Syracuse University Press, 1993.

Ip, John. "The Dark Knight's War on Terrorism." *Ohio State Journal of Criminal Law* 9, no. 1 (2011): 209–229.

Isikoff, Michael. "Bin Laden's Death Rekindles 'Enhanced' Interrogation Debate." NBCNews.com, May 2, 2011. Accessed October 22, 2011. http://www.msnbc.msn.com/id/42863247/ns/world_news-death_of_bin_laden/#.UD57idZlTYg.

Jamilla, Nick "Defining the Jedi Order: *Star Wars'* Narrative and the Real World." In *Sex, Politics, and Religion in Star Wars: An Anthology*, edited by Douglas Brode and Leah Deyneka, 147–163. Lanham, MD: Scarecrow Press, 2012.

Jancovich, Mark. "Modernity and Subjectivity in the Terminator: The Machine as Monster in Contemporary Culture." *The Velvet Light Trap* 30 (Fall 1992): 3–17.

Jasinski, James. "Heteroglossia, Polyphony, and the Federalist Papers." *Rhetoric Society Quarterly* 27, no. 1 (Winter, 1997): 23–46.

Javitt, Gail H., Kristen Suthers, and Kathy Hudson. *Cloning: A Policy Analysis*. Washington, D.C.: Genetics and Public Policy Center, 2005.

Kerslake, Patricia. *Science Fiction and Empire*. Liverpool: Liverpool University Press, 2007.

King, Geoff and Tanya Krzywinska. *Science Fiction Cinema: From Outerspace to Cyberspace*. London: Wallflower Press, 2000.

King, Martin Luther, Jr. "Beyond Vietnam—A Time to Break Silence." American Rhetoric Online Speech Bank, delivered April 4, 1967. Accessed June 12, 2013. http://www.americanrhetoric.com/speeches/mlkatimetobreaksilence.htm,

Kinnucan, Michelle J. "Pedagogy of (The) Force: The Myth of Redemptive Violence." In *Finding the Force of the Star Wars Franchise: Fans, Merchandise, & Critics*, edited by Matthew W. Kapell and John S. Lawrence, 59–72. New York: Peter Lang, 2006.

Kloppenberg, James T. *Reading Obama: Dreams, Hope, and the American Political Tradition*. Princeton: Princeton University Press, 2011.

Kolata, Gina. "Scientist Reports First Cloning Ever of Adult Mammal." *New York Times*, February 23, 1997, 1.

Kramer, Peter. "Star Wars." *History Today* 49, no. 3 (1999): 41–47.

Krauthammer, Charles. "The Truth About Torture: It's Time to Be Honest About Doing Terrible Things." *The Weekly Standard*, December 5, 2005.

Kristeva, Julia. "Word, Dialogue, and Novel," In *The Kristeva Reader*, edited by Toril Moi, 34–61. New York: Columbia University Press, 1986.

Lacy, Mark J. "War, Cinema, and Moral Anxiety." *Alternatives* 28 (2003): 611–636.

Lancashire, Anne. "*Attack of the Clones* and the Politics of *Star Wars*." *Dalhousie Review* 82, no. 2 (2002): 235–53.

_____. "The Phantom Menace: Repetition, Variation, Integration." *Film Criticism* 24 (2000): 23–44.

_____. "*Return of the Jedi*: Once More with Feeling." *Film Criticism* 8, no. 2 (1984): 55–66.

Lee, Burton J., III. "The Stain of Torture." *Washington Post,* July 1, 2005.

Leung, Rebecca. "60 Minutes II Has Exclusive Report on Alleged Mistreatment." CBSNews.com, April 27, 2004. Accessed April 10, 2013. http://www.cbsnews.com/news/abuse-of-iraqi-pows-by-gis-probed/.

Lev, Peter. "Whose Future? 'Star Wars,' Alien,' and 'Blade Runner." *Literature Film Quarterly* 26, no. 1 (1998): 30–37.

Levy Simon, Barbara. "Women of Conscience: Jeannette Rankin and Barbara Lee." *Affilia* 17, no. 3 (Fall 2002): 384–388.

Lopach, James J., and Jean A. Luckowski. *Jeannette Rankin: A Political Woman.* Boulder: University Press of Colorado, 2005.

Lubin, David. "Liberalism, Torture, and the Ticking Bomb." In *The Torture Debate in America,* edited by Karen J. Greenberg, 35–83. New York: Cambridge University Press, 2006.

McDonald, Paul F. *The Star Wars Heresies: Interpreting the Themes, Symbols, and Philosophies of Episodes I, II, and III.* Jefferson, NC: McFarland, 2013.

McDowell, John C. "'Wars Not Make One Great': Redeeming the Star Wars Mythos from Redemptive Violence Without Amusing Ourselves to Death." *Journal of Religion and Popular Culture* 22, no. 1 (Spring 2010): 1–60.

McVeigh, Stephen P. "The Galactic Way of Warfare." In *Finding the Force of the Star Wars Franchise: Fans, Merchandise, & Critics,* edited by Matthew W. Kapell and John S. Lawrence, 35–58. New York: Peter Lang, 2006.

Mebane-Cruz, Anjana, and Margaret Wiener. "Imagining 'The Good Reality': Communities of Healing in Two Works of Utopian Fiction." *Contemporary Justice Review* 8, no. 3 (September 2005): 307–320.

Merlock, Ray, and Kathy Merlock Jackson. "Lightsabers, Political Arenas, and Marriages for Princess Leia and Queen Amidala." In *Sex, Politics, and Religion in Star Wars: An Anthology,* edited by Douglas Brode and Leah Deyneka, 77–88. Lanham, MD: Scarecrow Press, 2012.

Meyer, David S. "Star Wars, Star Wars, and American Political Culture." *The Journal of Popular Culture* 26, no. 2 (September 1, 1992): 99–115.

Milbank, Dana. "Bush Seeks to Reassure Nation on Iraq." *Washington Post,* May 25, 2004. Accessed April 10, 2013. http://www.washingtonpost.com/wp-dyn/articles/A52711–2004May24.html.

_____. "The Chamber Meets the Force." *Washington Post,* May 20, 2005.

Morson, Gary S., and Caryl Emerson, *Mikhail Bakhtin: Creation of a Prosaics.* Stanford: Stanford University Press, 1990.

Murphy, John M. "Mikhail Bakhtin and the Rhetorical Tradition." *Quarterly Journal of Speech* 87, no. 3 (August 2001): 259–277.

National Bioethics Advisory Commission. *Cloning Human Beings.* Washington, D.C.: Government Printing Office, 1997.

Nikolaidis, Aristotelis. "Televising Counter Terrorism: Torture, Denial, and Exception in the Case of *24.*" *Continuum: Journal of Media & Cultural Studies* 25, no. 2 (April 2011): 213–225.

Norwegian Nobel Committee. "The Nobel Peace Prize for 2009." Nobelprize.org, October 9, 2009. Accessed June 12, 2014. http://www.nobelprize.org/nobel_prizes/peace/laureates/2009/press.html.

Obama, Barack. "Ebenezer Baptist Church Address." American Rhetoric Online Speech Bank, delivered January 20, 2008. Accessed May 21, 2015. http://www.americanrhetoric.com/speeches/barackobama/barackobamaebenezerbaptist.htm.

_____. "A Just and Lasting Peace." *Vital Speeches of the Day* 76, no. 2 (February 2010): 50–53.

_____. "Obama's Speech Against the Iraq War." *Npr.Org,* delivered October 2, 2002.

Accessed May 21, 2015. http://www.npr.org/templates/story/story.php?storyId= 99591469.

_____. "Remarks by the President on Winning the Nobel Peace Prize." whitehouse.gov, delivered October 9, 2009. Accessed June 12, 2013. http://www.whitehouse.gov/ the_press_office/Remarks-by-the-President-on-Winning-the-Nobel- Peace-Prize/.

Ott, Brian L. "(Re)Framing Fear: Equipment for Living in a Post–9/11 World." In *Cylons in America: Critical Studies in Battlestar Galactica*, edited by Tiffany Potter and C. W. Marshall, 13–26. London: Continuum International, 2007.

_____. "Set Your Cathode Rays to Stun(Ning)." *Flow* 1, no. 1 (February 2005). Accessed August 14, 2012. http://flowtv.org/2005/02/set-your-cathode-rays-to-stunning/.

_____, and Eric Aoki. "Counter-Imagination as Interpretive Practice: Futuristic Fantasy and the *Fifth Element*." *Women's Studies in Communication* 27 (2004): 149–176.

_____, and _____. "Popular Imagination and Identity Politics: Reading the Future in *Star Trek: The Next Generation*." *Western Journal of Communication* 65 (2001): 392–415.

_____, and Beth Bonstetter. "'We're at Now, Now': *Spaceballs* as Parodic Tourism." *Southern Communication Journal* 72, no. 4 (2007): 309–327.

_____, and Carl R. Burgchardt. "On Critical-Rhetorical Pedagogy: Dialoging with Schindler's List." *Western Journal of Communication* 77, no. 1 (January-February 2013): 14–33.

Pak, Chris. "The Dialogic Science Fiction Megatext: Vivisection in H. G. Wells's the *Island of Dr Moreau and* Genetic Engineering in Gene Wolfe's the Woman Who Loved the Centaur Pholus." *Green Letters: Studies in Ecocriticism* 12, no. 1 (October 2012): 27–35.

Parry-Giles, Shawn J., and Diane M. Blair. "The Rise of the Rhetorical First Lady: Politics, Gender, Ideology, and Women's Voice, 1789–2002." *Rhetoric and Public Affairs* 5, no. 4 (Winter 2002): 565–599.

Peach, Lucinda J. "An Alternative to Pacifism? Feminism and Just-War Theory." In *Bringing Peace Home: Feminism, Violence, and Nature*, edited by Karen J. Warren and Duane L. Cady, 192–210. Bloomington: Indiana University Press, 1996.

Peter, Lev. "Whose Future? 'Star Wars,' Alien,' and 'Blade Runner.'" *Literature Film Quarterly* 26, no. 1 (1998): 31–37.

Pohl, Frederick. "The Politics of Prophecy." In *Political Science Fiction*, edited by Donald M. Hassler and Clyde Wilcox, 7–17. Columbia: University of Carolina Press, 1997.

Pounds, Micheal Charles. "'Explorers'—Star Trek: Deep Space Nine." *African Identities* 7, no. 2 (May 2009): 209–235.

"President George W. Bush's Address on Stem Cell Research." CNN, August 9, 2001. Accessed May 28, 2015. http://edition.cnn.com/2001/ALLPOLITICS/08/09/bush. transcript/.

Randell, Karen. "'Now the Gloves Come Off': The Problematic of 'Enhanced Interrogation Techniques' in *Battlestar Galactica*." *Cinema Journal* 51, no. 1 (Fall 2011): 168–173.

Rankin, Jeannette. *"Two Votes Against War" and Other Writings on Peace*. New York: A. J. Muste Memorial Institute, 2001.

Reeves, Joshua, and Matthew S. May. "The Peace Rhetoric of a War President: Barack Obama and the Just War Legacy." *Public Affairs* 16, no. 4: 623–650.

Rehak, Bob. "Adapting Watchmen After 9/11." *Cinema Journal* 51, no. 1 (Fall 2011): 154–159.

Rose, Charlie. "George Lucas on the Meaning of *Star Wars*." YouTube, 3:33. October 17, 2014. Accessed October 23, 2014. https://www.youtube.com/watch?v=-pbRGt WkHWg.

Ruane, Abigail E., and Patrick James. "The International Relations of Middle-Earth: Learning from the Lord of the Rings." *International Studies Perspectives* 9 (2008): 377–394.

Rubey, Dan. "Star Wars: Not So Long Ago, Not So Far Away." *Jump Cut: A Review of Contemporary Media* 18 (August 1978): 9–14.

Ruddick, Sara. *Maternal Thinking: Toward a Politics of Peace.* New York: Ballantine, 1990.

Rushing, Janice Hocker, and Thomas S. Frenz. *Projecting the Shadow: The Cyborg Hero in American Film.* Chicago: University of Chicago Press, 1995.

Ryan, Michael, and Douglass Kellner. *Camera Politica: The Politics and Ideology of Contemporary Hollywood Film.* Bloomington: Indiana University Press, 1988.

Scahill, Jeremy. "The CIA's Secret Sites in Somalia." *The Nation*, August 1, 2011, 11–16.

Schrag, Calvin O. *Doing Philosophy with Others: Conversations, Reminiscences, and Reflections.* West Lafayette: Purdue University Press, 2010.

_____. *Philosophical Papers: Betwixt and Between.* Albany: State University of New York Press, 1994.

_____. *Resources of Rationality: A Response to the Postmodern Challenge.* Bloomington: Indiana University Press, 1992.

_____. "Rhetoric Situated at the End of Philosophy." *Quarterly Journal of Speech* 71, no. 2: 164–174.

Shactman, Noah. "CIA Chief: Drones 'Only Game in Town' for Stopping Al Qaeda." Wired.com, May 19, 2009. Accessed November 1, 2011. http://www.wired.com/dangerroom/2009/05/cia-chief-drones-only-game-in-town-for- stopping-al-qaeda/.

Silvio, Carl, and Tony M. Vinci, eds. *Culture, Identity, and Technology in the Star Wars Films: Essays on the Two Trilogies.* Jefferson, NC: McFarland, 2007.

Singer, P. W. "Robots at War: The New Battlefield." *The Wilson Quarterly* 33, no. 1 (Winter 2009): 30–48.

Sisco King, Claire. "Rogue Waves, Remakes, and Resurrections: Allegorical Displacement and Screen Memory in Poseidon." *Quarterly Journal of Speech* 94, no. 4 (November 2008): 430–454.

Smith, Norma. *Jeannette Rankin: America's Conscience.* Helena,: Montana Historical Society Press, 2002.

Sontag, Susan. "The Imagination of Disaster." *Commentary* 14 (October 1965): 42–48.

Sparrow, Robert. "Killer Robots." *Journal of Applied Philosophy* 24, no. 1 (2007): 62–77.

_____. *Wired for War: The Robotics Revolution and Conflict in the 21st Century.* New York: Penguin, 2009.

Spence, Rebecca, and Jason McLeod. "Building the Road as We Walk It: Peacebuilding as Principled Revolutionary Nonviolent Praxis." *Social Alternatives* 21, no. 2 (Autumn 2002): 61–64.

Stahl, Roger. "Why We 'Support the Troops.'" *Rhetoric & Public Affairs* 12, no. 4 (Winter 2009): 533–570.

Star Wars: The Clone Wars. Film. Directed by Dave Filoni. Warner Bros. Pictures, 2008.

Star Wars: The Clone Wars. Seasons 1–5. Supervising director Dave Filoni. Cartoon Network, 2008–2013.

Star Wars: The Clone Wars. Seasons 6. Supervising director Dave Filoni. Netflix, 2014.

Star Wars: Episode I—A Phantom Menace. Directed by George Lucas. 20th Century Fox, 1999.

Star Wars: Episode II—Attack of the Clones. Directed by George Lucas. 20th Century Fox, 2002.

Star Wars: Episode III—Revenge of the Sith. Directed by George Lucas. 20th Century Fox, 2005.

Star Wars: Episode IV—A New Hope. Directed by George Lucas. 20th Century Fox, 1977.

Star Wars: Episode V—The Empire Strikes Back. Directed by Irvin Kershner. 20th Century Fox, 1980.

Star Wars: Episode VI—Return of the Jedi. Directed by Richard Marquand. 20th Century Fox, 1983.

Suvin, Darko. On the Poetics of the Science Fiction Genre." *College English* 34, no. 3 (December 1972): 372–382.

Sweet, Derek R. "More Than Goth: The Rhetorical Reclamation of the Subcultural Self." *Popular Communication* 3, no. 4 (2005): 239–264.

_____. "We Are All Cylons: Battlestar Galactica and Fandom's Fitting Response." In *The Dynamics of Interconnections in Popular Culture(S)*, edited by Ray B. Browne and Ben Urish, 95–113. Newcastle: Cambridge Scholars, 2014.

Telotte, J. P. "Human Artifice and the Science Fiction Film." *Film Quarterly* 36 no. 3 (Spring 1983): 44–51.

_____. *Replications: A Robotic History of Science Fiction Film.* Urbana: University of Illinois Press, 1995.

_____. "Science Fiction in Double Focus: Forbidden Planet." *Film Criticism* 13, no. 3 (1989): 25–36.

Tenenboim-Weinblatt, Keren. "'Where Is Jack Bauer When You Need Him?' the Uses of Television Drama in Mediated Political Discourse." *Political Communication* 26, no. 3 (2009): 367–387.

Terrill, Robert. "An Uneasy Peace: Barack Obama's Nobel Peace Prize Lecture." *Rhetoric & Public Affairs* 14, no. 4 (Winter 2011): 761–780.

Thill, Scott. "Rebooted Darth Maul Closes Down the *Clone Wars*." Wired: Underwire Blog, March 15, 2012. Accessed March 20, 2012. http://www.wired.com/underwire/2012/03/clone-wars-darth-maul/.

Tigges, Wim. "Xena Rules: A Feminized Version of Antony and Cleopatra." *Feminist Media Studies* 10, no. 4 (2010): 441–455.

Tindol, Robert. "The *Star-Trek* Borg as an All-American Captivity Narrative." *Brno Studies in English* 38, no. 1 (2012): 151–158.

United Nations. "Convention Against Torture and Other Cruel, Inhuman or Degrading Treatment or Punishment." *United Nations Treaty Series* 1465 (December 10, 1984): 85–209.

van Zoonen, Lisbet. *Entertaining the Citizen: When Politics and Popular Culture Converge.* Lanham, MD: Rowman & Littlefield, 2005.

Vicaro, Michael P. "A Liberal Use of 'Torture': Pain, Personhood, and Precedent in the U.S. Federal Definition of Torture," *Rhetoric & Public Affairs* 14, no. 3 (2011): 401–426.

Vogel, Gretchen. "Cloning: Could Humans Be Next?" *Science* 291, no. 5505 (February 2, 2001): 808–809. Academic Search Complete, EBSCOhost (accessed November 1, 2012).

Walzer, Michael. "Coda: Can the Good Guys Win." *The European Journal of International Law* 24, no. 1 (2013): 433–444.

_____. *Just and Unjust Wars: A Moral Argument with Historical Illustrations.* New York: Basic Books, 1977.

Warren, Karen J., and Duane L. Cady. "Feminism and Peace: Seeing Connections." *Hypatia* 9, no. 2 (Spring 1994): 4–20.

"Weekend Journal." *Wall Street Journal*, May 20, 2005.

Weldes, Jutta. "Going Cultural: Star Trek, State Action, and Popular Culture." *Millenium—Journal of International Studies* 28 (1999): 117–134.

_____. *To Seek Out New Worlds: Exploring Links Between Science Fiction and World Politics.* New York: Palgrave Macmillan, 2003.

Westfahl, Gary. *Science Fiction, Children's Literature, and Popular Culture: Coming of Age in Fantasyland*. Westport, CT: Greenwood Press, 2000.

Young, Brian. "Why Aren't You Watching *The Clone Wars?*" *The Huffington Post*, March 30, 2011. Accessed March 31, 2011. http://www.huffingtonpost.com/bryan-young/why-arent-you-watching-th_b_841727.html.

Zagarri, Rosemarie. "Morals, Manners, and the Republic Mother." *American Quarterly* 44, no. 2 (June 1992): 192–215.

Zappen, James P. *The Rebirth of Dialogue: Bakhtin, Socrates, and the Rhetorical Tradition*. Albany: State University of New York Press, 2004.

Index